How to Measure Human Resources Management

Jac Fitz-enz

Second Edition

McGraw-Hill, Inc.
New York St. Louis San Francisco Auckland Bogotá
Caracas Lisbon London Madrid Mexico City Milan
Montreal New Delhi San Juan Singapore
Sydney Tokyo Toronto

Library of Congress Cataloging-in-Publication Data

Fitz-enz, Jac.
  How to measure human resources management / Jac Fitz-enz.—2nd
ed.
        p.   cm.
  Includes bibliographical references and index.
  ISBN 0-07-021259-7
  1. Personnel management.   2. Personnel departments.   I. Title.
  HF5549.F555   1995
  658.3—dc20   94-36439
                                                           CIP

7 8 9 10   FGRFGR   9 9 8

ISBN 0-07-021259-7

*The sponsoring editor for this book was Philip Ruppel and the production
supervisor was Donald F. Schmidt. It was set in Palatino
by TopDesk Publishers' Group.*

This book is printed on acid-free paper.

To My Parents, Kathryn and Art
Thank You

About the Author

Dr. Jac Fitz-enz is founder-president of Saratoga Institute, a performance measurement research and consulting company headquartered in Saratoga, California, with offices throughout Asia, the Pacific, the Americas, and Europe. Previously, he held the position of human resources vice president at Motorola Computer Systems, Imperial Bank, and Wells Fargo Bank. Since 1978 he has conducted workshops on staff performance management and measurement in 25 countries, and he has published three books and nearly 100 articles.

Contents

Section D: Supporting the Human Asset: How to Measure Employee and Labor Relations

12. Orientation and Counseling   167

13. The Hidden Costs of Lost Time   187

14. Labor Relations   205

Preface to the Second Edition

The marketplace has changed dramatically in the ten years since I sat down to write the first edition of *How to Measure Human Resources Management* (HTMHRM). The go-go 1980s, the Decade of Greed, has given way, and the pendulum has swung to the other side: a period of prolonged recession and slow growth. Instead of junk bonds and management buy-outs we now deal with massive restructuring, reskilling, and, more important, a search for a new organizational model that will work during an era of volatility.

There is both good news and bad news for the human resources profession. (For the sake of brevity I will hereafter refer to the human resources department or profession as HR.) The bad news is that many HR departments have not responded to the change. They are operating with exactly the same philosophy and self-image as they did in 1980. Some have even resisted the call for new methods, new ideas, and new responses for HR. I find many of the older types angry with their companies because the methodology they learned in the 1960s and 1970s is no longer appreciated.

The good news is twofold. First, in many companies management is finally walking their talk. They are truly turning to HR for help in running the business. There is a greater receptivity to HR when it comes in with business enhancing-programs. There is more recognition that the human resource is truly the critical variable. Along with that is the corollary that HR can and should play a management role. Second, many HR people are responding to the call. They have shifted positions from a defensive posture to an assertive one. They believe that they can add value and they are showing it.

Measurement Is Coming On

With the onset of quality, benchmarking, and reengineering programs, objective performance measurement has become an imperative. Early in the 1990s quality began a slow move toward the office. At this point in early 1995 all three are still predominantly focused in manufacturing, but are moving inexorably into staff functions. As they advance it will be obvious that departments like HR will have to learn how to develop hard data, analyze it, and report it.

There are two categories of performance measurement: internal and external. The first edition of this book focused primarily on internal measures. At that time HR was still largely an unmanaged function. By that I mean it was internally focused on running programs. Today, many in HR are still committed to contemplating their navel. Despite all the signs pointing toward a get-involved-or-get-out mandate, too many HR people are fighting the inevitable. If I told you some of the intensely stupid things that some HR managers are saying about their role you wouldn't believe me. The good news is that more HR types are beginning to look outside. The successful HR directors know that they need to transform their department into a business partner. This requires establishing partnerships with their customers and developing the ability to track the effect of their work on the outcomes of their internal customers.

New Features

This edition contains two new chapters: human resource information systems and labor relations. Ten years ago HR had only begun to install sophisticated data processing equipment. Its principal use was to automate employee records. Today, it is slowly, very slowly, moving toward becoming a management decision tool. Now it warrants a separate chapter of its own. On the other topic, union membership as a percentage of manufacturing employment has fallen from 40% just after World War II to about 15% today. Still, it is a factor within some companies, so I have expanded the employee relations section to include a number of labor relations measures. The section has been renamed "Employee and Labor Relations."

I've been working on performance measurement for staff departments since the early 1970s. In those twenty-plus years I've learned a few things. As my wife Ellen says, "If you open enough oysters sooner or later you find a few pearls." I'm passing on my pearls in the form of italicized quotes. They are scattered throughout the book wherever they seem appropriate. I call them Dr. Jac's Gems. I hope you will find them to be simple, yet significant points to remember.

Acknowledgments

I must thank our clients for continuing to challenge us and to share with us their ideas and experience. It is impossible to mention all their names, and to list just a few would do a disservice to so many others. We have learned a great deal from working with our global network representatives, particularly Peter Howes, Neil Peters, and Pat Foley in Australia; Alfonso Gonzalez in Mexico; Richard and Maurice Phelps in the United Kingdom; Abdul Rahim Majid in Malaysia; and the Ventocilla brothers, Elio and Jose, in Venezuela. Over the past five years my colleagues at the Saratoga Institute, Carol Walton and Barbara Jack, have been invaluable. And of course my greatest inspiration is always my wife, Ellen Kieffer.

Jac Fitz-enz

Preface to the First Edition

This is a book about success in organizations. To be more precise, it is about how to be more successful in running a human resources department in a modern organization. Success is built on your ability to do your job, the wisdom to spend your time on the issues that are important, and the skill to communicate your results. I believe that the management of people is the most important task of any organization. If that is true, then it follows that the professionals who are directly charged with building the systems to attract, pay, counsel, and develop employees ought to be esteemed members of the management team. In too many companies that is not the case. This book is designed to help you win a spot on the first team.

The Language of Business

If the language of business is dollars, then the alphabet is numbers. All organizations, whether profit or not-for-profit, depend on their ability to get the best possible return on dollars invested. Even some government agencies who thought they were immune from this basic law have found themselves severely cut back by an electorate who demand service in return for their tax dollars. Managers of human resources functions have long labored under the burden of lean staffs and tight budgets. Part of the reason for this has been their inability to communicate with management in the language of business.

The Approach

My method is experiential and very practical. There is little reference to theory and even less to statistics. Although we will deal with numbers throughout the book, the mathematics are very basic. The four functions of arithmetic will take care of 99 percent of the applications discussed. The design is the result of 12 years of running personnel and training functions. The last six of those years were spent developing and refining a total system concept for quantifying human resources management. Since 1978, I have conducted public workshops on this subject. The ideas, formulas, and reports you will find in this book are a result of my concept, enriched with the valuable suggestions of the hundreds of human resources practitioners, consultants, and college professors who have attended the workshops.

I believe this book represents the most comprehensive text on the subject available today. I do not expect that you will drop everything you already know and adopt this system. I hope that initially you will find the philosophical basis sound and that it might be a source of inspiration for you to rethink what your purpose is in the organization. Once you are secure in the knowledge of what you want to construct, this book is like a big toolbox. It can help you build the structure necessary to achieve your goal. I expect you will use the tools selectively, as this book is not intended as a panacea. Everyone's environment is somewhat unique. I cannot tell you what you need. I can only give you the toolbox and explain where and how to use each tool. You must decide which of the formulas and reports are useful in your situation.

The Style and Plan

My style is familiar and direct. I use the editorial "we" very seldom. I want to talk with you just as though we were in the same room together. I want to discuss common human resources issues with you and give you some ideas on how to deal with them. I have divided the book into an introductory section, four applications sections, and a short concluding section on the payoffs and rewards to be found in this approach.

Section A provides a short history of the human resources profession. It lays out the issues of measurability and talks about some of the fundamental questions of human resources management. The section concludes with a chapter on how to generate quantitative measures for the human resources department. Sections B through E provide detailed explanations with examples of how to measure the four main human resources functions: planning and staffing, compensation and benefits, employee relations, and training and development. Section F provides examples of organizational and individual payoffs, which are the result of the quantitative approach to human resources management.

My plan was to write a book that would be useful to people working at many levels within a human resources department. In addition, I wanted to provide a new perspective for the senior- and graduate-level college student of human resources management.

Acknowledgments

My first and most sincere thank you must go to the people who over the years told me that we cannot or should not quantify the work of the personnel and training departments. They challenged me to keep working on the conceptual and mechanical problems. By now, most people agree that we should be able to objectively evaluate our work. But those early doubters were a great inspiration. I want to thank Toronto consultant Tom Handley, Ida Meyers of Tektronix, Walt Whitt of American Express, Barb Schoneberger of Internorth, Ginny McMinn of Rustoleum, Harry Garner of Northern Telecom, Lon Boncyk of Computervision, Susan Bailey of Best Products, and Bert Mastrov and Bob Lopresto of Korn-Ferry for supporting my work and recommending it to others. In particular, I would like to thank Richard Israel for telling me repeatedly that I had a valuable concept and not to be discouraged by critics. Deep appreciation goes to the staff at the American Society for Personnel Administration—Marsha, Debbie, Shirley, Tom, Jeff, and retired executive director Len Brice—for supporting my workshop as we all worked to make it as effective as possible. I also want to thank the people I worked with from 1976 to 1982 at Four-Phase Systems' industrial relations department. They took my ideas, added value, and turned them into an excellent system. Special support came from Kathryn Hards, Pat Morton, Sharon Bue, Barbara Kuenzel, and Bob Coon.

Along the way many others contributed also, and I regret that I cannot mention all their names. One of the most important people in this endeavor is Esther Hunt. Esther did research, typed the manuscript, and offered whatever support was needed when it was needed. Finally, I would like to thank my wife, Ellen Kieffer, who put aside much of our social life for the past year so that I could spend the time it takes to write a book. She encouraged me to do it and provided loving advice all along the way. Without her it would have gotten done, but it would not have been as good a product.

Jac Fitz-enz

SECTION A

The Evolution of Human Asset Management

Prologue:
How We Got Here

Stage One: A Slow Start

In the late 1800s the industrial revolution overwhelmed the United States. In the space of two decades giant manufacturing complexes replaced the small business, cottage industry model that had been the focal point of commerce for hundreds of years. Paradoxically, only one hundred years later the arrival of electronic technology swung the pendulum back toward small business as a major production source. Nevertheless, as the giant steel, railroad, petroleum, and electrical companies grew, they spawned the first staff departments, one of which was personnel. The personnel department usually was formed to meet the need to recruit thousands of people to work the machines of the new age. It was staffed of necessity by employees from line functions, and there was no formal education for personnel work. Since the value systems of nineteenth-century industrialists focused on new ways to engineer and manufacture, the people function and the worker in general were not highly valued. Employees were treated like production parts and personnel like inventory clerks. Although most organizations are now more enlightened in their treatment of workers, this attitude has not totally disappeared. I remember vividly how the president of a company I worked for described the personnel department to a visiting VIP. He opened the door to the department, stepped in, and said to his guest, "This is where they keep employee records." The man nodded. They turned and left.

In time, personnel departments came to be staffed by individuals who could be released from the "more important" functions of manufacturing, sales, and finance. In effect, the department often became the dumping ground for the organization's casualties. When well-liked employees began to have performance problems, a decision might be made to place them in personnel rather than fire them. After all, the feeling was, "they can't hurt anybody there." There were some individuals who willingly chose personnel as a career field. Nevertheless, this was more the exception than the rule in the early days.

Stage Two: The Service Model

Between the two world wars, the personnel function began to develop. By the late 1940s it had become more than an offshoot of payroll. Besides being an employment service, it took the first step toward creating sophisticated compensation systems. Training blossomed during the postwar boom. The training technologies that had been developed in the armed forces began to find their way into industry. Labor relations had matured before most other functions. When the unions again flexed the muscles that they had voluntarily left unused during the war, labor negotiators became important.

Two traits characterized the changing personnel department. First, it was largely a reactive service; that is, there was not a great deal of forward planning. Although the organization might develop elaborate short- and long-term business plans, little effort was made to carry that over to the full range of personnel subjects. Some work was done to generate gross numbers of employees needed to meet the business plan. Still, most companies did not begin to think of manning tables and succession planning with its implications for training until well into the second half of the century. Personnel was often not privy to the highest management councils. Hence, it had little choice except to be reactive.

The second characteristic of the postwar period was a continuation of the attitude that labor was an adversary and not a partner of management. This supported the view that employees were an element of cost and not an asset. It was only during the 1960s that this view began to change. Given these attitudes and values, personnel work was directed toward a maintenance mode. The idea was that no news from personnel was good news.

Stage Three: Opportunity

The third and current stage owes its birth to government intervention into private business. As much as any other force, the federal government changed the way organizations related to and managed their employees. It is a rather consistent phenomenon that when any individual, group, or institution achieves a power advantage he, she, or it tends to guard that edge with great vigor. Change occurs when a greater power comes along. In this case the power was the federal courts and Congress.

The 1960s and 1970s saw the passage of the Civil Rights Act, ERISA, ADEA, and OSHA. This has continued into the 1990s with the ADA.

Each act found a different point of entry into the organization. In an effort to deal with these new realities, organizations placed the responsibility with the personnel group and staffed to meet the intrusion. The problem had created a need for competency. Along about this time the shift from personnel to human resources began. It looked like the opening of a new era for the people who worked the human side of the organization. Young people looked at it and saw an opportunity for interesting work and perhaps even satisfying careers. As they entered the function and began to show results, management came to see possibilities they had never before imagined could exist there. No other single force did as much good for the professionalism of personnel as did Uncle Sam.

Three other factors have also played roles in the recent development of the HR profession. The first was the evolution of the work force itself. A profound social change took place in the United States after World War II. The baby boom of the late 1940s and early 1950s threw a large number of young people into the labor market around 1970. Not only were they young, but they were also better educated than their parents. More important, their values were different. Being generally better educated than their parents and grandparents they were not content with just a job. They demanded meaning and satisfaction from their labors. Compounding this, many oppressed people began to find their voices. Women and minorities, with the support of zealous federal agencies, pressured for a piece of the action and demanded that organizations provide a wide range of welfare benefits and social activities in addition to simply employment. In the 1990s the full impact is finally being felt, with support programs such as child and elder care and parental leaves.

Another important factor was the rapid postwar growth of organizations themselves. Both in size and scope of markets, the industrial concerns of the 1970s dwarfed those of the 1930s. Today, some companies do as much business in the Pacific Rim as their predecessors used to do in the entire world. This has brought new requirements for specialists in areas such as expatriate compensation and intercultural training. Human issues arising from restructuring of multinational corporations are being delegated to HR for study and for a role in implementation.

Finally, most recently, the slowdown in the growth of industrial productivity has become one of the nation's most pressing problems. Many HR departments are becoming involved by designing new pay systems, conducting more training and organizational development interventions, and becoming involved in quality programs. It is here, within the productivity/quality dilemma, that HR has been handed its greatest opportunity. Some departments have taken advantage of it. In doing so they have moved from the reactive and peripheral mode of stage two toward a more involved and strategic position.

It is clear that the HR function is moving into the fourth and perhaps final stage in its evolution.

Stage Four: The Last Chance

In the past decade I have worked with a large number of HR pros who bear no resemblance to their predecessors. There is no whining about lack of resources or appreciation. There is no acceptance of second-class citizenship or exclusion from strategic planning. Of course, not everyone loves them and they have to face the normal percentage of idiots. But these talented, insightful people have gone on the offensive. They are deeply involved in the operation of the company. Their work is clearly affecting the performance of the company. Best of all, their numbers are growing daily.

On the other side of the fence there is a force growing in strength daily that is saying, "Outsource!" One after another of the staff functions are being outsourced in the name of cost effectiveness. Whether or not that is true is not the point. There is an unquestionable ground swell in favor of outsourcing staff functions. One of the reasons for it is that it is an apparently.simple solution. Management likes simple solutions, like layoffs. Outsourcing fits that criterion. MIS functions are being outsourced by even some of the largest high-technology firms. Transaction processing is another candidate. Payroll and benefits administration are two currently popular passengers for the outsourcing bus. I know a couple of companies wherein compensation has been put under accounting because the comp staff never did anything other than conduct surveys and plot salary curves.

By the turn of the century you will see three solutions to human resources management:

1. *Zombies:* The familiar, traditional staff as expense model continues with perhaps 30 to 50%. This is found mostly in the lagging companies, who don't manage any function in an especially enlightened fashion. Very often these are family owned or controlled by a small group of investors. They just milk the company and go to the country club every weekend. These are the types of companies that have very small pieces of the market. They pick up the leftovers. One venture capitalist described them as "the walking dead." A job in one of them is only slightly better than unemployment.

2. *Reactors:* The outsource-and-decentralize model with line managers taking most of the responsibility back that they had in the early decades of the 20th century constitutes perhaps 20 to 30%. These people have never seen a fully functioning HR professional, so in desperation they have reverted to the old model. At least they have control, even though they wish they didn't have to handle personnel matters. All in all, not a bad place to work if you don't have too much ambition.

3. *Confidants:* The outsourced processes model with a few trusted, talented, corporate HR people playing the role of internal advisor, consultant, and broker of outside services includes about 20 to 30%. This is what enlightened managers wish they had. In this model HR truly is a lever helping improve quality, productivity, and service, thereby giving their company a competitive edge in the market place. If you have what it takes to operate in this highly accountable situation, go for it. It will be the best job you'll ever have.

So you have a choice of careers. It is up to you to pick the situation that best fits your ambition and aspirations. If you choose correctly, you can be contented. The questions are, how hard do you want to work, what do you want to spend your time doing, and when you look back on your career will you be able to say, "I made the world a little better place in which to work and live?"

1

You Can't Measure What We Do

The Subjectivity Myth

Decades ago a mythology developed about the personnel function in particular and staff work in general. (Please note that I use the term *personnel* when referring to the traditional model. I use *HR* when referring to the value model.) It had to do with the nature and purpose of the work. More important, it dealt with the outcomes or results of the labor. The fundamental belief was that the true and full value of personnel's work could only be judged by those who perform it. Even then, the appraisal was limited to subjective criteria. There was a belief that business-type measures could not be applied to this function.

Whether the subjective position was valid or not was a key question to be sure. However, just the fact that it existed made it a major barrier to developing the organization's human assets. This view sets personnel apart from the rest of the organization. Line managers quickly learned that personnel had neither understanding of nor interest in business matters. Therefore, when there were meetings to review business performance or to plan future business moves, personnel was not invited to sit in. Many personnel managers resented this second-hand treatment, yet they did little to change it.

Reasons Why Not

A number of reasons account for the lack of objectivity in HR. Probably the most prevalent is that HR people simply do not know how to quantitatively measure their activity. In this regard they are not that different from many types of staff people. There were many routes into HR management. Few, if any, offered training in quantitative methods. Many senior people in HR today have worked their way up from clerical or specialist positions. Since the chances are better than 9 out of 10 that their predecessors did not have quantitative measurement systems, it follows that many contemporary managers were never exposed to a measurement methodology. Therefore, it is not surprising that many of them rely on subjectivity.

The hope lies in the newer generation, many of whom have business degrees and a familiarity with computers and numbers. Unfortunately, they aren't getting much help from within academia. Quantitative procedures have seldom been adapted to the creation of input-output ratios for measuring the HR function's results in college curricula. The reason for this is simple: Most academics have never applied themselves to the problem. Only lately have they begun to respond to this imperative and require objectivity in HR management courses. Promoters of public workshops have seldom offered sections on quantitative techniques. As of mid-1994, only the Saratoga Institute regularly offered public seminars in quantitative management of HR.

Top management bought the myth of subjectivity many years ago. Perhaps because there was little interest in the personnel function, the early captains of industry simply never asked the question. As time progressed, the tradition of nonmeasurability went unchallenged. Few chief executive officers (CEOs) have taken more than a cursory tour in the HR department during their careers. Human resources is often only a quick stop on the way to the executive suite. Just about the time they begin to get a feel for what might be accomplished, they are off to their next developmental assignment.

If the current condition is to change, top management will probably have to take some responsibility and act. There are two ways they can promote a change. First, they can demand that an objective reporting system be created by the existing HR department. In order for that to happen, they may have to focus on the function and review the level of resources committed to it. Second, they could hire a person who knows how to put a performance measurement system in place. There are companies who have such systems in various states of development. HR managers who have run these systems are usually upwardly mobile and willing to move. It is already obvious and clearly inevitable, given the demands that will be made on HR in the future, that measurement must become a part of the function. The payoff for creating a fully functional quantitative system will become evident as we proceed.

GEM #1   *Direction and control are impossible without data.*

Summary

The myth that one cannot measure human resources value has been refuted in so many cases that it is a wonder that there is anyone who still accepts it. I suspect it is because they don't want to change and become accountable. In today's market that is simply impossible.

Organizations cannot afford to support people who are not obviously contributing to the strategic goals of the enterprise. Top management has but two choices today. One is to turn HR into a value-adding function. The other is to outsource it and pay for specific services as needed.

2
The Pros vs.
the Cons

Success in Organizations

Success in organizations depends on three abilities. First, you have to be able to do your job. But just meeting the standards is not enough. Today, you must excel in your technology or you give away competitive advantage. I assume that you can do that, and I am not going to tell you anything about how to do the technical aspects of your job better. Second, you must excel in the right areas. That is, you need to focus your attention and energy on the issues that make a difference. This is a failing of many staff departments, because they look at their mission inside-out instead of outside-in. Inside-out refers to the "me-first" approach. The inside-outers look at what they want to do first and then try to bring the organization around to their values. Inevitably this fails. The outside-inners look at their client organization and ask, "What do they need from me?" Then, they structure themselves to provide that service or product. This does not mean that they give up their convictions, but they recognize that there are other valid viewpoints and that staff departments are in existence to support the mission of the organization, not vice versa. All of us on the staff side would do well to keep this pragmatic principle in mind. Finally, success depends on your ability to take measures of your performance and use them persuasively to obtain the resources you need and to work effectively as peers with your customers. This is the ability we will focus on in this book.

Performance measurement is a two-phase skill. First, you need to be able to develop data about your performance in a form that is meaningful to your audiences. I say *audiences* because there are several. One is your department. You must communicate with the people you work with in ways that inform, compliment, criticize, stimulate, and reward them, because without them you will achieve nothing. Another audience is the various departments and managers you interact with to service or to obtain cooperation to perform your responsibilities. Obviously, informative and persuasive communication is critical in these relationships. Yet another audience is senior management. This includes everyone in the system above your level. There is where the power is, and if you want to tap it you must be able to inform and persuade the people who hold it.

This leads us to the second phase. There is no getting away from it; we are all salespeople. Although few people realize it, more than 50 percent of our communications are persuasive in nature. Research has proved that many of the seemingly unimportant comments we make are really attempts to turn others to our way of thinking or to make them act according to our wishes. Test it if you like. Stand at the edge of any conversation and listen to how much of it is claims and assertions and how much is pure information offered with no desire to persuade.

To summarize, if you want to be successful over the long term, you have to do three things well: you have to excel at your job; you have to perform in areas that positively impact the mission and purpose of the larger organization; and last, but also very important, you have to be able to use information about your performance to prove to the organization that you are doing an excellent job and that you should be given whatever it is you are seeking.

The Name of the Game

Business is and always has been a numbers game. With the advancements in information processing technology, today's executive has access to a range of data that is nearly infinite in its depth and breadth. There is almost nothing that a computer can't process at incomprehensible speed. In the original edition of this book I predicted, "The price-performance curve on computers is declining so rapidly that before the 1980s are over desktop microprocessors will offer most of the capability that today's multimillion dollar corporate computer does." Was I right or not? If anything I understated the capability of computers, because not only have microprocessors doubled their capability every two years, software has added even more punch to the hardware.

Computers today are churning out numbers on sales volume, accounts receivable and payable, production efficiency, market penetration, and hundreds of other subjects, including projections for the future. The numbers tell management how much something costs, how many units are being produced and sold, and how long the lead time is for delivery of parts or products. They are not only descriptive, they are also predictive. In short, they drive the business.

Periodically, businesses report on their progress by issuing press releases and filing required public reports with the government. Probably the most widely read report is the annual public relations product called the annual report. This four-color, high-priced glossy document is generally divided into two parts. The first is a narrative section, which is devoted to a message from the CEO and a picture story covering company products, customers, and general activities. This is where you find the CEO's "people are our most important resource" statement. The second section is filled with financial data, numbers, and explanations of accounting treatments.

If you want to know how well the company is doing, you don't spend much time in the front of the report. Bankers and securities analysts, people who make their living by their ability to diagnose the health of a company, turn immediately to the back of the book. They want to see the numbers, because words are too imprecise. The government and the accounting profession have combined to establish what are called generally accepted accounting principles. Analysts, using these principles for clarification, can read the financial statement in an annual report and feel comfortable that they are learning the true condition of an enterprise.

There is no escaping numbers. Without them the line departments would have little idea of their performance, and there would be no way to attract investors. Also, it would be impossible to report to the stockholders. Top management cannot run a modern large corporation if it does not have numbers to work with. This being the case, how is HR to exist in the organization? Surveys have shown that, although they knew the number of employees in the company, a majority of major corporation personnel directors couldn't state the dollar volume of sales for their company, didn't know the profit level, and had little idea of the rate of return.[1]

Although that quote is now almost fifteen years old, it still holds true. Not two months ago I took a call from a senior HR official of a well-known multinational company. After he explained his reason for calling, I asked him what revenues were in his company the past year. He didn't know, and he also didn't know if the company was profitable or not. Business issues such as revenue, competition, profitability, and market share are all part of the daily life of the line manager. If your company has a 50-percent market share versus a 10-percent market share, this profoundly affects every decision made in the company. The conclusion is obvious: If we want to be effective communicators in business, we have to build rapport with our audiences. The most direct way to do that is by identifying with their values and using their language to communicate with them.

GEM #2   *You must understand the business if you expect to add value.*

Selling Your Staff

The first time you introduce the idea of developing a performance measurement system to your staff, you will probably be greeted with a mixture of reactions ranging from apathy to rebellion. The first objection is usually, "I don't need anything else to do. I am already overworked and underpaid." The next is, "What are you going to do with the data? Will it be used to compare one person to another so you can fire the poorest performer?" That comment is followed by, "I don't see any value in doing it," "I don't think it can be done," and finally, "What's in it for me?"

All of these are reasonable reactions. They reflect the fact that this is a new concept for many HR workers. People are fearful of change unless they see a good reason for it. The introduction of a measurement system is such a radical departure from the norm that it is bound to create fear, suspicion, and opposition. It is nothing to be concerned about, since there are very plausible answers to these objections.

The staff has to be convinced on four points: first, that there is a valid business reason for doing it; second, that it can be done; third, that it won't mean a lot of extra work; and last, that there is definitely something in it for them. We will discuss these points one at a time.

Number one: There is a valid reason for doing it. This department is part of a business organization, whether you are a profit or a not-for-profit corporation. HR is not so unique that it can be run under its own separate philosophy, with a somewhat introverted set of objectives and a method of management that does not fit in with the larger organization, which it supposedly serves. HR is part of an organization and derives its support from it. We operate according to the organization's philosophy and serve its objectives. We use its compensation system and its review and discipline policies. Like most staff departments, our work infiltrates the whole organization, and that body in turn absorbs us and sustains us. It is truly a symbiotic relationship. Therefore, since the larger organization runs quantitative methods, in order to be in sync with it we need to adopt its methodology for interfacing and reporting results.

The second objection is the belief that performance cannot be measured. The next chapter will provide an in-depth treatment of the manner in which the total HR function can be broken down into manageable and measurable pieces. A review of the preceding discussion of the myth of subjectivity may also be helpful in formulating an answer. The point is that it is already being done in small and large departments in other organizations. There are some techniques to be learned, but a measurement system is much less complicated than a salary structure or a recruitment program. Once in place, it does not need constant updating to remain competitive or to cope with short-term changes in the job market.

The third objection is difficult to disprove until the system is actually in place. At first glance, it does look like a lot of extra work. Data must be collected from who knows where, a collection method must be designed, and a reporting format must be created. And that is only the beginning. Once it's all ready to go, some poor fool is going to have to make it happen. All of this is true, but like any task there is an easy way and a hard way to do it.

The critical element of a measurement system is the collection of data. Once you have the data, the reporting system is relatively simple. The secret to easy data collection is to make it part of the job that generates it. That is, workers are responsible for the development of their own raw data. If your system is automated, the computer may do the job for you. If you are manually collecting the data, workers simply maintain a log of the activities you want to measure. You may design standard logs, or you may let them create and maintain their own. It doesn't matter, so long as the data is complete, accurate, and turned in on time.

However, some people will say that logs get in the way and slow down the work. With practice, that need not be the case. When an activity such as an interview, a counseling session, a training class, a new-hire record, an agency invoice approval, or a termination is completed, it takes only seconds to record that in a properly designed log. At the end of a reporting period—say, a month—employees total their data and forward it to someone who fills in a master report form. For six years I managed a HR department that ran a system that measured 30 to 40 activities. Most of our data was collected and recorded manually. We calculated that it took less than 5 percent of our total work time to maintain the system. That was not 5 percent of work time *added* to the day, it was part of doing the job and therefore soon became invisible. Every group, no matter how busy it is, has more than 5 percent wasted time lying around. The value of having the data far outweighs the labor. Every consulting firm requires that the professional staff maintain logs of their time applied to different jobs. If those people can do it, why can't yours?

This leaves us with the final question, "What is in it for me?" People have a right to know what the payoff will be for them. They will be the ones who will do most of the work. Fortunately, there are several rewards for those who make the system work. As you read through the book, look for payoffs from measurement. Discuss them with your staff. When you reach Section F, "The Payoffs," see if you have found as many as I list there. I'll bet you will have found many more.

The Semantics of Measurement

Before we go any further, it might be prudent to define some terms and discuss some fundamental issues of measurement. The objective will be to foster clarity and to avoid semantic debates. Humpty Dumpty pointed out to Alice the ambiguous nature of words. "When I use a word," Humpty said, "it means just what I choose it to mean— nothing more nor less." Words are by their nature only neutral symbols. People give them meaning, sometimes in a rather haphazard fashion. This practice is particularly true in the case of the words *efficient*, *productive*, and *effective*. In everyday conversation these terms are often used interchangeably, and even the dictionary definitions are similar. However, the terms connote slightly different outcomes.

Efficient vs. Productive vs. Effective

Productive is defined as "producing readily or abundantly." Synonyms for productive are *profitable*, *fertile*, and *fruitful*. The definition of *efficient* is "competent or adequate in performance or operation," which is similar to productive but implies something less potent. *Capable* and *causative* are synonyms for *efficient*. So, while both *productive* and *efficient* are positive terms, *productive* implies something beyond mere competence. The third word, *effective*, takes the notion of productivity and adds a notion of expectation or desirability. It is, as Peter Drucker puts it, "doing the right thing."[2] Another definition of *effectiveness* is, "having the desired effect or producing the expected result." With this as a foundation, we will use *efficient* to mean simply an acceptable level of throughput or performance. *Productive* means efficiency directed at activities that have real value. An example might be a case where a person performs a task very quickly and neatly and is therefore efficient. However, the task is one that adds nothing to the output of the department and cannot be described as a productive act. Drucker's definition of *effectiveness* as "producing the right thing in an efficient manner," will serve our purpose.

Direct and Indirect

Two other words will be used to describe different types of measures: *direct* and *indirect*. A *direct measure* is one that refers to cost. It could be the cost of hiring, the cost of a benefit plan, or the cost of a training program. An *indirect measure* is one that does not deal with cost. It could be a measure of time, quantity, or quality. In many cases indirect measures can be converted to direct measures through the introduction of a simple conversion variable. An example would be converting the indirect measure of the time it takes to interview into the direct measure of the cost of interviewing. If we know that on average it takes our interviewers 1½ hours to interview a managerial-level job applicant and we know the hourly pay rate of our interviewers, it is a simple matter to multiply that pay rate by 1½ to obtain the cost of the interview. This is a very simplistic example. Obviously, other costs are involved in an interview. Depending on how precise you want to be, you can add in overhead and benefit costs, or any other cost item that is appropriate, to obtain the total cost of the interview. The point is that knowing indirect performance data has a value in and of itself. It usually supplies part of the data needed to develop a direct measure.

Whole and Partial

A subset of both direct and indirect measures is the difference between whole and partial measures. In this case, the terms are self-descriptive. *Whole measures* describe the total issue. For example, the cost per hire, which includes every expense item, would be a whole measure. However, if you just want to calculate the cost per hire using a particular source, such as agencies, you would be working toward a *partial measure* of hiring costs. In that case you would probably take all other costs as givens and would want to know only how much agency fees amounted to per hire.

Whole measures are informative on a broad basis. If you want to learn where you are spending most of your time or money you will dissect the whole measure into two or more categories or parts. By breaking down total cost by source, department, job level, race, sex, occupation, or other categories, you can find out where the problems lie or where the opportunities for improvements are.

Precision Levels

Anytime the subject of measuring HR work comes up, it is interesting to listen to the wide range of perceptions held by our colleagues. Some show no concern for the complexity of the task and seem willing to jump into the middle of it without a moment's pause. Others fret over a multitude of minor, solvable issues, apparently looking for reasons why they cannot or should not attempt it.

In the latter cases, invariably someone brings up the point of accuracy or precision. Their point usually is that it is difficult, if not impossible, to accurately measure HR activities. They point out their lack of control over factors such as inflation and labor market conditions. They are right, but similar conditions prevail throughout the organization. The marketing department does not have control over the product or the customer, and the finance department does not control the cost of money. Yet both of them are able to quantitatively evaluate much of their work. Everyone knows that certain factors are not controllable. In fact, if we are willing to admit it, there are probably more issues out of control than in control within any organization. The task of management is to reduce the uncontrolled and install as much order as possible.

Management does not require accuracy at the .05 level of statistical significance. In research, precision is obviously critical. In pharmaceuticals or medicine, extreme care must be taken with procedures and measurement. Results are often required to be statistically valid beyond the .001 level. That is measurement with a capital M, but it is not what is required in operational measurement. We are not in a laboratory, we are operating in the field, with all the problems inherent in field research and experimentation. Accuracy is necessary, but precision is naturally limited by internal and external conditions. Even though we can't control the variables in the environment, we can still come up with usable numbers.

It is not necessary to introduce heavy statistics to play the numbers game. Performance measurement of the type we are advocating can be handled with the four basic arithmetic functions. Knowledge of statistical procedures is helpful for designing a measurement system that will have the most validity possible. Nevertheless, an acceptable job can be done by someone who simply has experience in the function, common sense, and the ability to add, subtract, multiply, and divide.

On one occasion a professor from a midwestern university complained that my method, although effective, was too simple. My reply was, "If you think these formulas are too simple a way to express the conditions they observe, how would you evaluate $E = mc^2$?" He replied, "I don't know anything about chemistry." I don't make up these stories. The woods are full of fools, and I just happen to meet a lot of them.

Any object, issue, act, process, or activity that can be described by observable variables is subject to measurement. The phenomenon can be evaluated in terms of cost, time, quantity, or quality. (The methods for accomplishing this will be described in Chapter 4.) The only real issue in applying measurement to the HR function is: What is worth measuring? Management will accept progress over perfection.

> **GEM #3**   *Measurement of operating results cannot and need not be as precise as laboratory research.*

Reporting

Most people who go through the effort of collecting data and measuring their activities want to report their accomplishments to management. Report design is an art form that is not fully appreciated. Many people believe that it is simply a matter of arranging data on paper or a film medium and presenting it to some audience. These people seldom have much success in moving their audience in any desired direction.

Reports have two purposes: They both inform and persuade. Whether or not they achieve either purpose depends on the skill of the reporter as much as on the data presented. Reports should tell your story and simultaneously convince your audience that you are a professional manager who is in control of your function. For this to happen, your audience will have to take the time to read or view your report. To grab and hold their attention you have to speak to them in forms that they comprehend and appreciate. Chapter 4 will cover reports in greater depth.

Remember, you can do a great job, but if you cannot tell your story effectively you will never get credit for your accomplishments.

Summary

Success is won by performance. Performance is more than activity. Each and every activity must be turned toward adding value. Most of those values must be measurable. In order to be able to measure, one must learn to handle simple arithmetic data. Business runs on numbers, not on feelings.

Many people are afraid of numbers. They will use every excuse they can find to avoid having to deal numerically. Unfortunately for them, there is no escape. It's almost a case of "Count or die!" Beyond the numbers themselves people fear how the data will be used...to hurt them, maybe. The irony is that numbers can be used very effectively to demonstrate just how well they are doing.

Although accuracy is imperative, precision is not. A business enterprise operates in an uncontrollable environment. There is no way that anyone can prove his or her worth. Even salespeople who make sales cannot prove that it was their sales capabilities alone that won the orders. Statistical proof is not the point. Management just wants to know two things: Are we moving in the right direction, and how do we compare to our competition?

3
The New Look in Human Resources

Human Resources as a Value Management System

The notion of quantitative evaluation of the human resources function is still such a radical change for many people that it is almost like starting over. It requires not only a new way of doing the job, but a new way of thinking about it. Many people join the human resources function because they like to work with people as opposed to things or numbers. There is so much more to human resources in today's organizational life.

An idea that has been very useful in helping us grasp the complexity of large, modern organizations is *systems theory*. You don't hear much about systems theory any more. That's because it is now accepted as a truism. A simple definition of a *system* is "an assemblage of parts put together in a somewhat orderly fashion to form a complex whole." Each system is usually composed of smaller systems, called *subsystems*, and is also part of a larger system. Systems thinking is not a twentieth-century concept. Nor is it the by-product of modern scientific technology. John Donne pointed it out over 350 years ago when he said,

No man is an island, entire of itself; every man is a piece of the continent, a part of the main.[1]

In their simplest form, systems take something from the environment, called an input, and change it through a process. Then they release the changed item back into the environment as an output that, it is hoped, has greater value than the inputs. The emphasis is on the word *value*. More complex systems have established goals or objectives toward which they process the input, plus a feedback mechanism to keep them on track. Complex systems not only receive inputs and make outputs to the external world, they also exchange inputs and outputs among internal subsystems. That is, the outputs of one sub-system become the inputs of another. There is an inherent interrelationship and interdependency between the parts of any large system. This is perhaps the most critical fact that human resources staffs have to learn if they are to survive and prosper.

The HR department is inherently a value-adding system, even though some people do run it that way. Its primary subsystems are staffing, planning, employee and labor relations, compensation and benefits, HRIS, training and development. Even casual consideration of the HR department in action shows that there is constant, necessary interaction among the subsystems. For example, inputs to staffing in the form of applicants are processed and output to the external organization as new hires, as well as to the HR department as input to the records. Later those new hires will be input to the orientation and compensation functions. Still later they will be picked up by training and perhaps employee relations. Each time employees are touched by one function within the HR department, they are transformed somewhat. Those transformed individuals then become input to another function. Therefore, the quality of work in one section affects the process for the next section in the system.

Feudal Management

Human resources work is often practiced in a fragmented fashion. Staffing groups focus on the job of providing qualified new hires. Compensation strives to maintain equity in pay and benefits for all employees. Training exposes people to new knowledge and skills. Each group seems oblivious to the work of the others. There is seldom any evidence of collective activities. This is not only inefficient for optimum organizational performance, it is often a sign of a much more dangerous illness in the departmental organism.

In order to establish and maintain a healthy, high-performing HR department, the function must be operated as a mutually supportive system. The department cannot ignore the intrinsic interrelationships among its parts and cannot be effective on a fragmented basis. Human resources is one department, one unit, inextricably bound together. Success and failure are collective, not individual, phenomena.

A Vision for HR

During the early part of the go-go 1980s it seemed we had found the secret to sustained prosperity. America frolicked in one of the longest-running periods of economic growth. Then, all of a sudden, the facade began to wear thin and we saw the first signs of a new wave. By the time 1990 arrived, we had already begun what now seems like an unending time of economic uncertainty. This flip-flop from expansion to contraction and stagnation has driven organizations to reassess what they are about.

The latest strategic game is the development and articulation of a new "vision" for the enterprise. John Rock of the Oldsmobile division of GM noted wryly:

> A bunch of guys take off their ties and coats, go into a motel room for three days, and put a bunch of friggin' words on a piece of paper—and then go back to business as usual.*

The truth of that notwithstanding, many companies are putting out vision statements. Slogans such as Motorola's "Total Customer Satisfaction" and Chevron's "The Best in the Business" are meant to communicate the dedication of management to employees and customers. HR departments also are coming out with their vision statements in an attempt to refocus their staffs in new directions that add more value. For many in HR this is a novel idea, yet it has been going on in some HR groups for over a decade. We used to call it a management philosophy. Whatever we call it, a vision is the essential foundation from which any function takes its direction.

It is much more effective for an organization to take the time to formulate and disseminate a vision than it is for the employee to have to search for and perhaps misperceive an organizational belief system. If an organizational vision already exists, it is easy to draw up an appropriate departmental statement. If it is not apparent, the task is still not too difficult. The type of thinking that forms the basis for an HR department's vision is as follows:

1. Human resources exists in an organization because it adds tangible value by providing necessary services at a competitive cost.

2. Human resources' mission is to enhance the productivity and effectiveness of the organization from the people side.

*Fortune, May 16, 1994, page 18.

3. Human resources should drive the organization's management in regard to people issues.

4. Human resources is a professional function, staffed by people dedicated to the development of employees in ways that are satisfying to the individual and beneficial to the organization.

Today's vision statements are usually short and very focused on the organization's goals. Typical examples are:

- Be a business partner.
- Help management build an environment of success.
- Facilitate positive change.
- Add value.

Position Messages

These visions of HR's raison d'être are typically followed by a message aimed at HR's customers. The message deals with values and traits that HR pledges to exemplify in its dealings with customers. In effect, they describe the types of behaviors that customers can count on. Words like *professional, competent, flexible, responsive, strategic,* and *caring* are used to convey HR's style of operation.

The exercise of establishing a departmental vision has been very useful in unifying HR departments that were operating in a feudal mode. One of the characteristics found in the best HR departments is the formal recognition of interdependence.[2] The best meet on a regular basis to share their plans and look for potential conflicts as well as synergy. If the process of visioning and valuing is carried out in a participative manner, the staff feels a sense of ownership and commitment to the product. Everyone is clear about what is appropriate. If they choose not to subscribe to the vision, they are free to look for an organization that is more compatible with their style. As a result, whether people buy it or not, the most fundamental principles of operation have been promulgated and no one can claim not to know what their purpose is.

Service, Support, or Partner?

The issue of positioning, or repositioning, HR is a question of self-perception. In order for a new way of thinking and acting to become institutionalized, it must be consistent with the individual's view of self. For many years the human resources department has been viewed as a service function. Service can be defined as "performing labor for the benefit of others." The inferior attitude implied in this definition seems to have infected many people, both in management and in the HR department. People who have an inferiority complex communicate it verbally and nonverbally to those around them.

I suggest we drop the words *service* and *support* as descriptors for the HR department and instead use the term *partner*. *Partner* implies two or more people who view themselves as equals pursuing a common goal. This is a more appropriate and efficient way to operate in these highly competitive times. The question is, "Is management willing to accept HR as a partner?"

A number of studies have shown that the HR department and management do not see eye to eye on what the HR department's role is, should be, or could be. The door is open to HR, but many don't know how to get through it. A study by Wm. Schiemann & Associates and *Quality* magazine[3] reported that 60 percent of more than 800 executives claimed that inferior internal service adversely affects their ability to compete effectively. Only 24 percent gave HR a favorable rating. Among those rating their internal services unfavorably, the following were cited as problems: lack of leadership, inappropriate organizational culture, lack of perceived need for improvement, and ineffective organizational structures. When asked for effective practices they cited measuring operations, productivity, and delivery system efficiency as the most important practices. The next two success practices were measuring structures, roles, and jobs, and measuring employee capabilities. The authors of the study, Mary Azzolini and John Lingle, suggest six steps staff executives should take to improve internal customer service:

1. Develop an improvement plan that integrates ongoing initiatives and business strategy.

2. Assess customers, staff, and suppliers to pinpoint gaps in service performance.

3. Align work processes, structure, systems, culture, and capabilities with business strategy and customer expectations.

4. Secure commitment, and clearly define roles and responsibilities.

5. Provide continuous performance improvement through communication.

6. Establish ongoing measures for tracking and monitoring service performance.

A University of Michigan study[4] asked senior managers what they viewed to be the key skills for HR in the 1990s. The responses showed that management wants HR to be more involved, provided they acquire certain business management and change management capabilities. On the business side management wants to see HR gain competence in technical, strategic, and financial areas. To play a role as change managers, it was recommended that HR learn how to diagnose situations, analyze data, and influence. Clearly, the exercise of those skills would bring HR into partnership with its customers.

The key difference between support and partnership is found in the question asked of the customer. The support person asks, "What (which) services do you want from us?" The partner asks, "What is happening with you?" The focus shifts from products to objectives. In the first case the customer does not often know which professional service is most needed. In the second case both parties are putting their minds to solving problems and attaining goals.

HR is at a crossroads. On one side there are very definite trends toward downsizing, outsourcing, and even eliminating the HR department as we've known it. I know several cases where the department has been reduced by 90 percent and the function delegated to line management. As the word gets around that management can run an organization without a defined HR department, many CEOs will follow the trend.

On the other side, CEOs are looking for strong, talented, pragmatic people to build a value-adding people-management function. Management won't accept a function dominated by paper pushers and huggers. They want someone on the management team who can show them how to leverage people.

GEM #4   *Successful people build partnerships.*

Management Experts on Performance Measurement

There is ample support for performance measurement in the management literature. Peter Drucker, perhaps the top management philosopher of our times, speaks about the issue of measurement in several of his writings. He makes two basic assertions. First, he states that few factors are as important to the performance of the organization as measurement. Second, he laments the fact that measurement is the weakest area in management today. The late W. Edwards Deming, a pioneer in statistical methods for quality control, pointed out that in

Japan great emphasis is placed on statistics for business managers. It was partly the application of the statistical techniques taught by Deming that turned postwar Japan from a manufacturer of cheap imitations to a worldwide leader in quality products. Tom Peters, the currently popular management maven, has said in a dozen ways that objective data is necessary to manage a function. Practically every management book author has lamented that measurement is critical to success and that most American managers don't have adequate quantitative skills. The following are a few of the claims made regarding measurement.

You can't manage what you don't measure. —Peter Drucker

Measurements are key. If you cannot measure it, you cannot control it. If you cannot control it, you cannot manage it. If you cannot manage it, you cannot improve it. —James Harrington in *Business Process Improvement*.

If you don't measure it, you're just practicing. —Robert Galvin, former CEO of Motorola.

If you don't measure it, people will know you're not serious about delivering it. —James Belasco in *Teaching the Elephant to Dance*.

I could fill a chapter with quotes supporting performance measurement. There is no question that it is justified and required of all people who choose to have an effect on their organizations. The only questions are how to do it and do it well, and what effect doing it well can have on your staff.

In the face of this overwhelming evidence, some people persist in the notion that they can survive without performance measurement. They blame the rest of the people in the organization—their customers—for not understanding that their function is somehow different from all the other organizational entities, who depend on quantitative analysis. Dr. Deming died a very frustrated and angry man because of people just like this, who would not accept the need for fundamental reassessment of the need to change.

The Bottom Line

Measurement has a central role to play in your system as the Schiemann/Quality study showed. It does more than simply evaluate performance. A measurement system provides a frame of reference that helps management carry out several important responsibilities.

1. *Focuses the Staff on Important Issues.* Organizations are complex, intense places. Many forces compete for attention and energy. If a measurement program is designed as a management decision tool, it will differentiate tasks for the staff according to higher and lesser priorities. If cost reduction is a major issue in an employment group, data helps recruiters decide how to source applicants. For trainers, it tells them the return on investment of a training program. Fundamentally, the staff learns that cost, time, quality, quantity, and human reactions are trade-offs around which decisions and actions take place.

2. *Clarifies Expectations.* A measurement system is neither inert nor reactive—it is directive and clarifying. Once objectives are set for cost, time, quality, quantity, and customer satisfaction, the staff understands what is expected of them. Standards of performance and acceptable levels of deviation from those standards are known. If objectives are set to reduce hire costs, third-step grievances, and training time, or to increase record-processing efficiency and turnaround time on application forwarding, the staff knows what is acceptable performance.

3. *Involves, Motivates, and Fosters Creativity.* In my experience, once a measurement system is in place, the staff begins to compete to meet or exceed the objectives. When the system is fully functioning, people bring forth new and important issues that can be measured, along with ingenious ways of doing it.

Since the human resources staff occupies slots at different levels from management, their view is correspondingly different. Therefore, they find items that can or should be handled, which the director of human resources might never see. All employees enjoy bringing something to the boss that has not been thought of before, so long as they are recognized for it. Once measurement objectives are promulgated, people naturally focus on the issues therein and as a result often find something truly valuable that has been overlooked.

4. *Brings Human Resources Closer to Line Departments.* One of the most consistent complaints of line management is that the human resources staff does not seem to be interested in the important issues of the organization, namely return on investment (ROI).

One of the criticisms most heard in a Saratoga two-year study of HR customers was, "HR doesn't understand the business." Obviously, HRM systems should include factors that relate to organizational quality, productivity, services, and profitability. Tracking and reporting hiring costs can be useful, but connecting a new hiring strategy to an improvement in operational quality, productivity, and service is much more compelling.

Summary

Human resources is a system within a system. Everything that happens within HR, to one extent or another, affects the larger system. Even if HR *seems to* have no positive effect—that, in itself, is an effect. However, HR does have an effect on the organization through the service it provides its customers within the organization.

In order to function at an optimal level, HR needs a vision of what it is about. The vision unifies the staff and provides a foundation on which to make future decisions. Knowing what you are about is one thing. You still have to communicate it to your customers. We call that *positioning*. Every supplier or vendor occupies a position within the mind of its customers—whether or not either party realizes it. HR needs to position itself as a value-adding partner rather than as a servant. This is a much more efficient and useful position to occupy for both parties.

You can't just declare yourself to be a partner. You have to earn partnership by acquiring the skills necessary, and by demonstrating to the customer partner that you truly have something of value for them. When you start to operate that way you build visible links between your work and the bottom line of the company. How to show that is the subject of the rest of this book.

4

Designing Your Measurement System

The National Standards

In mid-1984 Saratoga Institute (SI) assembled 15 human resources professionals under the sponsorship of the then American Society for Personnel Administration (ASPA, now Society for Human Resource Management [SHRM]) for the purpose of developing the first set of formulas to measure the work of HR functions. The purpose was to establish standard ways of talking about our work. I had been advocating this since 1980 without support. Finally, with ASPA's help we put together a set of approximately thirty measures. Over the years there have been minor changes and some additions. These measures are the human asset management benchmarks that form the basis of the annual SHRM/SI Human Resources Effectiveness Report (HRER). The formulas as of 1994 are as follows (all employee figures are in full-time equivalents):

Revenue per employee	HR department expense as a percentage of company expense
Expense per employee	HR headcount ratio—HR employees : company employees
Compensation as a percentage of revenue	HR department expense per company employee
Compensation as a percentage of expense	Supervisory compensation percentage
Benefit cost as a percentage of revenue	Workers' compensation cost as a percentage of expense

Benefit cost as a percentage of expense	Workers' compensation cost per employee
Benefit cost as a percentage of compensation	Workers' compensation cost per claim
Retiree benefit cost per retiree	Absence rate*
Retiree benefit cost as a percentage of expense	Involuntary separation*
Hires as a percentage of total employees*	Voluntary separation*
Cost of hire*	Voluntary separation by length of service*
Time to fill jobs*	Ratio of offers made to acceptances*
Time to start jobs*	

These data are sorted and reported by industry, size of company, region and growth rate. In 1994, data was obtained from approximately 500 companies. Now in its ninth year, this report constitutes the national standard report on human asset management.

The Most Important Measure

In the course of this book I will describe in detail over fifty ways to measure cost, time, quantity, quality, and human reactions. Important as these are, the most important measure is none of them. Every business depends on its customers for survival. Peter Drucker hit the nail on the head when he pointed out that the purpose of a business is determined, not by the producer, but by the customer, through the needs that the customer satisfies when purchasing the business's products or services.

That truism applies to staff functions as well. Staff departments are businesses within a market, namely the organization that the staff serves. When your internal department customer is dissatisfied with your service, you have a problem. Today, many staff services are being outsourced because management believes it is a better way to provide the service. If you want to keep your customers, you need to know not only what they truly want from you, but how satisfied they are with your services and products and what you can do to increase their level of satisfaction.

---

* Reported as exempt, nonexempt, and total

Measuring Customer Satisfaction

From 1985 to 1990 a research project was carried out for the purpose of learning about customer satisfaction as it related to services.[1] The researchers at Duke and Texas A&M studied several service industries—including banks, credit card companies, brokerage firms, and repair businesses. Five factors were uncovered that accounted for customer satisfaction. The factors, in descending order of importance, were:

Reliability—dependable and accurate performance

Responsiveness—willingness to help and provide prompt service

Assurance—skills and knowledge displayed that generate trust and confidence within the customer

Empathy—caring, individual attention

Tangibles—appearance of facilities and staff, and appearance and usefulness of the published materials

At Saratoga Institute we have applied these factors to internal customer satisfaction for human resources' customers. In addition to asking for satisfaction levels, we also asked how important each factor was. We constructed a 20-item survey (four questions per factor) and provided scales to respond to both satisfaction and importance. Then we added another section, which dealt with specific HR products, and incorporated in the instrument a third general comments area. The survey has been administered to several thousand supervisors and managers. Essentially, we confirmed Zeithaml's findings with minor variations.

One of the more interesting variations we found is that in many cases assurance is becoming the second most important factor. This is a positive sign, since it indicates that HR's customers are looking for professional advice from the HR staff. Apparently, supervisors and managers view HR somewhat as they do legal and financial professionals. In short, your customers depend on the quality of your advice to keep them out of trouble and to know the best way to handle people matters. This view is a welcome change from the "necessary evil" image that personnel used to carry.

Another surprising development was the emergence of a sixth factor. Comments suggest that your customers now want HR to anticipate their needs. Given a very uncertain marketplace, people want their vendors to do more than simply respond. They want the vendor, in this case HR, to look ahead to changes in job skill availability, costs, time frames, and other human-asset-related items. We believe that this need has emerged because the issue of customer service is so prevalent today. People have heard so much about customer service that their expectations have increased. Now customers want more than they did in the past. In terms of relative importance, anticipation usually ranks about fourth or fifth among the six factors.

The Value Chain

A decade ago I described the subjectivity myth, which claimed you cannot measure HR's work. Fortunately, that myth has disappeared from the minds of most HR staffs. Although many still don't know how to objectively measure HR, most people are at least open to the possibility. Over the past decade I have experimented with various ways to simplify the measurement process. Now, instead of laboring through some complex method, I have reduced the process to the examination of just four points. These points are the linked components of the value chain. They are:

process -> outcome -> impact -> value added

All processes are entered into for the purpose of adding value. Any other purpose would be wasteful. Our objective is to develop ways to measure and evaluate changes in processes, outcomes and their resulting value. An example of processes and outcomes in the various HR functions are shown in Figure 4.1.

For every improvement in a *process* there should be a better result. We call the result an *outcome*. The difference between this outcome and the outcomes before the process improvement is the *impact*. The dollar improvement represented by the impact is the *value added*. An example would be to change the sourcing method in hiring (process), which shortens the time to fill jobs (outcome). As jobs are filled faster, there is less need to use temporary or contract workers. The cost avoidance can be calculated and a dollar savings computed. If through HR's efforts jobs are filled faster, not only does the company save the operating expense just described, the cost of the product or service is lowered and it is gotten to market faster. Lower product cost and shorter delivery time creates a competitive advantage in the marketplace, thereby increasing your company's market share. That is the tangible

Function	Processes	Outcomes
Staffing	Interviewing Job offers	Hires Acceptances/rejections
Compensation	Job evaluation Salary processing	Number of positions graded Time to process
Benefits	Claims processing	Process cost Number processed Error rate
Employee Relations	Employee counseling	Number counseled Time spent counseling Problems solved
Labor Relations	Grievance processing Contracts negotiated	Number resolved Wages rates in new contract
Training	Program design Program delivery	Cost of training Hours of training provided
Organization	Problem solving	Time to solve
Development	Team building	Efficiency levels

Figure 4.1. Sample Human Resource Processes and Outcomes

value added to the organization as a result of an improvement in an HR process.

Results Orientation

The definition of a manager is one who gets things done through working with people. The focus is working with people to get *results*. Many people in staff jobs fall in love with their process. A description of their work might be something like, "hires, pays, and trains people." I know a company that dissolved its HR function because there was a lot of movement but no visible value added. Their focus was on activity. I want to fix your attention on results.

As you read through the following sections you will study many activities, tasks, and processes. You want to view them, not for themselves, but for their instrumental value. That is, how to improve them so that you will achieve positive results in terms of cost, time, quantity, quality, or human values. One way to keep focused on results is to do a functional analysis on each of the major HR department functions. Figure 4.2 is a partial example of a functional analysis of staffing, one of the many HR activities.

There are many tasks and processes in acquiring a new hire. You will measure some of them to the degree that they can tell you how efficient your staff is, but the variable that ultimately makes or breaks you is results or outcomes.

Function	Staffing		
Activities	General recruitment	College recruitment	Transfers
Tasks/Processes	Write and place ads	Contact placement offices	Post jobs
	Contact agencies	Schedule campus interviews	Screen
	Promote employee referrals	Interview on campus	Counsel
	Schedule interviews	Invite to visit company	Interviews
	Interview	Etc.	Etc.
	Refer		
	Reject		
	Make offers		
		Impact on production and profits	
Results	Hires	Hires	Placements Counselings

Figure 4.2. Function Analysis—the Staffing Function

- What did it cost?
- How much time did it take?
- How many hires did you accomplish?
- What was the quality of the hires?
- How did it impact organizational profitability?
- How do these hires compare to previous periods?

These are the things you need to pay attention to. When you can prove that you achieved positive results in key areas, you will have established yourself as a valued member of the management team.

Reporting More Than Just Data

I will conclude this section with a few points about reports. The issue is communication and persuasion. You can do a marvelous job, but if you cannot communicate your many worthwhile achievements, no one will ever know what you have done. If you want recognition for your results, it is almost as important to be an effective report writer as it is to be an effective manager.

Report generation is often approached as though it were either a weak piece of fiction or a textbook. In the first case, there are a lot of unsubstantiated statements, loosely connected, leading to a conclusion that is all too apparent. In the latter instance, there is a massive dump of information, seemingly with no form or direction, that challenges the reader to find something—anything—of value in it.

Every report has a purpose and an audience. If both of those are not clearly defined before the data is assembled and the format chosen, the chances for a meaningful document are lessened. Reports are not sterile descriptions of inorganic chemistry. They describe, or should describe, the results of often large numbers of human beings who are expending resources to achieve predetermined objectives. As such, they deserve a spark of life and a hint of personality. They should be interesting as well as informative. Dull reports bore readers; and what's worse, they don't get read.

A report cannot be a neutral document. It must say something that causes the reader to make a decision. Even basic monthly reports of operation cause the reader to do something because a problem is evident, or to do nothing because all seems well. Project and investigative reports usually evoke more action than conditional reports. Whatever the type, the report writer should keep in mind that a report must have a specific, value-adding purpose.

The purpose of a business communication is to inform and persuade. If a report is primarily informational it displays the following characteristics: clarity, conciseness, accuracy, and appropriateness. Whether you are using words or graphics, remember that this is not meant to be a mystery story. Ask someone who is not involved in the process being reported to read the report for clarity. If they, who know nothing about the topic, can understand what you are trying to say, the chances are good that your reader will understand also. If you use some type of chart or graph, remember that graphic formats have special attributes and certain limitations. Keep the graphs simple and uncluttered. Do not try to report too much on them. Use charts for illustration, and use words for explanation. Be concise. Most business people are busy. They want to get the information quickly and go on with their work. Get to the point, make it, and get out. Above all, be accurate. Sloppy, careless, or just plain wrong data will destroy your credibility. If you are not good with numbers, have someone who is check your work before you publish it. Those who disagree with you will be looking for a bad number. If they find one, you can bet everyone will know about it. Finally, be relevant. Report what people want to know about, what you want them to know about, and what is important. Hopefully, these will all be the same. It does more harm than good to report something that no one cares to know. All it does is clog your report, make it harder to follow, and add to the fatigue of the reader.

Your report is intended to do more than inform. It is your chance to persuade. If you want to sell your idea, you must understand the buyers. Are they interested in the topic? How do they generally feel about it? Is it enough for them to merely agree with you or do you want them to act on it? Persuasive efforts always proceed from a central idea that the audience can comprehend. Points are made in a logical, cause-and-effect sequence, which leads the reader along in an orderly manner from the central idea toward the desired conclusion. To show cause-and-effect relationships, it is usually necessary to have demonstrable, supporting evidence. This is where the power of numbers is so strong. The argument should proceed to the point at which the conclusion becomes self-evident. Two surrounding issues that help to shape your persuasive outline are the situation and the audience. Ancient rhetoricians studied only the discourse between the speaker and the audience. However, modern systems theories and holistic psychology have made us appreciate the impact of the environment on the persuasive event. You must consider how activities and events in the general area surrounding your point will influence it. If you are asking management to commit resources to a project, make sure that the financial condition of the organization will permit such an expenditure. If you want your boss to do something, make sure that it is something that top management does not oppose.

Audiences (buyers of your ideas) are diverse. Organizations make the mistake of viewing their employees as a monolith. That is, they tend to communicate with their people as though there were only one personality for the whole group, yet every individual has a different combination of interests, values, attitudes, and needs. You can communicate effectively if you take this into consideration. The questions are simple and straightforward. Think of them in terms of Interest, Value, Attitude, Need (IVAN).

1. How interested are your readers in the subject?
2. How much value do they place on it?
3. What are their individual attitudes toward it?
4. Do they feel a need for it?

Assuming that your readers are interested enough to read the report, what format do they relate to best? Some people like a lot of detail. They want to see tables of numbers, sometimes out to two decimal places. Other readers prefer the big picture. They will accept bar charts or trend lines, which are not so specific but give a quick impression of the situation. There is no way to persuade a big-picture person to plow through tables of numbers. Likewise, the accountant type feels insecure with only a slashing line across a graph. If you want people to read, comprehend, and react favorably to your recommendations, you must do the courtesy of providing them with the data in the form they prefer.

GEM #5   *Reports are your opportunity to sell your point of view.*

Summary

Measurement starts with the conviction that you can and should evaluate your work in both qualitative and quantitative terms. Without some type of objective review, it is very difficult to improve performance. For the past nine years a national report has been published that constitutes the standard measures for the HR profession. Beyond that the most important measure is what the customer says about your work. For you to be successful, your customers must be satisfied.

Management wants to know how you are performing. In order to impress the top executives, you have to use terms that they understand and appreciate. This means numbers describing costs per unit of service, cycle times of various processes, quantity or volume of work completed with a given level of resources, the quality of the result, and the level of satisfaction of your customers. In order for management to know that you are doing something more than raising a lot of dust, you will want to show value added. After all, that is what management pays for: value added. By following the logic of the value chain, you can find the potential and actual value of nearly everything you do.

The last factor in the success formula is communication. You can do great work—I'm certain you *are* doing great work—but if no one knows it, you will be devalued within the organization. You can overcome this potential problem by structuring your reports so that your audience will understand and appreciate what you have contributed. Keep in mind that reports are meant to persuade as well as inform. Don't dump ten pounds of activity data on your readers. No one cares how hard you worked. Instead, give them a few examples of results and the value added by those results.

SECTION B

Acquiring the Human Asset: How to Measure Planning and Staffing

5
Acquiring
Human Assets

People are assets. We established that earlier. So, let's look at your work from the standpoint of human asset managers. It is your job to lead the organization in the acquisition, maintenance, development, supervision, and measurement of human assets and the results of their work; namely quality, productivity, service, and sales. The subject of this chapter is acquisition. Just like capital equipment, supplies, and energy, people have to be acquired. You call it hiring. A great deal of the value-adding potential of all functions in your organization depends on how effective are the human assets you help them acquire. Everyone acknowledges that people are the key assets in the new world market. All other assets are nothing more than commodities that can be purchased at market prices. Once purchased and delivered, the others are inert, depreciating assets. Only the human asset has potential to learn, grow, and contribute. This chapter deals with the first step in asset management: acquisition.

The First Input

Planning is the first formal input in the human acquisition process. The planning section's job is to take data from the business plan, the strategic plan, and the marketplace, and put it together in ways that meet certain needs of the organization. Like any other function, planning's role is somewhat predetermined by the style and values of the organization's management. Years ago a computer company president told me there was no need to plan. He said, "We just stay very close to IBM, and whichever way they go we try to follow and leapfrog them occasionally." I suggested to him that if such were the case, he should create a spy unit instead of a planning function.

Planning has several purposes. The more central ones are to prepare data that assists management in making decisions about the future direction of the company. Supplying pertinent information about the future lessens uncertainty and risk. HR planning promotes efficiency and effectiveness in the acquisition of human resources. Although planners use numbers to communicate their story, there is more to the job than just statistics. A forward-looking group might work in the compensation section to audit the job structure of the organization. The reason would be that there is no point in projecting work for jobs that are becoming obsolete, redundant, or inappropriate. This is particularly appropriate today, as team-oriented structures and cultures are emerging. Following that, planning could come up with an algorithm to convert the business plan directly into a staffing plan.

Planners have talents that are usually unique among human resources professionals. In recent years I see more planners coming out of their ivory tower and engaging the organization. A planner can be a catalyst. Grahn[1] described how one planner did just that.

The planner in question converted the sales projection for the upcoming year into the number of invoices to be processed. Then, once she knew how many invoices could be processed per person per day, she showed the order processing manager how many new people would be needed to handle the increased sales. Beyond the discovery of interesting information, she worked out a plan with the manager to increase the productivity of the order-processing function. The result was that the staffing growth curve leveled out in comparison to the sales growth curve.

Another approach to the planning function is to turn the planner into a coordinator. I once gave my planner the task of bringing together people from staffing, training, career development, and organizational development to create a model of effective management. The idea was that once we knew what kinds of skills, abilities, aptitudes, and interests were typical of an effective manager in our company, we would then be better able to recruit, counsel, and develop people according to their best fit in the organization and their maximum personal potential. The planner was excellent at this, for she had a better overview of the organization than did most people and she was more experienced at handling the type of data that was collected.

Linking HR and Business Planning

Practically every issue of HR planning journals has an article about tying the HR plan to the business plan. It is so obvious that it hardly needs stating. The key point is that HR planning normally cannot be traced directly to tangible business outcomes. If you looked at the average HR workforce plan there would be no prima facie evidence that the plan could add value. However, an accurate plan helps management avoid costs, optimize productivity, and beat the competition to market.

The way to do this is to start with the strategic vision and business initiatives of the organization. One corporation had set targets for productivity, quality, and growth that would allegedly help them become more competitive and hence regain market share. The HR plan listed how many of which types of people would be needed if the targets were to be met. However, it did not investigate or suggest that there might be ways to control headcount growth through automation, reengineering work processes, or other means of improving efficiency. It was half a plan.

In my opinion, planners have the tools to make significant contributions beyond planning. The best of them play central roles in business operations. Others simply crank out documents.

Profiling and Projecting

One of the difficulties in trying to measure the work of planners is that their output is primarily a plan of the future. By definition, we will not know for a year or two how accurate their predictions were. In addition, no one is capable of predicting future events, and therefore it is not fair to blame the planner for the unforeseeable. It is impossible to measure the value of a long-term plan in the short term. Planners thus often feel frustrated because they cannot prove their worth with concrete evidence. Those who work from a value-adding perspective don't suffer this deficiency.

Basically, planning does two things. It profiles the current state of the employee population, and it projects future needs or conditions regarding that population. Since it is difficult to measure the effectiveness of projection, it might be better to look to profiling for evaluation purposes.

If the prime output of the planning group is a human resources plan, each year we will be able to measure whether or not the plan was published on time and whether it met any preset conditions and specifications. This is simple, obvious, and not very exciting. However, in order to produce the annual plan, certain data on the employee population must be developed. This data can be used for other projects that have some measurable short-term payoff.

The employees of an organization come in all sizes, ages, sexes, races, levels of education, experience, and performance. Planning can do distribution studies, which correlate different variables. For instance, Fig. 5.1 shows a distribution of employees by age, performance level (high ratings), and turnover. In this hypothetical example it is easy to see that there may be current and future problems. If you trace the profile of performance versus turnover, you find that the high performers are between 25 and 40 years of age, and turnover is highest among that same age group. In fact, from 25 on, those two curves correlate almost perfectly. If you follow the age line, you see that this organization has an aging population. The fact that age and high performance do not correlate at all is one more indicator of a problem. From this simple graph we can find enough work to keep the department and line management busy for some time.

There are many types of demographic studies that a planning section is equipped to handle. It can study sourcing history for the staffing group. It usually has data that the EEO people could use. It can trace turnover and development patterns of identifiable employee groups such as MBAs or other designated groups. It can look at promotion patterns versus hiring patterns at middle management positions. There are few limitations put on planners by others. If planners will get involved in issues, such as those just described, it will be

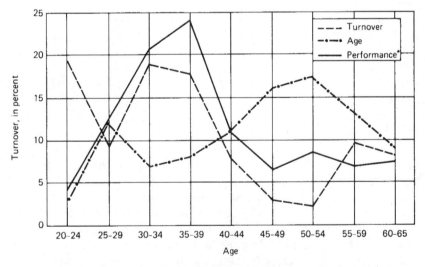

*High performers only: i.e., employees with 5 or 6 ratings on a 6-point scale.

Figure 5.1. Age-Performance-Turnover Relationship

much easier to find ways to measure their productivity and effectiveness. The question is, if you have that piece of information how would you use it to add value?

   GEM #6   *Planning is effective when it adds value.*

The Acquisition Process

Up to now planning usually makes its mark in its work with the staffing group. Planning can be an extremely valuable function. The hiring decision is often taken too lightly; few organizations have stopped to figure out just how costly the decision to hire a new employee actually is.

In the early 1980s the Upjohn Company computed the career cost of an employee to be 160 times the first year's salary.[2] What is startling is that by 1990 Upjohn had recalculated the career cost and found it was 117 times the initial year's salary. This figure assumes a 30-year career. The fact that many employees do not stay with a company 30 years does not lessen the importance of the acquisition decision. Even if the average person spends less than 10 years with one organization, we cannot ignore the importance of the selection process. Motorola believes this so strongly that they consider any turnover to be a quality problem.

Before buying capital equipment it is customary to detail the desired specifications and capabilities. Then a cost-benefit study is conducted to determine whether or not the equipment should be purchased. There are usually several choices to consider, since machines come with a range of speeds, weights, capacities, and options. The task is to select the one machine that is best suited to the operation.

It is the same with people. Each individual job applicant offers a unique combination of education, experience, aptitudes, skills, interests, needs, values, goals, and qualities. The selection process is not simple. Whether to fill a vacancy with an existing employee or to institute an outside search is the first and often one of the most critical decisions.

Internal and External Sources

The employment or staffing process has been thought of as the first step toward finding a replacement for an employee who has recently vacated a job. There are two potential sources of replacement: the outside labor pool and the existing internal work force. Until the past couple of years, this second source was not fully utilized. As we saw in the previous chapter, the replacement process starts with a human resources planning system. When the skills inventory and succession planning subsystems are operating, by definition they are providing candidates for many openings. The need to look outside is diminished, and the internal reservoir of applicants supplies qualified candidates.

In recent years, with massive downsizings, companies have given more attention to promoting from within. It helps to show employees there is hope and is usually less costly, unless relocation is required. Strangely enough, in a 1992 study of hiring costs, the cost of internal placements was higher that of external hires in many cases.[3] It turned out that many of the internal transfers included relocation costs.

In many organizations, the urge to seek candidates from outside the organization is more prevalent for higher-level openings than it is for lower-level ones. This is more often the case in young, fast-growing companies than in older, slow growing firms. Nevertheless, it occurs with enough frequency in both cases to support the generalization. Paradoxically, most organizational structures would suggest the opposite situation. Since they are pyramidal structures, the logic of mathematics tells us that there should be a larger number of employees below each level than there are above it. Hence, some, many, or in ideal cases, all of those below a given opening might be qualified and interested in filling the spot. The HRIS data bank can be sorted to locate available individuals and present those who most closely match the requirements of the position.

In the perfect situation, we would want the system to be operating at a level of efficiency whereby it could provide a fully qualified and interested candidate from the internal work force for each position. As one job is vacated by an employee moving up to fill a higher-level job, the system would provide a qualified candidate for that job. As the second and still lower-level job opened up, the system would yield yet another appropriate candidate. The process would cascade level by level until only entry-level jobs had to be filled from outside. The only exception would be unforeseeable or cataclysmic events. Examples could be an acquisition, which would have to be staffed, or a catastrophe such as a fire or a plane crash, which would take several key people suddenly.

There is one problem with this idyllic process: filling all jobs from within leads to incestuous thinking. There has been a good bit of research into what is labeled "groupthink." Simply described, it is a situation where the individuals who make up a group achieve a state of shared experience and values to the point that they cease to function cognitively as individual minds and begin to accept, without challenging, virtually all ideas put forth by a member of the group. A high level of comfort, security, and certainty develops within the group. The "not-invented-here" syndrome ("If we didn't think of it, it must be worthless.") takes over and blocks any novel ideas not presented by a group member. The amount of stimulus reception drops to a dangerously low level, and the group simply recycles the thoroughly processed ideas of the past. Such a case certainly speeds up decision making, but it completely shuts down the creative process. Recent American industrial history provides several textbook cases of this syndrome.

The railroad barons who fought each other for control of intercontinental traffic in the late 1800s concurrently developed a cadre of likeminded subordinates who carried on their myopic perception of the purpose of railroads. Within twenty years after World War II, as commercial jet aircraft took away passenger traffic, several American railroads went bankrupt. A slightly newer, but nearly as ossified, industry was the automobile business between World War II and the late 1970s. Americans were selecting Volkswagens, and later Nissans and Toyotas, by the hundreds of thousands while Detroit insisted it was only a passing fad. It took twenty years of diminishing market share plus the action of a small group of sheiks to finally convince the Detroit triumvirate that the V-8 was no longer the American dream.

There were similar cases of myopia in banking, mainframe computers, and other industries. The problem developed not due to lack of capital, material, or equipment. It overran them because incestuous value systems would not allow accurate perception of a changing world. The lesson for human resources planning systems is that they need to do more than project numbers. The systems should be designed so they can identify the values, aptitudes, and creative abilities needed in the changing market. The staffing problem of the 1990s is not only a matter of numbers, but more important, a matter of fit. Time frames have shrunk, the impact of decisions has increased, and risk has grown proportionately. Hence, recruitment and selection must become a more scientific process.

Until we reach the point where the human asset planning system can provide for all needs, we will continue to depend on outside sources for applicants. Everyone knows that we can manage our internal resources to meet some of our replacement needs. However, many managers don't make any attempt to manage the outside resources. They simply accept what is apparent in their labor market and turn to it as needed. The problem is compounded when there is no central control over the use of outside media or sources. The message of the company goes out in a confusing and sometimes conflicting manner. Then problems over fees develop, public relations suffers, and budgets are overrun. In short, no one is in charge.

The New Free-for-All Sourcing Strategy

There is a growing trend to source new hires through whatever method is most cost-effective. This includes bypassing the company's internal staffing department in favor of external vendors. Employment departments, along with other staff functions, have been given warning that they now have to compete for business.

Top management is under such pressure to control operating expenses and at the same time improve sales and service that many staff functions have been outsourced. Their work has been given to outside service bureaus and consultants. This trend will not reverse itself in the foreseeable future.

At IBM they have gone so far as to move the staffing function outside and turning into a separate business. Now, Employment Solutions, as it is called, must compete for staffing assignments from IBM departments.

The Make or Buy Decision

Organizations have two choices in acquiring human assets. They can train internal people for greater responsibility (make it), or they can go to the market and hire someone (buy it). One of the fundamental variables in the make versus buy decision is cost. It takes money to run organizations, and it doesn't matter if it is a profit or a not-for-profit business. Money has to come from somewhere, and it is usually in finite supply. The principle of most businesses has been: The less you spend on acquisition the more you can put into products or service. Ironically, the acquisition process has a wider range of effects on the organization than is generally realized. The cost-effectiveness of any given hire doesn't stop when the offer is accepted. That's actually when it starts, and it can be traced all the way through the new employee's career until the day that person becomes a turnover statistic. The issue of turnover cost really starts with selection. Turnover is as much a problem of the right hire as anything else. Some companies with historically high turnover rates have cut them by 50 percent or more simply by working on improved selection programs. Granted, changes in the organization after the fact can hurt the best of selection efforts. Nevertheless, a system that employs modern hiring tools and techniques can have a long-term positive impact.

Until the 1990s, when a manager was being replaced with an outsider, the new hire often came in at a higher salary than the predecessor. That's no longer so prevalent. Nevertheless, add the acquisition costs, training costs, and learning curve losses—the loss in productivity that occurs while the new employee learns the job—and you see hiring can be a costly process. Employees are investments. They should be treated as investments and not as expenses. They provide a return on the money spent to sustain them and thereby qualify as an investment. We spend a great deal of time in business studying potential returns on investments in capital equipment. However, we do not take the same care in scrutinizing a job candidate whose cost may be 10 to 50 times the cost of a new machine. A basic change of attitude toward the selection process is the first step in managing hiring costs.

The Death of Jobs

With more people working on process and project teams, the notion of fixed jobs is fading. This is forcing a new view on workforce planning. Instead of jobs the issue is competencies. Some companies have taken this to heart and started to amass and pay for skills. This means that as employees acquire new skills the organization pays them for that gain in potential. The problem is that in many cases the skills are never used, and the company finds itself putting out money and getting nothing but potential in return.

The McBer Company, a division of the Hay Group, has built its reputation on methods for identifying and developing competencies. They agree that fixed positions are slowly being eroded by the demand for flexibility. But competency is more than skill acquisition. Their view is that developing competencies is a matter of identifying those behaviors and characteristics necessary for top performance. McBer's leader, Lyle Spencer, asserts that competencies should be more than a set of skills. Any and every capability must be directly linked to producing superior results. I believe that the evolution toward competencies versus jobs will be slow but steady. By the end of the decade human asset acquisition will look quite different than it did in the century leading up to the 1990s.

The First Measure

In order to make an intelligent decision regarding the trade-offs between promoting from within or hiring from without, we have to know the relative cost of each. In this chapter we will start with what is often thought of as the first measure, cost per hire (CPH). Cost per hire applies whether we talk about internal or external sources. Internal placements do not require all the types of expenses that external sourcing does, but there are still costs and they need to be calculated.

At first blush we tend to think of CPH as the direct cost for advertising and agency fees. However, when you dig deeper you begin to realize the multitude of expenses generated by the replacement process. There are several types of replacement expenses. They fall into the following categories:

Type	Expense
Source cost	Advertising and agency fees paid to generate applicants; hire and/or referral bonuses.
Staff time	Salary, benefit, and standard overhead cost of your staff to meet with the manager to discuss sourcing; work with the media and/or agency to commence the search; screen applications; call applicants in for interviews; interview applicants and check references; review candidates with the manager and schedule interviews; make or confirm the offer.
Management	Salary, benefit, and standard overhead cost of the requesting department time management to plan sourcing, discuss and interview candidates, and make a hiring decision and an offer.
Processing cost	Manual or automatic data system cost of opening a new file; cost of medical exams; cost of employment and record verification (mail or telephone), security checks, etc.
Travel and relocation	Travel and lodging costs for staff and candidates; relocation costs.
Miscellaneous	Materials and other special or unplanned expenses. The cost of new employee orientation may be included or considered part of the training expenses. Reference checking, physical examinations, drug screen and bonding checks are other examples.

In its simplest yet most complete form, CPH could be expressed as shown in Formula S-1.

Cost per Hire

$$CPH = \frac{Ad + AF + ER + T + Relo + RC}{H} + 10\% \qquad (S\text{-}1)$$

In 1986, the first SHRM/Saratoga Institute Human Resource Effectiveness Report was published using this formula. Over the next eight years this formula proved itself to be accurate within 1.5 percent. That is, the sum of all other costs has been between 9 percent and 10.5 percent. From this experience has come the knowledge of how to collect valid reliable data with a minimum of effort.

Source costs are divided into four types: advertisements, agency fees, employee referrals, and no-cost walk-ins. We will ignore this last one, but hires from this source are included in the denominator of the formula above. Hiring costs are rather straightforward, since the invoices from the advertisements and the fees from agencies are unequivocal, and fees paid to employees are well-known. When you run one ad for one position, it is easy to ascribe the cost of the ad to that hire. However, quite often combination ads that showcase two or more jobs are run. Sometimes a blanket ad calling for an unstated number of applicants is placed. An example of the first ad would be one that calls for a supervisor of accounting, senior accountants, and bookkeepers. A sample of the second would be an ad stating simply, "Assemblers Wanted." In both cases, you are hoping for multiple hires from one ad.

In the assembler ad it is fairly simple to divide the ad cost by the number of assemblers hired to obtain an average ad cost. However, the accounting ad is a more complicated decision. Assuming you were to hire a supervisor, one senior accountant, and three bookkeepers from this ad, how would you apportion the cost among the five hires? Is it fair to divide the cost of the ad by five? That would make it seem that it's as easy to hire supervisors as it is to hire bookkeepers. You could weight the charges by the salary level of each hire. In that case, should you use actual salary, entry-level salary, or the midpoint of the salary range?

Questions such as these become important if you are attempting a detailed analysis of your CPH. They are also issues if the cost of the ad must be charged back to user departments. There are occasions when two or more departments will agree to pool their resources to place a large ad for people who could be employed in several departments. A common example of this is the job of programmer. Today, many departments have programming staffs, and they are almost always in need of programmers. For instance, quite often a programmer may be able to function in both market research and corporate planning. If you are looking for junior and senior programmers for two different departments, the problem of cost allocation is compounded. It is important that you establish the ground rules ahead of time, because when dollars are on the line, manners disappear. Also, you do not want users to think that they were treated unfairly. If they do, they are not likely to be as cooperative the next time you want to optimize your return on the corporate advertising dollar. The issue in cases like these is not, what is the right way? There is no prescribed rule to follow. The question is, what is the best way for all concerned at this time? If you are going to calculate CPH over an extended period of time, which is the only worthwhile way, then you must have some consistency in your methodology. If you allocate costs one way this month and another way next month in an effort to keep everyone happy, your month-to-month results will not be comparable.

Agency fees cover all types of outside agency sourcing. Executive search, employment agencies, and even temporary workers who are converted to permanent are all applicable agency costs. In the case of executive search, the fee can run into the tens of thousands. This along with relocation is usually one of the largest costs. It is precisely why so many companies have a policy of never or seldom using agencies.

Some companies have employee referral bonus programs that pay current employees a bounty if they bring in qualified applicants who are subsequently hired. When the labor market becomes particularly tight for a given job, some organizations have gone so far as to offer hiring bonuses to people who come in directly without going through an agency. Whether this is a short-term or long-term phenomenon is irrelevant. There will always be some kind of special expense that eludes the best plan. The point is simply to keep your eyes open and be sure that it is included.

Expenses associated with travel and relocation are significant. A managerial candidate flown from the midwest to either coast, fed and lodged for a day or two, and flown home can easily cost the company over a thousand dollars. And that's only for the first trip of one candidate. By the time you do that for two or three visits, bringing the finalist's spouse out to look over the territory, and top it off with a house-hunting trip, you have watched several thousand dollars disappear. And you haven't even begun relocation yet. In the 10 years between the first and second editions of this book the average relocation cost has quintupled. Quite often management positions are filled without incurring any significant travel or relocation expenses. Then all of a sudden you may spend $25,000 or more on one hire. If you simply throw that one in with the 10 preceding it, where you may have spent less than $5,000 total, the ensuing average CPH will be skewed. The number will be misleading and totally non-indicative of what has happened over the last 11 hires.

The $25,000 must be added to the total cost of hiring for the month. However, it will probably be appropriate to report two sets of figures. One would be those hires that did not require relocation. The other would be those in which there were relocations. Not only is this more truthful, it provides management with an appreciation for the impact of relocation expenses on the bottom line. Your job is not only to show management how effectively you are managing your department, it is also imperative to show them how the job could be done better. If you can come up with a plan to avoid having to hire people who require relocation, you can probably get support for it.

Our studies have shown that the recruiters' salary and benefits costs multiplied by the number of hours spent per job is the sixth important cost variable. All other staff time—e.g., clerks, hiring department staff, and management—is part of the 10 percent miscellaneous cost variable. As such, we don't recommend that you spend a lot of time working it out. However, if you feel you must, here are some tips.

The calculation and allocation of staff time can also quickly become an indecipherable mess unless you establish an accounting method and stay with it. The simplest way to reduce this problem to a manageable and understandable variable is to introduce standard labor costing. By borrowing a leaf from manufacturing's book, you can determine the normal cost of an employee hour of work and set that as your standard rate. For example, an employment clerk's standard rate could be determined in the following manner:

Salary (converted to hourly rate)	$8.25
Benefits (30% of salary)	2.93
Overhead charge (space, equipment, etc.)	4.65
Total	$15.83

The standard rate you will apply to all staff time calculations where an employment clerk is involved is thus $15.83

In time you will be able to develop an average number of hours that a clerk puts in on a given class of hires. Let us say, as an example, you find that the clerk spends 1½ hours on the average per direct labor hire. If you multiply $15.83 times 1½, the product is $28.75, which becomes the standard cost of an employment clerk's time for each direct laborer that the clerk assists in hiring. Multiply $28.75 times the number of hires that month and you have one component of the total month's cost of hiring. The same process is then applied to recruiters, receptionists, record clerks, and anyone else in your department who is involved in hiring. You may even choose to allocate a portion of the employment manager's time.

The process may need to be recomputed for different types or levels of jobs. It usually takes more time to hire managers than laborers. Hence, although your standard labor rates will not change, the amount of time each person devotes to the hire may change by job. Therefore, the multiplier changes. The most dramatic changes are usually with the recruiters. At the nonexempt level, recruiters may have to spend on average half an hour per applicant interviewing for each hire. At the exempt level, that could jump to two or three hours per applicant. In addition, the number of applicants seen per hire may also vary significantly. This will strongly influence your CPH when calculated by job level. It takes time to set standard rates and to establish a realistic time multiplier. It is up to you to use what is the most appropriate to your situation. You are free to choose, so long as you are consistent.

The last thing to keep in mind when you employ standard labor rates is that rates change over time. The cost of a clerk or recruiter today is about 50 percent higher today than it was in 1984 when the first edition of this book was published. You need to check your costs periodically. It is usually sufficient to do this on an annual basis. To do it any more frequently would cause confusion in your monthly comparison of CPH statistics. Remember, the real reason for measuring is to find out if you are doing an effective job of managing the function. This is not an exercise in statistical precision, but a tool for managing.

The allocation of employee orientation costs is a question that currently does not have a definitive answer. Some HR managers think it is a cost of hire because it usually occurs before the person actually assumes the job. Even if it comes a week or a month later, they believe it should be charged to hiring because the information presented is aimed strictly at easing the induction of the new person into the organization. Another opinion is that orientation takes place after the hire and therefore is part of an individual's training. To date, this argument has not been resolved. In my opinion, until we adopt a generally accepted set of accounting principles for our field, it is a moot point. Account for it on either side and let it stand by itself. The only rule that always applies is to be consistent.

Breaking It Down

The true value of the measurement system becomes apparent only when you dig into a dependent variable such as cost per hire. The bottom line number, CPH = $X for a given month, is the starting point for what can be a very enlightening tour of the employment function. Whether you have an automated or a manual system, you can divide CPH by any of the types of expenses we have discussed. Furthermore, you can mix and match those independent variables in just about any combination. The net result is a chance to discover in great detail just where you are being extraordinarily effective and where you can improve.

It is very easy to cut your CPH by source. You can compare the average CPH using the cost of advertising versus the cost of agencies. You can throw in other sources, such as employee referrals, and make multiple comparisons. Another fundamental cut is level. You can look at CPH by exempt, nonexempt, and hourly wage earners. You can cut it finer if you combine level with job groups—you can look at the difference between the CPH of entry-level, junior, and senior programmers, for instance. Of course, in order to be able to make those cuts you have to remember to collect that data at the time of hire.

Figure 5.2 shows a three-dimensional analysis matrix. It is a graphic way of considering the many subsets of cost per hire that are obtainable. This concept could be designed for a database program. Each cell in the matrix contains the cost per hire of a given type of employee in a given department using a given source. For example, cell 1 would display the cost of hiring an exempt employee for department A using advertising, and cell 7 would show nonexempt employee costs for department A using agencies. Moving back into the third dimension, cell 50 would show costs for hourly workers in department B using not-for-profit agencies.

1. *Source Analysis.* In the analysis block, standard costs for staff and management time, travel, relocation, and other costs were taken as givens. The outcomes, the costs in each cell, were only the sourcing costs. The process of holding certain costs constant and calculating certain others is a good way to isolate and emphasize trends. The basic equation is seen in Formula S-2.

Source Cost per Hire

$$\text{SCPH} = \frac{\text{AC} + \text{AF} + \text{RB} + \text{NC}}{\text{H}} \qquad (\text{S-2})$$

where   AC   = advertising costs, total monthly expenditure (e.g., $48,000)
        AF   = agency fees, total month (e.g., $29,000)
        RB   = referral bonuses, total paid (e.g., $4,500)

NC = no-cost hires, walk-in, nonprofit agencies, etc. (i.e., $0)
H = Total hires (e.g., 63)

EXAMPLE

$$SCPH = \frac{\$48,000 + \$12,000 + \$4,500 + \$0}{63}$$

$$= \frac{\$81,500}{63}$$

$$= \$1,294$$

The basic formula can be varied by changing total hires (H) to include only exempt hires (EH), or nonexempt hires (NEH):

$$SCPH = \frac{AC + AF + RB + NC}{EH} \quad \text{or} \quad SCPH = \frac{AC + AF + RB + NC}{NEH}$$

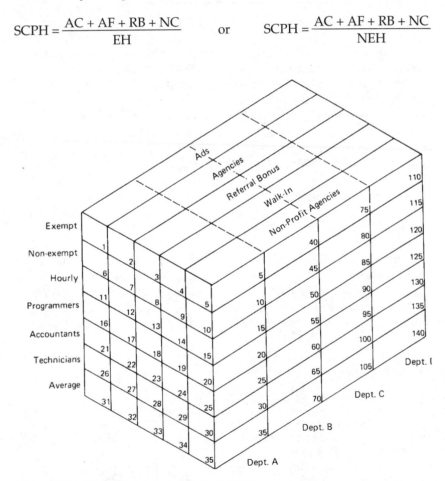

Figure 5.2. Three-Dimensional Analysis Matrix.

Once you have the basic formula, you can change the denominator to any group of hires and recompute cost per source just for that group. For example, you could look at source costs for exempts versus nonexempts, or for technical, administrative, sales and marketing, and EEO classes.

For reporting purposes it is enlightening to show the comparative costs of each source of hire. To do that, simply separate the variables in the numerator and do separate computations:

$$SCPH = \frac{AC}{H} + \frac{AF}{H} + \frac{RB}{H} + \frac{NC}{H}$$

A sample report based on this type of cost analysis is shown in Fig. 5.3.

2. *Special Recruiting Programs.* It can be useful to evaluate the costs and outcomes of ongoing programs on a periodic basis. For college recruitment programs or national recruiting campaigns the costs can be identified and separate calculations performed. Staff and management time may be included or not, depending on your objective:

$$SCPH = \frac{AC + AF + T \& R (+ ST + MT)}{H}$$

The result can be compared to other methods of recruitment as one input to a cost-benefit analysis.

3. *Interviewing Costs.* You already know how to calculate standard labor costs for your staff and for outside management. Observations will disclose how long, on the average, each interview takes. The cost of interviewing (C/I) as a component of the total cost is a simple, two-step process:

Step 1: Interviewing Cost

$$C/I = \frac{ST + MT}{I} \qquad (S\text{-}3)$$

where ST = staff time, total staff time spent interviewing (e.g., $18.60 per hour standard cost times a half-hour per interview times number interviewed)

MT = management time, total management time spent interviewing (e.g., management time is based on a $26.60 hour standard labor cost times one hour per interview times number interviewed)

I = number interviewed, total number of applicants interviewed (e.g., 494)

(a) April: Cost of hires by source, in dollars

	Agency			Ads			Employee referrals			Nonprofit other	
	Number	Total cost	Cost per hire	Number	Total cost	Cost per hire	Number	Total cost	Cost per hire	Number	Cost
Exempt	6	47,500	7,916	8	24,375	3,047	5	1,500	300	1	00
Non-exempt	1	624	624	24	10,078	420	24	2,400	100	9	00
Total	7	48,124	6,875	32	34,453	1,077	29	3,900	134	10	00

Total number hired	Total cost	Cost per hire
20	73,375	3,669
58	13,102	226
78	86,477	1,109

(b) Year to date: Cost of hire by source, in dollars

	Agency			Ads			Employee referrals			Nonprofit other	
	Number	Total cost	Cost per hire	Number	Total cost	Cost per hire	Number	Total cost	Cost per hire	Number	Cost
Exempt	21	83,512	3,977	28	43,282	1,546	16	4,800	300	3	00
Non-exempt	8	2,843	355	91	26,270	289	69	6,900	100	17	00
Total	29	86,355	2,978	119	69,552	584	85	11,700	138	20	00

Total number hired	Total cost	Cost per hire
68	131,594	1,935
185	36,013	195
253	167,607	662

Year to year

1978	712
1979	662

Figure 5.3. Source Cost per Hire Report: (a) April, (b) Year to Date

EXAMPLE

$$C/I = \frac{\$4,594 + \$13,140}{494}$$

$$= \frac{\$17,734}{494}$$

$$= \$35.90$$

Step 2: Source Cost per Hire (per Interview)

$$SCPH = \frac{IC + AC + AF + RB + NC}{H} \qquad \text{(S-4)}$$

where IC = total monthly interviewing costs, by using the formula of cost per interview to calculate total interviewing costs (e.g., $17,734)

AC = advertising costs, total monthly advertising expenditures (e.g., $38,000)

AF = agency fees, total monthly agency fees paid (e.g., $26,000)

RB = referral bonuses, total monthly referral bonuses paid (e.g., $6300)

NC = no-cost hires, nonprofit agencies, etc. (e.g., $0)

EXAMPLE

$$SCPH\ (P/I) = \frac{\$17,734 + \$38,000 + \$26,000 + \$6,300 + 0}{119}$$

$$= \frac{\$88,034}{119}$$

$$= \$739.78$$

This example reflects the cost of the fact that, although there were only 119 hires, it was necessary to interview 494 applicants.

Special Event Analysis

At some point in their careers most staffing managers find themselves in a position of having to perform some special recruitment magic. There may be an immediate need for a large number of a certain type of employee, such as retail clerks or assembly workers, or perhaps a given job group—programmers, for example—is in extremely short supply. Whatever the particular need, the manager may decide to conduct some type of special event designed to recruit a relatively large number of people in a very short time. This may take the form of an open house. Open houses are often day-long or evening events where both recruiters and line managers are on hand to expedite interviews and offers. A media blitz takes place for a week or so in advance of the event. Refreshments are often served, and door prizes or favors may even be given away. Essentially, the manager marshals all the company's resources and concentrates them on this one important day, with the hope that it will attract a large number of qualified candidates and fill most of the open requisitions.

When the event is over, the staffing manager will want to evaluate its effectiveness, based on the ROI. There is a simple method for calculating that which consists of four steps.

1. Make a list of all expenses on the left side of a sheet of paper. These include ad costs, management time costs for both the HR staff and the involved line department, refreshments, door prizes and other incentives (if used), and all other types of costs shown on Formula S-1. Total these at the bottom of the column.

2. Write the number of people hired (assuming in this case they are all of one type—for example, programmers) on the right side of the page. If you were looking for several unrelated job groups, such as accountants, technicians, and secretaries, it will be difficult to precisely divide the costs among the different types. If separate ads for each type were run, their costs could be assigned to each group. General expenses, such as refreshments, could be prorated according to the number of applicants for each job group. Therefore, you may have to prepare more than one analysis sheet.

3. Divide the total expenses by the total number of hires to obtain CPH for this event. This tells the manager what the absolute ROI was, but it does not tell if it is better or worse than the cost would have been using conventional means. In order to answer that question one more step is required.

4. Referring to the most current data on cost per hire for similar jobs, compare the open house CPH to the staffing department's monthly report on cost per hire. This final step tells the manager if the open house hires were less expensive or more expensive than hires obtained by the other method. Normally, well-planned and well-executed special events yield a better CPH than standard methods. Focused attention and high levels of cooperation usually yield high ROIs. Even if the event's CPH is higher, there is a trade-off in time spent. In a few days of preparation and action such an event usually fills more open positions than weeks of standard recruiting. If there is a premium for quick results, the special event almost always delivers.

On the question of hire quality, we have found that special events produce applicants of about equal caliber to those obtained through conventional methods. Ways of assessing the quality of hires will be discussed in the next chapter.

GEM #7   *The value of anything becomes clear when you understand its purpose, even if takes several steps to find the purpose.*

Summary

Evaluating the cost-effectiveness of the employment process is one of the easier judgments to make. Costs are mostly visible in the form of invoices for advertisements, fees, and travel. The less apparent expenses, such as the cost of someone's time, can be found quickly. The only difficulty human resources staffs consistently complain of is their inability to get their hands on the cost data. In some companies, the bills are sent directly to the hiring manager for approval and then to accounts payable for payment, bypassing the HR office completely. When that is the habitual pattern, a deal can be made with the accounting department.

Sometimes the accountants receive bills on which they have little or no information. They spend a good deal of their time tracking down the source of the bill or the person who submitted it in order to get an explanation or an approval signature. If you are being bypassed, tell the accountants that if they will pass all employment-related bills to you, you will verify the amounts, relate them to a given event, and obtain the necessary approvals. The controller will thank you for taking an onerous, time-consuming task off the accounting staff's backs, and you will then be in control of the process, rather than a passive spectator.

No human resources department can claim to operate efficiently if it does not know how much it is spending to hire people. Acquisition costs are important whether you are talking about machines or employees. Fortunately, these costs are easily obtainable, powerful tools for proving that you are maximizing the organization's recruiting ROI.

6
Responding to Customer Time and Quality Priorities

There are other staffing considerations beyond cost. Issues of timeliness, completeness, and quality may be more important in the eyes of the hiring manager, your customer. Keep in mind that the customer is focused on achieving his or her operational objectives. The decision point may shift among time, cost, and quality as outside pressures change. In a fast-growing company, having a warm body in place may be the key requirement. Without sufficient staff, the customer can't meet his or her production and service objectives. As growth slows, a manager can take more time, be more selective, and opt for quality. Knowing where the customer's priorities are or are likely to be will enhance your service. This is just one more example of the value of establishing partnerships with our customers.

All performance measures, whether direct or indirect, can be used for at least two broad purposes. One is to help you manage and control your organization, and the other is to work with people outside of your group. You will develop a database that can be used to report your activities and results. Someday you may be required to defend yourself against criticism of your work. By maintaining your database you will be able to demonstrate that the claims are unfounded. Some managers like to have an unreasonably large number of candidates from which to choose. In their zeal to defend their lack of decisiveness, they may claim that they never see more than one or two qualified people. By referring to your applicant-tracking system you can prove that, on the average, they had perhaps 6 to 10 acceptable candidates from which to select.

Let's pause at this point to establish once and for all a fundamental issue regarding the qualifications of the job applicants you refer to management for interviewing. If you have dealt with the types of criticisms of timeliness and quantity we have just discussed, you may then have to answer for the quality of your referrals. Indecisive, overworked, or mediocre managers may concede upon proof that you have met the tests of time and volume. Then, in a face-saving attempt, they may, "Yes, but" you and accuse you of referring inferior or unacceptable individuals. There is only one way to effectively deal with this, and your position must be absolutely inflexible. You only refer one type of applicant: a qualified applicant—period! You can prove it by matching the specifications on the requisition to the qualifications of your applicants. You do not send out teasers, loss leaders, straw men, shock troops, or any other type of quasi-qualified or unqualified individuals. If you ever admit to offering management anything but a suitable candidate you will destroy your credibility and undermine your position forever. There is absolutely no other stance to take, period—end of discussion.

By far the more important use of your database is continuous improvement. By keeping track of what's going on internally and externally you can manage rather just oversee staff activity. Knowing your trends and market forces related to costs, time factors and labor availability you will run a more efficient and cost effective shop. You will also be able to counsel your customers regarding changes and possible effects of the workforce market on their operation.

Time Factors

Basically, there are three time issues in the recruitment process. One has to do with how long it takes to develop qualified candidates and refer them to management for interview. We call this *response time*. This is the period over which you have the most control. Another is how long it takes to fill a job requisition (have an offer accepted). We call this *time to fill*. Once you refer an applicant, your degree of control begins to lessen. I will discuss the recruiter's responsibility after referral when we come back to this second issue. The third is *time to start*. This ends when the new hire actually shows up for work. You have little control here. But as far as your customer is concerned, until this happens everything else is activity without result.

Response time is defined as the time from the day you have a signed, approved job requisition in hand to the day on which you call or visit the requesting manager and announce that you have at least one qualified candidate ready to be interviewed. This is an important issue. Although it does not mean that you have completed your assignment, it does show how quickly your procurement system works. Formula S-5 shows the response time calculation. In this case it is not a ratio, as we are accustomed to working with in cost measures, but a subtraction problem.

Response Time

$$RT = RD - RR \qquad \text{(S-5)}$$

where RT = response time
       RD = date of first qualified candidate referred for interview (e.g., January 22)*
       RR = date of receipt of job requisition (e.g., January 4)

EXAMPLE

$$RT = 22 - 4$$
$$= 18 \text{ days}$$

Adding total days to respond and dividing by total hires gives an average response time.

This formula came in very handy for me one day when I was managing the staffing department. I received a call from a high-ranking person in our company who proceeded to chew me out for the alleged slow response time of my recruiters. Since I did not know offhand what our current rate was for the job classification he was angry about, I told him I would look into it and get back to him. After he hung up I went to the lady who maintained our manual applicant tracking system (in the olden days we didn't have PCs) and asked her for the log she used. I was frankly concerned that there might be some justification for the complaint because the jobs he pointed out were computer programmers. At the time programmers were a very scarce commodity in our marketplace. I was hoping that we had at least maintained a reasonable response rate over the year. The worst situation would be if each month our time to respond had increased. Within a few minutes I was able to draw out of the log the average response time for programmers over the past 10 months. I constructed a simple chart and

---

*If the referral date is in a different month than the requisition date simply count the intervening dates. For example,

    RT = February 20 – January 4
        = 27 days until the end of January + 20 days in February
        = 47 days

plotted the results on it. An example of what it looked like is shown in Fig. 6.1.

As you can see, it showed unequivocally that the recruiters were doing a superb job. In a bad market they were managing to respond more quickly each month throughout the year. You can imagine my pleasure when I called the gentleman back and said, "John, I don't know where you are getting your data, but my records show that our current response time is only about 14 days. Over the year it has gotten better, not worse." He replied that he found my numbers rather hard to believe. So I suggested he come over to my office and take a look at the books for himself. To make a long story short he came, he saw, and he stormed out of my office vowing vengeance on his managers. I learned later that he went back to his department and verbally assaulted his staff for lying to him. The problem had been that they were not making their schedules and were unfairly blaming it on staffing for not filling the numerous open requisitions.

You probably know what was happening. The managers were claiming that, for a wide variety of highly imaginative reasons, they did not have time to see the candidates we were referring. By the time they came back to us and said they were ready, the candidates had found jobs in other departments in our company or in other organizations. The recruitment process had to start all over again. This resulted in jobs being open for many weeks and work not getting done. When put under the gun by their boss, they sought a scapegoat in the staffing department.

This is a fairly typical example of how the human resources department can be given the blame for a line department's problems. The lesson is clear. If I had not had the data to set the record straight, I proba-

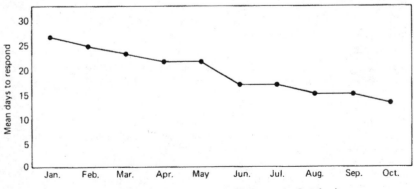

Figure 6.1. Response Time for Programmers (January to October)

bly would have had to take the blame for the problem. I call that bag holding—one manager will walk into another manager's office and make an accusation. In effect, the accused is handed a bag of garbage. Unless the accused can muster a defense based on facts, he or she will usually have to take the bag. Human resources staff members have more than their share of garbage bags tossed through their doors. When they have a measurement system that demonstrates their performance, they can tell the bearer to take the garbage and put it where it belongs.

Time to Fill

The second time issue is time to fill. The lay person has the notion that the recruiting process is a relatively simple matter. The perception is that a requisition is delivered to staffing, an ad is run, applicants are screened, and a few are selected for interviews by management. In fact, the process has about 30 separate steps to it. Time to fill measures the total number of days between the delivery of an approved requisition to staffing and the date on which an applicant accepts your job offer. The calculation is exactly the same as it was for response time. The only difference is that the referral date (RD) is replaced by the offer (accepted) date (OD). The formula for time to fill is shown in formula (S-6).

Time to Fill

$$TF = RR - OD \qquad \text{(S-6)}$$

where   TF = time to have an offer accepted
RR = date the requisition is received (e.g., January 4)
OD = date the offer is accepted (e.g., February 20)

EXAMPLE

$$TF = January\ 4 - February\ 20$$
$$= 47$$

Time to Start

The third time measurement is time to start. It is calculated exactly as is time to fill except that it shows the additional number of days between acceptance and start. Start date refers to the day the new hire reports for work. Thus, Formula S-7 for time to start is start date minus requisition receipt date.

Time to Start

$$TS = RR - SD \qquad\qquad (S\text{-}7)$$

where　TS　= time till the new hire starts
　　　　RR　= date the requisition is received (e.g., January 4)
　　　　SD　= date the new hire starts work (e.g., March 10)

EXAMPLE

$$TS = \text{January 4 - March 10}$$
$$= 65$$

A staffing manager who is looking for opportunities to improve the time to fill or time to start record does not have to look hard. I told you that there are about 30 steps to the recruitment and selection process. A system can be set up to monitor the more significant points in that 30-step process. Any large-volume recruitment function should have an automated applicant and requisition tracking system. With such a system in place, an ongoing audit of efficiency is easy. Figure 6.2 is an example of how one might look.

Select the key checkpoints that you want the system to record. In this example I have chosen 10 checkpoints. This system can be programmed to run as part of the core function of an applicant tracking system. Spreadsheet or database software can be used to define checkpoints and can calculate them automatically.

There is another way to record these events. In the event date cell put the number of days or elapsed time since the last event. For example, on the first requisition from manager J. Jones the line would read:

Event	1	2	3	4	5	6	7	8	9	10
Date	9/1	1	7	5	6	9	6	1	7	33

Event 1 is the receipt of the requisition; the starting date for the process. You could put 0 for elapsed time. However, the starting date is more worthwhile. Since event 2 took place on 9/2, there is 1 day of elapsed time and the number 1 is entered. Event 3 was on 9/9 which is 7 days later, and so on across the line. This approach has the advantage of showing immediately how much time has been lost between steps. For the manager who is looking for places to cut response time and time to fill, the delays are very apparent. The largest opportunities are at events 3, 6, 9, and 10.

Requesting manager	Event* and date									
	1	2	3	4	5	6	7	8	9	10
J. Jones	9/1	9/2	9/9	9/14	9/20	9/29	10/5	10/6	10/13	11/15
F. Koontz	9/2	9/4	9/11	9/17	9/22	9/30	10/7	10/9	10/10	11/1
L. Smith	9/7	9/8	9/16	9/22	9/30	10/9	10/20	10/21	10/30	11/15
G. Mack	9/7	9/9	9/19	9/30	10/15	10/25	11/10	11/12	11/18	12/7
E. Kieffer	9/8	9/9	9/15	9/30	10/9	10/16	11/5	11/7	11/14	1/2

*Event numbers:

1—Requisition received; 2—Sourcing started; 3—First applicant responds; 4—First screening; 6—First management interview; 7—Hiring decision made; 8—Offer made; 9—Offer accepted/ rejected; 10—New employee starts work.

Figure 6.2. Hiring Track

In place of "requesting manager," the job title can be entered. In a computerized system you would have both because you do not have the space limitations of a manual log. When you have too little space, the best solution is to show job title and department number.

Time is the enemy of the ambitious recruiter. By keeping track of response time, time to fill, and time to start, the recruiter and the manager will know for themselves how they are doing. They will also be able to defend themselves if necessary. Finally, they will be able to go to line management with the facts to obtain cooperation in speeding up the process.

Referral Rate

One large company in the northwest for many years was the major employer in its region. The staff members had become accustomed to taking their time in recruiting and enjoyed the luxury of having many applicants for each vacancy. As a result, managers developed the habit of looking at as many as 10 candidates before they made a hiring decision. Late in the 1970s other organizations around the country began to see the advantages of locating plants in the northwest. Within a year or two, several large- and medium-sized plants had been built within 15 miles of the *grande dame*. Suddenly there was competition for qualified personnel. However, the managers of the first company continued their habit of waiting for staffing to produce 7 to 10 candidates. When they began to go for weeks without filling jobs, they complained loudly to staffing. After viewing the evidence, they finally accepted what they had been told before: The old game had changed. They could no longer expect more than two or three candidates for most positions. For certain jobs, they would be lucky to have one. Today, after nearly a decade of market turmoil, people are more amenable to the notion that they have to change. Twenty years ago they were more rigid.

As market conditions change, referral rates generally change accordingly. In the case just described, management's expectations and practices had to change if they wanted to fill their jobs. One of the ways that the staffing manager can keep on top of the change is to compute a referral ratio. In order to avoid confusion with the RR symbol from the response time formula, we use RF to stand for the referral ratio and we call it the *referral factor*. The ratio is shown in Formula S-8.

Referral Factor

$$RF = \frac{R}{O} \qquad (S\text{-}8)$$

where RF = referral factor, relationship of candidates to openings
       R = number of candidates referred for interview (e.g., 76)
       O = number of openings (e.g., 22)

EXAMPLE

$$RF = \frac{76}{22}$$
$$= 3.5$$

This data can be collected by job group or work unit to show how many qualified candidates, on the average, are being developed. A variation on this formula is to substitute hires for openings. Not all openings result in hires. Sometimes conditions change between the time that an approved job requisition arrives and a hire can take place. The difference is subtle, but perhaps meaningful in some situations. A realistic referral factor will always be a combination of management demand and market conditions. No matter which one predominates, the staffing manager should know what the ratio is, otherwise it can't be improved.

Job-Posting System

In the career development chapter of Section E I will deal with the job-posting system as part of the career development effort. At this point we will look at it solely from an administrative standpoint.

Three views of job posting are the employees' use of the system, the rate of hire generated by the system, and the role of the system in the total hiring scheme. Each perspective provides opportunities for measurement.

Periodically jobs are posted for employees to see and apply for. In terms of this discussion, it does not matter which job levels are posted or how long jobs are left on the list. Posting systems vary widely among industries and in different parts of the country. Management philosophy, union status, and other issues dictate how a system will be run. So long as the system rules do not change, valid measurements can be conducted over time. No matter what the style of the system is, the first question to ask is, how are people responding to it? When you post a job, what happens? Are you flooded with employees anxious to transfer? Does anyone at all show up? The basic measurement is the job-posting response rate (JPR), which indicates how many responses are received per job posting. Formula S-9 shows the measures used to calculate JPR.

Job-Posting Response Rate

$$JPR = \frac{A}{PJ} \qquad \text{(S-9)}$$

where   JPR = job-posting response rate
        A = number of applications received at the job-posting desk (e.g., 348)
        PJ = number of posted jobs (e.g., 65)

EXAMPLE

$$JPR = \frac{348}{65}$$

$$= 5.4 \text{ applications per posting}$$

People may apply for several jobs simultaneously, realizing that they can only be successful in obtaining one of them. Nevertheless, count applications rather than applicants, because this tells what the system is generating. The fact that some people are chronic applicants or have other idiosyncratic reasons for applying is an issue outside the system itself. Sorting through hundreds of applications in search of multiples from one person is just not worth the effort. Pulling those few out of the pile probably will not make a significant difference in the numbers.

Job posting, if monitored, can yield much more than a list of applicants for open positions. Assume that there is a flood of applicants for a particular job or for all jobs. What could that mean? The answer can be found somewhere among the reasons people apply for transfer. A few are

- Desire for advancement
- Escape from a bad supervisor
- Disinterest in current job (boredom)
- Escape from a bad interpersonal situation (co-workers)
- Better pay
- Move to a new location (geographic)
- Change of shift
- Family or health problems

An analysis of the source of applications and the reasons given by applicants often helps pinpoint an organizational problem. If the people who run the posting system develop rapport with the employees, they will tell your job counselors the real reasons for their application. Poor supervision, boring jobs, unsafe or unhealthy environments, inequitable pay, or other sources of employee unrest will surface. Then you will have a chance to investigate and decide whether or not the complaints are reasonable.

Assume that very few employees respond to postings. What could that imply? It may mean

- There is a consistent history of rejection in favor of outside applicants.
- There is no visible support from management.
- There are threats from supervisors about applying for other positions in the company.
- Your department has done a substandard job of dealing with applicants.
- Only low-level jobs are posted.

In my experience, all of these occur. But unless you are monitoring your responses, you will never become aware of potentially serious organizational problems. Consider as just one example the consequences of supervisors threatening people who apply for posted jobs. Immediately you recognize the possibility of unfair labor practice charges or discrimination suits. Besides playing the traditional role of a transfer mechanism, the job-posting system can also be an early warning device. If you have your antenna up and scanning, you just might see something coming over the horizon in time to intercept it.

There are variations on the basic JPR formula, one of which is how to calculate how many posted jobs were responded to, as in Formula S-10.

Job-Posting Response Factor

$$JPRF = \frac{PJR}{PJ} \qquad (S\text{-}10)$$

where   JPRF   = ratio of jobs posted to jobs responded to
          PJR   = number of posted jobs responded to (e.g., 58)
            PJ   = number of posted jobs (e.g., 65)

EXAMPLE

$$JPRF = \frac{58}{65}$$

$$= 89.2\%^*$$

This gives you a picture of the spread of responses. In the first formula, you may have a large number of applications per posting, but they may be for only certain jobs. Averages can be deceiving, so there is a measure in statistics called *standard deviation*. It tells you how broadly the numbers are spread from the mean. In a sense, that is the type of function which this measure performs. It tells you whether or not all of your jobs are being applied for. If the number is less than 100%, you can make a note of which jobs are not drawing applicants. If those jobs continually fail to turn up any interest, you can look into the reasons and do whatever is appropriate.

Another way to track responses is by job. It may be worthwhile to know which jobs are drawing the largest number of applicants. This is not discovered by use of a formula; it is a logging task. You can set up a log, either manually or automatically, that looks like Fig. 6.3. Applications are tallied by job and the story tells itself. Again, follow-up will uncover the reasons for abnormally high or low responses.

The second test of the job-posting system takes the process of application one step further. It deals with the number of hires or placements which result from the system. The formula used here is called the job-posting hire rate (JPH). It is seen in Formula S-11.

Job-Posting Hire Rate

$$JPH = \frac{H}{JP} \qquad (S\text{-}11)$$

---

*The maximum percentage can never exceed 100%.

Job name or number	Number of applicants
Accounting clerk	11111 11111 1
Assembler II	11111 11111 11111 11
Senior buyer	11111 111
Personnel representative	11

Figure 6.3. Applicant Log

where JPH = percentage of jobs filled through job posting
       H   = number of hires made from internal applicants
              (e.g., 54)
       JP = Number of jobs posted (e.g., 65)

EXAMPLE

$$JPH = \frac{54}{65}$$

$$= 83.1\%$$

This measure follows the same logic as the job-posting response ratio and carries the process to its conclusion. If a high rate of response is coupled with an equally high rate of hire, the system would appear to be fulfilling its mission. If both factors are not in an acceptable range, it is a sign that the system should be reviewed for defects. This is what people in business like to call the bottom line. After all is said and done, what is the result? Obviously, the objective is to fill a large percentage of the posted jobs. You may not want to fill every position from internal sources, for this could lead eventually to organizational incest. Fortunately, most industries have learned their lesson and no longer expect or want all promotions to come up through the system.

Some companies set targets or goals for internal replacement rates. This is probably a healthy thing to do. It lets everyone know what the expectation is. If it is communicated well, employees will understand and support it. A formula for measuring that is called the internal hire rate, shown in Formula S-12.

Internal Hire Rate

$$IH = \frac{IA}{H} \tag{S-12}$$

where IH = percentage of jobs filled internally
      IA = jobs filled by internal applicants (e.g., 49)
      H = total hires (e.g., 76)

EXAMPLE

$$IH = \frac{49}{76}$$
$$= 64.5\%$$

I know one company that encourages supervisors and managers to support the job-posting program through a cost transference mechanism. It works like this. Department A decides to accept the transfer request of an employee from department B. A then must pay B, through a cross charge, $X to cover the cost incurred by B to recruit a replacement. The amount is determined at the beginning of the year based on the average cost of hiring either an exempt or nonexempt employee. If B replaces their lost employee from another internal source, then the charge passes to that department. Eventually, whoever has to go outside for a replacement is compensated for that expense. If the last department in line does not choose to replace, it still gets the money as a reward for having developed a good employee and for having found a way to operate more efficiently. Given today's drive to operate more cost-efficiently, this method can be a stimulant for managers to practice continuous improvement.

Job-posting measures are a good example of the inherent value in measurement. These seemingly secondary issues yield information well beyond what appears on the surface. In the process of obtaining data on one subject, the procedure and the results cause another set of questions to be asked. Gradually the holistic, interrelated, systems nature of the human resources function reveals itself. Time and again we will see how one process connects with another. In this one small series of job-posting measures we have discovered how job counselors are connected to affirmative action, employee relations, compensation, and labor relations. As we work through each of the main functions of human resources, the many rewards for measurement will become overwhelmingly clear.

Recruiting Efficiency

In order to describe the performance of a recruiter we have to look at more than just how many applicants the recruiter helped to turn into hires. Some recruiters believe that hires are the sole criteria of their efficiency. However, like everyone else, recruiters work in a group as part of a team. How they handle their total job responsibilities is as important as the number of hires they effect.

I believe that it is better to measure recruiters as a team than as individuals. Few people truly work alone anyway. This principle holds true, wherever possible, for other functions as well. If people feel that they are constantly under the gun to come up with good numbers, they are liable to succumb to the temptation and give you what you seem to want: numbers rather than results. When employees start to manufacture numbers the system is worse than useless, it is fraudulent. Treat your recruiters as a team. Pool their data and report their results as a group. Since we started talking about human resources as a system, we have emphasized the team aspect. Teaching your staff to work together and report results together takes away individual threat and promotes cooperation. When you set team objectives and team rewards, you get teamwork.

Let's start by looking at the recruiters' efficiency. How productive are their interviewing habits? What is the average length of interview for given types of jobs? How many interviews does it take to develop a list of qualified candidates? How many does it take to make a quality hire? Ratios for all these issues can be created, if that would be useful. The most basic is average length of interview, as shown in Formula S-13.

Interview Time

$$AIL = \frac{h}{HI} \qquad \text{(S-13)}$$

where   AIL   = average length of interviews*
           h   = total hours spent interviewing (e.g., 6)
        HI   = total number interviewed (e.g., 5)

EXAMPLE

$$AIL = \frac{6}{5}$$

$$AIL = 1.2 \text{ hours}$$

This can be accumulated for all recruiters and measured on a daily, weekly, or monthly basis and by exempt, nonexempt, or hourly job classification.

---

*AIL is computed by determining the total amount of time a recruiter spends interviewing and dividing by the total number of people interviewed.

This figure is needed as an input to other equations. It is a prerequisite to cost of hire measurement when staff time is involved, and it is necessary for measuring the cost of interviewing. It is also used in other indirect measures of recruiter efficiency and effectiveness.

Along with interviewing time, some staffing managers like to know how much time recruiters are spending on administrative duties. There is no clear definition of administrative time. Is it all activity other than application screening and interviewing? Does calling on sources of applicants, such as schools and not-for-profit agencies, count as recruiting time or administrative time? I know managers who insist that their recruiters spend at least 15 percent of their time out of the office cultivating low-cost sources of applicants. Usually they consider this administrative time, but it is up to you to call it whatever you like. The point is that recruiters should be doing that kind of work and you might want to track it occasionally. A simple log kept by either the recruiter or the recruiter's assistant (clerk) will provide the data.

There is another efficiency measure that yields information about both your recruiters and your sources of applicants. It is called hire ratios. At first glance it looks very complicated. Although it is complex in appearance it is quite simple to follow, since there is a natural sequence to it. Formula S-14 lays it out.

Hire Ratios

$$HR = \frac{I}{A} \ \frac{R}{I} \ \frac{H}{R} \ \frac{H}{A} \qquad (S-14)$$

where HR = hire rate
      A = applications received (e.g., 120)
      I = interviews (e.g., 30)
      R = referrals (e.g., 10)
      H = hires (e.g., 4)

EXAMPLE

$$HR = \frac{30}{120} \ \frac{10}{30} \ \frac{4}{10} \ \frac{4}{120}$$
$$= \ 25\% \ 33\% \ 40\% \ \ 3\%$$

Hire ratios trace the process from the point of application to the point of hire. They show how the original pool of applicants is cut at each step. These computations can be made for all hires, or they can be done separately by source for different levels, job groups, or locations.

The first issue to look at is the ratio of applications to hires. Hypothetically, one could say that an advertisement that produced 120 applications was very effective. However, if you only obtained four hires, was it really effective? Consider the time, and therefore the cost, of processing those 120 applicants. Thirty got interviewed after someone plowed through 120 applications. Ten got a second interview by the line manager. That second interview might have been repeated by several other people in the requesting department as well. When the process was finally completed, with four hires, probably 50 to 60 hours of labor had gone into it. Was that satisfactory?

I vividly recall the occasion when one of the field sales forces of the computer company I worked in started a new sales training program. Without seeking advice from the staffing group, they placed an ad and got over 300 responses. At that point we received a panicked cry for help. They only wanted to hire four people initially. As they plowed through the ever-growing stack of applications, it was evident that anyone who had ever considered a sales career was applying. One might say that 300 applications was a great response. In fact, it was only a large response. The first screening eliminated over 280, and that was being generous. It took four people better than a day to accomplish the first cut. That is not my idea of a productive ad.

The second issue that the hire ratio brings out is the efficiency of your recruiters' selection criteria. In the example, they screened 75 percent of the applications out, and after interviewing 30 people they referred 10 to management. Management selected four. That means that only 3 percent of the applicants actually got hired. None of these numbers has an intrinsic "rightness" or "wrongness." As you read the numerators, the denominators, and the percentages from left to right, you begin to get a feel for how the selection process is working. You may know how acceptable they are at first glance, or you may have to collect this data for a period of time until you can develop norms of acceptable practice. Either way, this measure can be a very helpful tool as part of your criteria for recruiting efficiency.

Another measure that tells you something about how productive your recruiters are is called the *hit rate* (HO). Simply stated, hit rate is the ratio of job offers made to job offers accepted, as shown in Formula S-15.

Hit Rate

$$HO = \frac{OA}{OE} \tag{S-15}$$

where   HO = percentage of offers that result in a hire
         OA = offers accepted (e.g., 42)
         OE = offers extended (e.g., 50)

EXAMPLE

$$HO = \frac{42}{50}$$

$$= 84\%$$

It is helpful to have an acceptable standard for this ratio. Under normal circumstances, you should be able to have perhaps three or four out of five offers accepted. College recruiting typically is an exception to this rule.

If a recruiter knows the client manager's idiosyncrasies, comprehends the subtleties of the requesting department, does a good job of screening and interviewing, and sees to it that the right salary and conditions are offered, it is not hard to reach at least a 80-percent hit rate. As the job market shrinks you will see hit rate increase. It is a direct reflection of supply and demand. With fewer job opportunities available the candidate is more likely to accept your offer.

None of the criteria just mentioned are unreasonable. They are the knowledge and skills that a competent professional recruiter must have. The value of having a standard is that with a quick glance the staffing manager can tell how it is going. It will not be necessary to wait for someone to complain that you can't seem to hire people.

There is probably nothing more irritating, frustrating, and wasteful than an employment offer that is rejected. After your staff and the hiring department have spent many hours talking with candidates, checking references, comparing strengths and weaknesses, and preparing an offer, it is very disheartening to be turned down. If it happens very often you will have very unhappy customers and a demoralized recruiting staff.

The value in tracking your hit rate is, as always, to generate a signal telling you that performance is unacceptable. When the signal flashes you can investigate and take steps to remedy the problem before your client senses it. For that reason it is important that your standards of performance be set higher than your client would demand. If, for example, your line managers feel that a 70 percent hit rate is acceptable, you will want to set your goal at 80 to 90 percent. This way you can drop to 75 percent, catch the signal, identify the problem, and act on it before the rate drops to 70 percent. You always want to solve your problems before they become visible to the client. Your professional image depends on a high standard of performance.

Average hit rates in the SHRM/Saratoga Institute Human Resource Effectiveness Report have been 80 to 90 percent for the past nine years, and they haven't moved more than a few percent either way from year to year. Typically, you will find a low hit rate isolated in one group. This makes it easy to correct. If it is widespread, this usually means your pay or benefits packages are not competitive or there is some other general organizational problem (such as a negative reputation).

Two Ways to Quantify Quality

Up to this point we have been looking at ways to measure efficiency and productivity in the recruiting corps. But what about effectiveness? Effectiveness implies something beyond productivity. It embodies an expectation of desirability. It is not only doing something well; it is doing the important thing well. This issue of importance brings up the subjective nature of quality and makes it more difficult to measure than productivity. The fundamental struggle in organizations has been between human resources people who see their work as purely qualitative, and management, which wants some hard data to analyze. The key to closing this values gap depends on our ability to describe qualitative results with quantitative data.

For centuries, alchemists tried to turn lead into gold. They wanted to exchange the properties of one matter for those of another. Our job is much easier than that. We are not going to change anything; we are only trying to communicate a result through the medium of numbers rather than words.

Usually when people think about quantifying HR work they look at the total function, which may encompass nearly a hundred seemingly discrete tasks, and wonder how they can ever measure it. There are ways to attack this problem. Quality is a function of use over time. When an employee joins the organization and begins to work you can assess performance, but that requires waiting. How do you approach quality rating in the short term?

I have already demonstrated that the way to do that is to break the function down into those individual tasks that are in themselves quantifiable. That process of dividing a complex issue into identifiable parts is one method we use to determine the quality of new hires. The only difference will be that we will build a quality measure not by defining tasks, but by selecting specific results that reflect the quality of the new employee. As always, the objective must be results, not activity.

Surely one of the most critical indices of a recruiter's effectiveness is the quality of the individuals who are hired. Recruiters may do many tasks well, but if they cannot produce good candidates they must admit failure. The new hire is the end product of everyone's labor. The staffing manager, the recruiter, the administrative assistants, and the line manager are all involved in the process. Ultimately, the recruiter is the one who is held accountable for the quality of the end result.

The path to assessing new hire quality runs down two tracks. First, we must acknowledge that quality is time-bound. We don't really know how good something is until we have contact with it over some period of time. Therefore, the problem is how do you judge the quality of a new hire at the time of hire—-before the person starts working? I'll give you the answer to that shortly.

The second path to quality assessment is easier. It is found when you answer the question, "How do we describe a good employee?" Performance is the first indicator that comes to mind. Is that the only criterion? No. Promotability and stability also come into play. You may have others in mind to add to the list. For the sake of a simple example, I will work with these three. Recruiters deal with many applicants and generate many hires. In order to have a fair measure of the results of their labor, we should do a periodic evaluation of all hires. A semiannual review is a fair system to use for this purpose. There is usually enough activity in six months to smooth out any uncontrollable factors.

Patience is a prerequisite to measuring quality. We want to avoid flash-in-the-pan assessments. As you know, some new employees look great for the first few months, until they feel secure. After about six months the true nature of the individual becomes visible, and evaluations made thereafter are normally more reliable.

Performance on the job, promotion to higher levels, and stability are all issues that cannot be measured for a minimum of six months. Only if an employee leaves in a short time can we assess stability. From a management standpoint, this may be disturbing. However, quality is inherently a long-term issue. Whenever we think about product quality we expect that the item will not only do what it is supposed to do, but that it will last. We have a right to expect a product to perform its function for a long time before we allow the manufacturer to proclaim its quality. Likewise, it is unreasonable to expect a qualitative assessment of a new employee in less than six months, and a full year is an even better appraisal period. With this as a basis of assumption, let us look at a quality of hire (QH) measure, as shown in Formula S-16.

Quality of Hire

$$QH = \frac{PR + HP + HS}{N} \qquad \text{(S-16)}$$

where QH = quality of the people hired

          PR = average job performance ratings of new hires (e.g., 4 on a 5-point scale)

          HP = percent of new hires promoted within one year (e.g., 45%)

          HS = percent of new hires retained after 1 year (e.g., 90%)

          N = number of indicators used (e.g., 3)

EXAMPLE

$$QH = \frac{80 + 45 + 90}{3}$$

$$= \frac{215}{3}$$

$$= 71.7\%$$

The resulting percentage, 71.7 percent, is a relative value. It will be up to the person constructing the equation to decide if that number represents high, medium, or low quality. The decision can be based on historical comparison, preset performance standards or objectives, or management mandates.

Having said all that, we are now faced with the reality that performance ratings, promotions, and turnovers are beyond the control of the recruiter. A perfect hire can be driven out by a poor supervisor, lack of promotional opportunity, job market conditions, and many other phenomena that have nothing to do with the recruiter or the recruiting process. Business, no matter whether it is profit or not-for-profit, is an influenceable, not a controllable, activity.

A less objective but more valid procedure for establishing a quality criterion is to ask the receiving department. You could ask the hiring manager to rate a new hire at the time of hire. Before the person goes to work, the hiring manager rates, and ranks if you like, this hire against all other hires during a given time period. The rating can be along a scale, say—1 to 5 or 1 to 10. The ranking procedure is based on a comparison. A list would have to be maintained, and the receiver would insert the newest hire into the list in the appropriate slot. There are problems associated with establishing the validity of these types of opinions. Nevertheless, the measures are arrived at systematically, which implies some degree of reliability and objectivity.

That is the most complete and arduous way to measure quality. It works, but probably the best measure is the simplest. Compare the specifications on the requisition—e.g., education, experience, required skill levels, special abilities (language), etc.—to the qualities of the new hire. If they match, you have a high-quality hire. What happens after that has nothing to do with the recruiting and selection process...with one exception. Success on the job depends on fit as well as skills. If the recruiter knows the hiring manager and the department in which the new person will work, a good fit should occur.

Recruiter Effectiveness

In order to answer the broader qualitative question of recruiter effectiveness, we will follow the same procedure but employ some different indices. The place to start is to ask, "What do recruiters do that makes the most difference?" Effective work is not performing one task, is it? It is the sum of many important things done well. So, if we want to know how effective a recruiter is, we have to talk about several key tasks. As an example, let us say that an effective recruiter sources, screens, recommends, and assists management in the hiring of good employees. Beyond that, effective recruiters respond quickly, fill jobs promptly, cut hire costs to a minimum, maintain a high hit rate, and find quality candidates. Effective recruiters may do a few more things that make a difference, but for the sake of example let's stop there.

The following is a list of important issues for recruiters:

- Response time
- Time to fill jobs
- Cost per hire
- Hit rate
- Quality of hires

When you do this you are free to select your own list. There is no mandatory group of tasks or results that add up to effectiveness in all situations. Qualitative terms are by nature open to subjective definition. All you need do is agree on the variables with the other people who are going to judge recruiter effectiveness. Assuming that you were to agree with my sample, the next step is to put them together so that they add up to effectiveness as shown in S-17.

Recruiter Effectiveness

$$RE = \frac{RT + TF + HR + C/H + QH}{N} \qquad \text{(S-17)}$$

where   RE   = overall recruiter effectiveness
        RT   = response time (e.g., 9 days)
        TF   = time to fill (e.g., 34 days)
        HR   = hire rate (e.g., 80%)
        C/H = cost per hire (e.g., $884)
        QH   = quality of hire (e.g., 71.7%)
        N   = number of indices used (e.g., 5)

You can decide to simply take the resulting numbers at face value and make a judgment of relative effectiveness. This is often sufficient, but if you want more objective data you can compare each number with a predetermined goal. If you perform the percentage test on all indices, you will have converted the data to a common base. Then you can add all the percentages and divide by N to come out with a percentage of effectiveness, as shown in Fig. 6.4.

Proceed carefully in calculating percentage of goal achievement. In response time, goal is divided by result because the objective is to respond in 8 days or less. For time to fill and cost per hire, the objective is to fill in 45 days or less, at a cost of $1,000 or less. In both cases this was achieved, so performance exceeded 100%. In quality of hire, result was divided by goal because the objective was to exceed 75%. The question of which is the divisor and which is the dividend depends on whether you want the result to be a higher or lower number than the goal.

If you believe that one measure is more important than another, you could weight the measures to correspond to your evaluation. You might say that time to fill is 1.5 times more important than response time or hit rate. You might also say that cost per hire is two times and quality of hire is five times more important. Then you can multiply these factors times the percentages, add all five products, and divide by the sum of the weights. Mathematically, this is more proper than

Measure	Result	Goal	Goal achievement, weighted percentages
Response time	9 days	8 days	88 × 1.0 = 88
Time to fill	34 days	45 days	132 × 1.5 = 198
Hit rate	80%	80%	100 × 1.0 = 100
Cost per hire	$884	$500	113 × 2.0 = 226
Quality of hire	71.7%	75.0%	96 × 3.0 = 288
			900 ÷ 8.5 = 105.9

Figure 6.4. Recruiter Effectiveness

averaging simple percentages. Your result is a weighted evaluation of recruiter effectiveness. This is probably the most thorough computation you would consider. One step less would be to eliminate the weighting and simply compute an overall average percentage of effectiveness. The simplest and most common procedure would be the first one, a face value check of the actual raw data result.

Whichever method you choose, the fundamental principle is the same. Any subjective issue can be quantified by collecting and calculating data on a few key activities or results. Quality is an issue that requires more than one criterion, and it can be quantified.

> **GEM #8**   *A little useful information is more valuable than a mountain of irrelevant data.*

Summary

Cost is not the only issue in staffing. Time to fill jobs and quality of hires are also key performance indicators. Time can be measured along a continuum that starts with the receipt of an approved requisition and ends when a new hire arrives at work. Quality programs call this cycle time: the time it takes to complete a process. There are several points at which time can be measured and evaluated. You can even break down the total process into its key steps and monitor them. If you have an automated applicant tracking system, this is easy. The driving criteria around what to monitor is a function of which factors are most important at this point.

There are many activities involved in staffing, all of them subject to assessment and valuation. Monitoring the job-posting system can give you ideas on how much it costs to hire and move internal personnel compared to external hires. It can also give you ideas on how to improve the process or how to help employees use it more effectively. If you have a goal that a certain percentage of jobs should be filled from within, this will help you check your record.

The most perplexing problem for some people is the measurement of quality. There are several ways to go about this. One is to ask for ratings of the new hires by the hiring managers. You can also check the requisition specs against the qualifications of the new hire. The key thing to remember is that once a new hire shows up for work, other factors within the work environment can confound an otherwise good hire.

Recruiter effectiveness has long been a topic of discussion. This chapter provides a multidimensional form for measuring how well a recruiter is doing. Recruiter effectiveness represents a microcosm of the whole measurement issue. The process has many steps, and there are five ways to measure outcomes: cost, time, quantity, quality, and customer satisfaction. An effective measure is one that balances the need to know specifically what is happening against the need to spend a minimum of time on measurement. This is where knowing what the HR function's vision and customer relations goals are helps decide what will be the most useful set of data.

People often ask me, "Doesn't it take a lot of time to run a measurement system?" It does if you want to monitor 20 or 30 activities. But if you start with a small number, learn shortcuts and spread data collection out to the people who do the work, no one will feel it is oppressive. When the data comes in and your people begin to see what they can do with it, the objectives vanish.

7

Planning in a Volatile World

Forecasting Through Uncertainty

The purpose of planning and forecasting is to increase an organization's options and to reduce the penalties incurred by inappropriate actions. The success of forecasting depends on the reliability of the data put into the system, the choice of models and methods used, and most important, the linkage between the planners and forecasters and the line organization. In the best of all possible situations three conditions prevail. First, the planners are professionally competent and are respected for their ability to translate esoteric models and mountains of data into usable management information. Second, line management wants the planning system and will devote time to making it work. Third, the marketplace is stable and predictable. Given these times of instability, planning is a very precarious art. Planning cycles have come down from five years to sometimes no more than the upcoming year. Everyone recognizes that the long-term planning routines practiced from 1950 to 1990 are extinct.

Human resources forecasting deals with the internal and external sources of people needed to make the current business plan. The human resources plan profiles the existing work force, predicts the turnover rate, and projects the company's staffing needs by type, place, and time. Burack and Mathys[3] detailed the factors, both internal and external, that impact forecasting. Internal factors affect the availability and utilization of personnel throughout the group, while external factors impact the recruitment of people. Figure 7.1 lists some of the variables in each category.

Internal	External
Budget restrictions	Competition
Production levels	Contract bidding
Sales/service levels	World trade
Organizational structure	External labor markets
Policy/manpower management allocations	Demographics
Internal labor market	Unions
Manpower planning competency	Education/skills
Contract services	Laws
Communications (openness of job info)	Economic climate
Organizational goals	Technology
Mergers or acquisitions	Work methods
Organizational climate	Equipment
Personnel programs	New products or services
Training	
Compensation	

Figure 7.1. Factors Affecting Forecasts

In all, there are over 25 inputs, any one of which can skew the results of a forecast. Despite the development of predictive techniques and better sources of information, it is clear that forecasting is anything but a precise science. The future is still unknown and unknowable. Stable industries and stable economic conditions increase our ability to predict, but stability is a thing of the past. Volatility is the norm for the foreseeable future. Because of this unpredictability, it is very difficult for the staffing manager to plan even for the staffing department itself. The issue is, given the uncertainty, how does a staffing department prepare itself to respond promptly to the demands made on it? Our view of the planning model looks like Figure 7.2. The guiding principle is that each step should be connected to some type of identifiable and measurable value. Too much of planning focuses on providing bodies; that is the activity. We want planners to focus on how they are adding value.

Most companies will not allow staffing to carry excess employees. That is, you're one in a million if you have the luxury of maintaining a 110-percent staff complement in order to be ready for any emergency. Since you have to try to operate with no more, and probably less, than the number of people you need at any given time, and because you know from experience that periodically you will be inundated with unplanned and unexpected recruiting demands—what can you do to

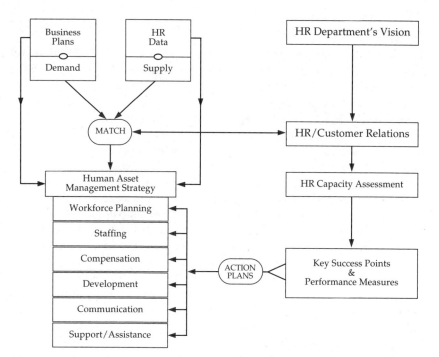

Figure 7.2. Strategic Human Asset Management Planning System

mitigate the stress that will be put upon your staff while maintaining an acceptable level of recruiting support?

The answer to this question lies in selecting those variables that are most affected by changes in recruiting demand. The most common variables are your requisition inventory, the workload of your recruiters and their assistants (expressed by the number of requisitions they are handling), the expected number of hires that can be attained by your recruiters and assistants in a given time period, and your past history of projected openings versus actual openings. All these are mitigated by market changes and volatility. These variables are also influenced by your support systems and the nature of management's needs. If you redesign the work flow or automate, it should make a difference in the number of requisitions your staff can handle. If you choose to source through agencies versus advertising, it will impact your workload. If the ratio of exempt to nonexempt or professional to managerial requisitions changes, that may affect your response time and time to fill. Your ability to predict the future depends on your knowledge of the past, your perception of the present, and your skills in forecasting.

Requisition Inventories

The first issue that the staffing manager needs to grasp is the size and variability of the requisition inventory. Requisitions are like orders: They come in, they are filled, and they go out. In a layoff environment such as we've experienced since the late 1980s, replacement requisitions are down and add requisitions are almost nonexistent. Yet even in unstable, cost-cutting times there are seasonal fluctuations in the requisition flow just as there are in the order flow. For instance, you know that more people quit their jobs and move during the summer. This causes the replacement requisition flow to increase. Some businesses, such as food processing, hire to meet the need to harvest and process different crops. Retailers increase their staff for the Christmas season. Manufacturers of consumer goods direct their output to supplying different buying seasons. These cycles all dictate an uneven load of requisitions.

The staffing manager could predict with some amount of confidence that the cycles will repeat each year. Except when the economy is in a deep recession, the cycles follow their normal patterns—only the amplitude changes. Of late the market defies traditional analysis. Nevertheless, we have to keep trying. Failure is also a great learning opportunity. Staffing can track the number of requisitions opened each month and the level of requisitions at the beginning or end of each month. The measurement of this type of ebb and flow is accomplished by a simple addition process. A ratio may be used later, when you compare time periods to each other or when you look at the number of new requisitions compared to the number filled or the number still in inventory. The three variations on this basic measure are shown in Formulas S-18 to S-20.

Requisitions Opened

$$RO = E\,RO + SNE\,RO + h\,RO \qquad\qquad (S\text{-}18)$$

where   RO   = number of requisitions opened per month, by level
    E RO   = number of exempt requisitions opened (e.g., 35)
  SNE RO = number of salaried nonexempt requisitions opened (e.g., 104)
   h RO   = number of hourly requisitions opened (e.g., 128)

EXAMPLE

$$RO = 35 + 104 + 128$$
$$= 267$$

In this example we tracked openings by level, but they could also be tracked by department, job group, or other criteria. This information could be recorded on a spreadsheet and updated each month. After one year the business cycle would be complete and cyclical fluctuations, if any, would be apparent. The next two measures would be calculated the same way.

Requisitions Filled

$$RF = E\ RF + SNE\ RF + h\ RF \qquad (S\text{-}19)$$

Requisition Inventory

$$RI = E\ RI + SNE\ RI + h\ RI \qquad (S\text{-}20)$$

These three indicators could be displayed on one table, as shown in Fig. 7.3. They could also be plotted on a trend chart and shown as three lines with months on the x axis and number on the y axis.

It is obvious that a manager of a staffing department needs to be able to predict the rate of incoming requisitions with some degree of accuracy. If there was no foreknowledge of the anticipated workload, it would be impossible to maintain a consistent level of service. One month the department might be overstaffed and the next woefully understaffed. If that were the pattern, the internal customers—that is, line and other staff managers—would turn to outside sources to meet their recruitment needs.

Requisition flow is only part of the picture, however. The staffing managers also must know how efficient the recruiters are. In the previous chapter we discussed a few measures of efficiency and productivity—for example, length of interviews and hit rate. When we examined recruiter effectiveness we also discussed response time and time to fill. It is helpful as well to know how many requisitions a recruiter and the recruiting assistant can effectively handle; that is, how many requisitions they can work on in an efficient and effective manner. Observation of past performance will show, within a range of values, what the optimum requisition load is for each recruiter and for the overall group in your organization. The manager also will want to have data on the hiring rates for different jobs. Some jobs are blessed

	Opened			Filled			Remaining		
Month	E	SNE	h	E	SNE	h	E	SNE	h
Jan	35	104	128	21	95	126	14	9	2
Feb	41	109	136	35	107	131	20	11	7
Mar	43	101	95	52	104	100	9	8	2

Figure 7.3. Requisition Activity

with an overabundance of applicants. This is most often true for entry-level, blue-collar, and white-collar positions. Other jobs go begging because there are more openings than there are applicants. This is the case with several scientific and technical occupations. Because the total job market is characterized by such variability, the staffing manager cannot maintain an optimum work force without knowing the profile of the requisition load and the efficiency and productivity levels of the recruiting staff.

Optimum Staff Ratios

First we looked at the size or volume of the incoming workload, namely the flow of requisitions. Now we want to learn how the recruiting staff reacts to that flow. Obviously, people can handle as many as 100 requisitions if all they have to do is funnel resumes and applications to the requesting departments. However, if the job entails screening incoming paper, interviewing, checking references, and conferring with the requester, then 100 requisitions is surely an unrealistic workload.

In 1992, Saratoga Institute managed a benchmarking project in which 36 companies investigated best staffing practices. We found that the ratio of recruiters to requisitions in those companies ranged from 1:3 to 1:50 depending on the variables just mentioned as well as expectations of service levels.

GEM #9   *The "right" or "best" number depends on conditions and expectations; there is no absolute answer.*

Since one of the notions underlying the term *productivity* is that the production is long term, let us use that as a working title for this question of optimum staff loading. The only way to arrive at an optimum factor is to track the hiring record of the recruiters and assistants over a long period of time. Seasonal fluctuations can distort short-term measures. During demand peaks and valleys the manager shifts people around to meet needs. As a minimum, I believe that you will have to have at least six months of production history before you can come to any conclusions. It is better to have the whole year to review, but if you do not have historical data and do not want to wait a year, then six months is a reasonable minimum.

The fundamental questions are, how many hires did the recruiters produce during each month? How many recruiters and how many administrative assistants did you have on staff in each of those months? Putting those facts together you can come up with the average monthly number of hires per recruiter and per assistant. This is the basic measure, and a table as shown in Fig. 7.4 could be constructed.

This table shows the average number of hires per month throughout the reporting period. The optimum number is not necessarily the highest number. For example, November produced 38.3 hires per recruiter and 28.7 hires per assistant. This was the highest monthly average for both groups. However, issues of cost, quality, and customer service are also important for a department that is more than a paper funnel. The staffing manager will take several factors into consideration before deciding which months were the optimum service months. In this case the staffing manager reviews hire quality, cost per hire, and recruiter effectiveness measures and concludes that the months 7 to 10 were the most effective recruiting period. During those months the recruiters generated an average of 25.8 new hires while the assistants supported 26.5 hires. Since the projection is for 1052 open positions in 1995, the staffing manager divides that by 12 and finds an average of 87.7 openings per month. Dividing that number by the production record of the previous year, the manager finds a staffing level of 3.4 recruiters and 3.3 assistants.

Month	New hires	Number of recruiters	Average per recruiter	Number of assistants	Average per assistant
Jan	37	4	9.2	4	9.2
Feb	40	4	10	5	8
Mar	57	4	14.2	5	11.4
Apr	78	4	19.5	5	15.6
May	88	5	17.6	5	17.6
Jun	79	5	15.8	4	19.7
Jul	104	5	20.8	4	26
Aug	114	5	22.8	4	28.5
Sep	108	4	27	4	27
Oct	98	3	32.6	4	24.5
Nov	115	3	38.3	4	28.7
Dec	61	3	20.3	4	15.2
Averages		4	20.6	4.3	19.2
Total	979				
New hires planned	682				
Attrition*	370				
Needed for 1995	1052				

*Turnover projections predict 370 openings due to voluntary and involuntary terminations.

Figure 7.4. Staff Productivity Record

Of course, this calculation is oversimplified. It ignores the variability of the recruitment year. You know that there will be seasonal fluctuations of all types that will affect your requisition flow. You have a business plan for the organization that translates this into a projection of hiring needs. You probably have high and low periods of turnover, which imply different levels of openings. All of these bits of information go into your estimate of new openings by month. Those 12 numbers would be the dividends, and the hiring production record (i.e., 25.8) would be the divisor. This set of computations will give you a base staffing level for each month throughout the coming year. By having people cross-trained, you can shift resources back and forth between functions and maintain an optimum level in your recruiting force.

As you track this recruitment function over a period of time, you may find changes occurring that are not seasonal. General business conditions, such as a recession, usually help recruiters improve their time and cost factors because more people are calling, writing in, or coming in off the street looking for jobs. On the other hand, the arrival of a new company in town may create more competition for jobs and thereby make each hire more difficult. This adds time and money to the process and may also negatively impact the quality of hires due to scarcity of good labor. A staffing manager has to be aware of these unforeseen factors if an accurate staff-level projection is desired.

Actual Versus Projected Results

I pointed out before that in order to project the future it helps to know the past. If Shakespeare was right and the past is prologue for what is to come, then we could use a convenient vehicle to record the past. The form that I propose illustrates the accuracy of the human resources planning system, as well as the organization's ability to accomplish its recruitment goals.

The form shown in Fig. 7.5 divides the data into two basic categories: additions to staff and replacements for existing jobs. Within those categories I have chosen to look at the data by the subdivisions of exempt, nonexempt, and hourly. As I have noted before, the subdivisions are a matter of personal choice. You may want to do it by occupations or by EEO categories. As always, it is up to you. The form provides space by category and subdivision to show the projected figure and the actual placement figure.

At the end of a reporting period—either monthly, quarterly, or annually—you can check the correlation between the actual and the

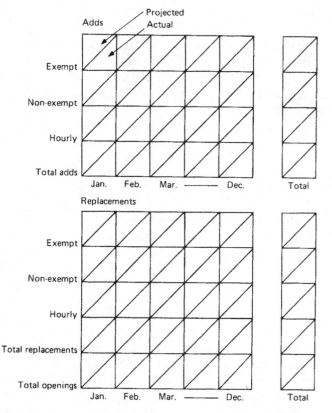

Figure 7.5. Actual versus Projected Hires

projected figures. Knowing how you have done by subdivision can help you strategize future recruitment efforts. For example, you may find that a given department, such as marketing, tends to project its needs either too high or too low. If this is a consistent pattern month after month, you might suspect that unless you can counsel them on projection techniques, you will have to inflate or deflate future projections by a certain amount. The market may change, but personalities seldom do. People have levels of skill and optimism that lead them to be a little high or a little low. Furthermore, this does not seem to change without some intervening event, such as training. Therefore, according to my experience as staffing manager, I could take the annual projections and inflate some while deflating others. The result was that my actual results came closer to my projected than they had before I bothered to study the patterns and make adjustments. This helped me plan my staffing levels more accurately. And whenever a new player got into the game, I would start my observations over again.

All successful people I know exhibit the habit of planning. It seems that they always have the time to study and plan before they act. On the other hand, the people whom I would classify as moderately successful to unsuccessful seem to spend more time acting and less time planning. They are the personification of the notion that they do not have time to plan, but they do have time to do it over when it goes wrong. Perhaps there is a lesson to be learned from these two approaches.

Summary

We have looked at the staffing function and measured it with the five basic indices: cost, time, quality, quantity, and customer service. I pointed out that the most important measure is customer satisfaction. Without it, you are out of work. The examples given were not meant to be all-encompassing. Rather, they were samples of what I consider, based on nearly ten years of managing a measurement system and a dozen more as a consultant focused on measurement, to be the most important tasks to measure. Do not use all the sample formulas. Choose a couple that have particular value for your situation. Furthermore, feel free to modify the sample to fit your needs. The way these formulas are expressed is not the only acceptable form There is a national standard system, the one endorsed by SHRM and used in the annual SHRM/Saratoga Institute survey. Nevertheless, you might have special needs within your company. Consider your environment, your staff, line management, business conditions, organizational objectives, and anything else that may impact your staffing function. Then design a set of measures and reports that will help you meet the twin goals of effective management and persuasive reporting.

SECTION C

Maintaining the Human Asset: How to Measure Compensation, Benefits, and Information Systems

8

The Pay System

No HR function is changing as much as compensation. Compensation professionals who insist on running their operation in the traditional structure and process orientation will face one of two destinies: termination or outsourcing. Processing functions are perfect places to apply principles of total quality management, benchmarking, and reengineering. Each of those three tools has different applications. TQM looks at the process and asks, "How could we do it better?" Benchmarking searches for the best process in another company and asks, "What can we adapt from that to our situation?" Reengineering looks past the process to the objective and asks, "What's the best way of doing it?" And if none of them work—the process is being outsourced. The smart "pay people" are learning that their future rests in managing the compensation system for value, not for activity.

The Most Popular Topic

Compensation is the one subject within human asset management that everyone wants to talk about. It is sometimes difficult to involve managers and supervisors in studies of planning, training, recruitment, or employee relations programs. But let it be known that you are going to review and revise the compensation system and you will find people knocking down your door to be on the project team. This is quite reasonable. Everybody, no matter how talented or limited they are, understands two factors in life: pain and pleasure. They view their pay as either one or the other. Most of us can always use more money, and when someone brings up the subject we are usually anxious to talk about it. We want to lobby for a bigger share of the pie or, in the worst case, protect what we have. The challenge for the compensation manager is not to get people interested, it is to convince them that the system is equitable and they should use it rather than subvert it.

If I ask you how you determine if your compensation program is doing its job, what would be your answer? The answer to that, of course, is, "It depends." What does it depend on? It depends on what it is supposed to be doing. This is not just a verbal jousting match. Tell me, what is the purpose of the compensation system? Whenever I ask that question the reply is usually something like, "Compensation's mission is to assist in attracting, retaining, and motivating employees." That answer is two-thirds right. Technically speaking, motivation is an inherent trait of human beings. You cannot motivate a person; you can only stimulate or incent employees. It is a small point, but for the sake of precision and education of managers, I believe it is worth noting. The implication of incent versus motivate is profound when applied to managing people. However, this is not the place to go into it in depth. In this case, we need only the notion that motivation is internal and incentive is external.

Compensation's New Challenge

Designing compensation programs is a complex process. There is much more to it than doing a salary survey and spreading some numbers across a form. In the olden days—pre 1990—the compensation department had to understand the processes for planning, projecting, and administering. It also needed to be comfortable with statistical procedures. In addition, it needed to be able to synthesize data from many sources and shape it into a structure that everyone could understand and use. That structure had to meet the reasonable needs and demands of employees, as well as mesh with the philosophy of the organization and its ability to pay. All of this could not be attained through haphazard methods. It required the development of a system. As I pointed out before, people understand the value of money in their lives. They will put up with a lot of managerial ineptitude except when it comes to pay.

The paradox is that in today's more fluid and informal organizations job structures are changing. The traditional heavily structured compensation systems are falling out of favor because they do not suit the times. Compensation professionals are feeling the pressure to be more responsive and flexible. What is becoming clear is that jobs as we've always known them are going away and being replaced by competencies. The new organizational forms are requiring people to spend more time on teamwork and projects. Thus, old job descriptions linked to pay grades are becoming obsolete. Just how and how fast this will come about is anybody's guess. However, when old systems give way to new ones, the need to monitor and objectively measure the emerging system's performance becomes critical.

By tracing the processes indigenous to a compensation system and the results that the system yields, we can find points to assess. The potential trap lies in measuring the usage and outcomes of the system and implying that this equates with the productivity or effectiveness of the compensation department. In some sense it does, and in another it does not. The point is important, and the issue is complex enough that we need to spend time now clearly establishing the rationale for our different measurement criteria.

First, referring to our definitions of *productivity* and *effectiveness*, you recall we said that productivity relates to levels of performance in valued activities. Effectiveness is doing the right thing—getting the desired result. The two issues are semantically discrete but pragmatically inseparable. It is hard to imagine effective performance that is carried out in an unproductive fashion. Nevertheless, I will offer a way of looking at the compensation department from both a productive and an effective viewpoint.

The compensation department attempts to fulfill its organizational role of assisting in attracting, retaining, and incenting employees by focusing on the following:

1. It builds a system of performance appraisal and pay that suits the evolving needs of the organization.

2. It controls the cost of the pay program not just by monitoring the dollar cost, but also by influencing how supervisors and managers exercise the program.

3. The compensation staff tries to communicate the pay and performance appraisal system to the employees so that they will understand how and why it works the way it does.

4. The compensation department strives to convince employees, by monitoring management pay practices, that the system is just, equitable, and competitive.

The way to judge the compensation department's productivity or effectiveness is to look at each of the focal activities separately, starting with system design. Point one is, does your pay system serve the changing organizational structure and management philosophy? As markets and organizations change, pay systems have to be redesigned. This was not a problem until the early 1990s. By then, it became apparent that something new was required. Along came broad-banding and pay for skills. Already companies are finding that it is counterproductive to pay for skills that are seldom used or don't contribute to value creation. It is blatantly obvious that compensation specialists will have to acquire new skills if they are to meet the challenges of the twenty-first century.

Cost control is an activity of the compensation department. However, the results of that activity are external to the department. Costs are, to be sure, a function of how system components are handled. For example, writing job descriptions and leveling jobs impact salary expenses. You can measure productivity by calculating how long it took the compensation analyst to write a job description (JD) or level a group of jobs. However, you measure the effectiveness of the work by what happens when managers use those descriptions and pay grades. The work is performed effectively if managers can attract, retain, and incent people, and still stay within the salary budget. By definition, if a system meets its objectives and does so with an acceptable level of employee satisfaction, it is effective. The second part of that definition leads us to the third focal point of measurement in compensation.

Employee satisfaction is a phenomenon totally external to the compensation department, yet it depends in part on the work of the compensation staff. A number of vehicles are available to the department for explaining their system to employees. The most direct methods are meetings and written communiqués—both electronic and on paper. However, the one that counts above all others is the manner in which an individual's supervisor utilizes the system. The role of the compensation manager is to make sure that those in supervisory positions are handling the system in the manner intended. The best way to determine that is through employee surveys and exit interviews. When it comes to pay questions, people are seldom reticent to tell you what they think and feel. A less formal but easily accessible source of effectiveness data is daily feedback. Your staff usually knows how people feel about their pay. They hear about it all the time if they are maintaining good contacts with the employees as a whole. If employees understand and feel good about the pay program, it is fair to claim that your staff has done an effective job.

In summary, it is relatively easy to measure your compensation staff's productivity. Primarily, this requires a judgment of how efficiently they are carrying out their tasks. Several examples will be presented in this chapter. *Effectiveness*, since it is a subjective term, is more ambiguous. In order to have a good measure of effectiveness, it is necessary to create a composite consisting of several external outcome variables. In Chapter 6 we did that to judge recruiter effectiveness. Although composites are not as neat as a single unequivocal measure, they are the best and only way to generate a useful indicator.

Maintaining a Moving System

Salary structures usually start with the development of job descriptions. Following closely on job descriptions is the job evaluation and leveling process. The result of the interaction between the description and leveling processes is a salary structure. One of the truest statements about structures is that they cannot stand still, but must be dynamic. In the 1980s and before, that usually meant an annual review of pay grades. Structures changed only if some significant event came along. Today, and in the foreseeable future, structures are becoming less permanent. With organizations attempting to manage pay costs, experiments are in vogue. Its interesting to watch organizations move to seemingly new methods such as broad-banding and then gradually modify them. Eventually, they look suspiciously like the old structures.

With the trend toward more teamwork, the components that hold a salary structure together must be monitored constantly. Since jobs change, job descriptions have to be broadened or rewritten constantly. The proactive manager thinks ahead to structural changes and trends, and writes descriptions that don't have to be reviewed every couple of months. To keep on top of the moving market, standards should be set for auditing job descriptions. The achievement of those goals can be monitored and quantified, as shown in Formula C-1.

Job Description Factor

$$JDF = \frac{JD}{J} \qquad (C\text{-}1)$$

where JDF = percentage of jobs having formal, current job descriptions
JD = number of jobs with current descriptions (e.g., 312)
J = total number of jobs in the system (e.g., 339)

EXAMPLE

$$JDF = \frac{312}{339}$$

$$= 92\%$$

Auditing the job description is just part of the task. It helps recruiters who need up-to-date information to fill jobs. However, unless it is followed by job evaluation and leveling, the salary structure does not benefit. Thus, system maintenance is a two-step process. Once job descriptions are rewritten, then job evaluations are conducted and the structure is releveled. Just as maintenance goals are set for descriptions, so should they be set for evaluation and leveling. Formula C-2 gives the job evaluation factor.

Job Evaluation Factor

$$JEF = \frac{JE}{J} \qquad \text{(C-2)}$$

where JEF = percentage of jobs that have been evaluated and leveled
      JE = number of jobs evaluated and leveled (e.g., 308)
      J = total number of jobs in the system (e.g., 339)

EXAMPLE

$$JEF = \frac{308}{339}$$
$$= 91\%$$

Another way of looking at the vitality of the system is to approach it from an exception standpoint. How many exceptions exist within the structure, or how often do we have to make adjustments in order to achieve a worthwhile objective? Two examples of this are salary range exceptions, commonly referred to as "red circles," and salary adjustments, usually made for a group of jobs.

In the first case it is worthwhile to know what percentage of your employees have salaries that exceed the maximum for their grade or salary band. The calculation is simple, as shown in Formula C-3.

Salary Range Exception Factor

$$SO = \frac{EX}{e} \qquad \text{(C-3)}$$

where SO = percentage of employees over salary grade maximums
      EX = number of excesses (e.g., 3)
      e = average number of employees (e.g., 71)

EXAMPLE

$$SO = \frac{3}{71}$$
$$= 4.2\%$$

A growing incidence of excesses may reveal an aging and stagnant employee population. Although with the early retirement programs that started in the late 1980s that is hard to imagine. But whatever the reasons, a number of people may have "maxed out" and are not able to move up to the next higher grade. Besides being a structural problem, this also creates an abnormally high labor cost. In today's intensely competitive marketplace, most companies cannot tolerate salaries above the maximum for the range. Another question that may be brought out is poor salary management. Managers sometimes use salary dollars to try to solve interpersonal problems. For example, they may have employees who should be counseled about lack of effort to qualify themselves for promotion. Instead of facing the issue, the manager requests a salary increase above range maximum. Keeping track of the excesses is one means of monitoring the system. This also pays off by pointing out organizational or managerial problems.

A second example of exceptions has to do with requests for salary adjustments. Even with the pressure to keep costs down, it may happen that some market perturbation takes place and forces an unplanned adjustment in a specific job family. Take the case where you suddenly learn that a competitor is now paying programmers 15 percent more than your company does. You can choose to hold the line, and predictably it will be more difficult to recruit programmers. You might also begin to experience unwanted turnover in that group as they learn what is being offered elsewhere. If jobs are truly available, more often than not your management will choose to adjust the salary range or the salaries of your current programming staff.

That kind of a situation can and does come up in every organization from time to time no matter what the organization's needs might be. However, if you find that it seems to be happening with great frequency, it might signal the need to audit the structure. It sometimes happens that a company forgoes a structural review because they believe that they can safely go another six months without moving the ranges. Then they begin to experience a rather constant stream of requests to make adjustments. In this case they have miscalculated or ignored information that might have predicted the need to adjust. Adjustments for a specific group may have an unsettling effect on the larger organization. If another group hears about it, and they always will, they begin to look for reasons why they, too, deserve an unscheduled raise. Soon a ripple spreads out across the organization, and the compensation department finds itself under severe pressure to meet both supportable and insupportable demands. In such cases, the management of the system has been taken away from the department.

There is no need to create a formula to track the frequency of adjustments. The point is to note that adjustments are exceptions to a system; and if there are too many exceptions, this implies that the system is no longer functional.

Cost Control

Periodically, all employees are entitled to a review of their performance. In a study of organizational communications, it was found that employees were much more interested in performance and career opportunity information than in any other topic. There has probably been as much research and speculation on performance reviews and appraisals as on any managerial subject. Operating philosophies have been created to inform and support managers so that they can do a more credible, constructive job. Elaborate procedures have been developed to help managers review their employees, management by objectives being the best example of that approach. And yet, even with all this very few companies are happy with their review systems.

As a last resort, some organizations have gone to setting up a standard profile by which they expect managers to distribute the performance appraisals in their group. Some insist on using the bell-shaped curve. With this they say, in effect, that most issues, activities, and outcomes are naturally distributed on the curve. Therefore, we would expect that the performance scores you give your group will be more or less normally distributed. That is, a very small percentage will receive the highest possible rating, a slightly larger number will receive the next highest rating, most of the people will be about in the middle, and the remainder will be spread down the backside of the curve. Management may sometimes become very specific and say that no more than 10 percent can receive the top rating, the second level should include about 20 percent, 40 percent should set a middle rating, 20 percent a low one, and 10 percent should probably be on probation. With today's low salary increase budgets, when an employee brings their increase to the bottom line, there will be very little dollar difference between any two adjacent points on a scale.

Nevertheless, one way to display the distribution data for several groups is to put it on a table. On the y axis, or side, list the departments and the number of employees. On the x axis, along the top, place the performance levels so that they are column headings. It is helpful to show both the number of people appraised at a particular level and the percentage of the whole which that represents. Figure 8.1 is a sample performance appraisal table.

It is relatively easy to see both how each department did against the goal and how they compared to each other. Was one consistently high? Was another consistently low? Either way, if the differences are significant they can act as precursors of organizational problems.

A quicker evaluation can be made if you plot those percentages as curves on a graph. Using a color display, five or six groups can be shown on the same chart without confusion. If you have set a desired

Division	Number of employees	Performance level 5		Performance level 4		Performance level 3		Performance level 2		Performance level 1	
		#	%	#	%	#	%	#	%	#	%
A	885	15	1.7	566	64.0	231	26.1	71	8.0	2	0.2
B	565	42	7.4	329	58.2	168	29.7	26	4.6	0	0
C	590	38	6.4	220	37.3	272	46.1	60	10.2	0	0
D	260	20	7.7	113	43.5	95	36.5	32	12.3	1	0.3
E	178	22	12.4	110	61.8	38	21.3	8	4.5	0	0
F	134	24	17.6	86	64.7	20	14.7	4	3.0	0	0
Corporate total	2612	161	6.2	1424	54.5	824	31.5	201	7.8	3	0.1

Figure 8.1. Performance Appraisal Distribution

distribution curve, you can also plot that. Then everyone can quickly see the correlations and deviations between the standard and the actual.

Salary increase patterns can be handled in the same manner. Many organizations set increase standards; for example, they may decide that the average increase should be 4 percent in the coming year. Within that parameter, they may allow managers to distribute increases as they see fit. Other organizations may structure the process by dictating minimum and maximum increases throughout the system.

No matter which way the system is set up, the results can be displayed to show how they compare to the standards. The principle is the same for salary increase displays as it was for performance appraisals. When a tabular format is used, the vertical axis shows the departments, set in a column along the left side. The elements to be reviewed are placed across the top as column headings. For example, the columns may be levels—i.e., hourly, nonexempt, and exempt—or job groups—i.e., programmers, engineers, accountants, and secretaries. The average salary increase percentage is then recorded in the appropriate position on the table.

Increase patterns can also be shown in a bar chart format. The percentage increase is placed on the vertical y axis from 0 up to a maximum of your choice. The groups to be viewed are arranged across the horizontal x axis. Be aware that the larger the y scale, the less the differences between groups will appear to be. For instance, a percentage range of 20 points will make the differences between measured groups smaller than a range of 15 points. A wide range lessens the visual impact. So, if your maximum recorded increase is 14 percent, use a 15-percent scale. The difference between the lengths of bars will be more dramatic than if you use a 20-percent scale. Always keep in mind the fact that a report is supposed to both inform and make a point. So, construct a chart which tells your story as effectively as possible.

Another goal-type measure is quite common, and most organizations have it: the salary budget. Budgets are constructed from different perspectives, but they all end up at the same point—they tell managers how many total dollars can be spent on salaries. Most budget systems kick out a monthly or quarterly report that shows the variance between actual and budgeted figures. Somewhere in the accounting system the salary account is subtotaled by department and then totaled for the whole organization. Simply divide those numbers by the budgeted figure and see what the variance is. If you do it on a month-to-month basis, you can see loosening or tightening trends across a range of departments. Your results can be reported in either dollar or percentage variance.

Distribution Patterns

The last section, where we looked at increase patterns, is a precursor to a discussion of distribution patterns. The underlying issue in both is, how are managers using the system? I pointed out earlier that we cannot design systems and then disavow how they are used. I believe that our job is to guide management in the proper utilization of the programs we develop. This is not always easy, as you know from experience. Nevertheless, it is our obligation not only to design the vehicle and train people how to drive it, but also to monitor their driving habits and point out faults and hazards as we see them. This is where the concept of effectiveness comes in. Just as bad driving habits are dangerous to the safety of driver, occupants, and bystanders, so inappropriate and improper use of a salary program can be unfair to employees and dangerous for the organization. When pay is distributed incorrectly, some employees will benefit while others suffer. Furthermore, the organization is jeopardized. Poor pay practices usually lead to higher turnover, lower morale, and in some cases legal actions against the organization. Americans sue at the slightest provocation. There have been many cases in recent years where class-action suits have resulted in multimillion-dollar back pay awards. And for every case that makes it to court, there are undoubtedly dozens that are settled quietly and privately.

Compensation managers have a mechanism that they can use to study the distribution of individual salaries within a salary grade. If a salary structure is set up so that there are four subdivisions to each salary grade, it is called a *quartile structure*. The method that is used to calculate the distribution pattern reveals how many people have a salary within each quartile of a given grade. When those figures are plotted, it is called a *maturity curve*. From a technical standpoint this is a very valuable measure for the compensation department. It tells them how well their structure is aging. That is, are there too many people high in the grade? It could mean that the employee population is stagnating and an excessive number of people are "topping out." This is already showing up as organizations go toward broad-banding.

You want to look at salary distribution from an equity point of view. You can be certain that there is no case of intentional or unintentional discrimination. There are at least two ways of doing this. The more precise method is to use a variation of the maturity curve calculation described earlier. In this case you would look at salary distribution across quartiles of each grade for each of the groups you wanted to examine. For EEO purposes, you would do it for each affected category. Obviously, this is a very complex and time-consuming calculation, which cannot be performed easily without computer assistance. If you choose to do it, you have to construct a separate table for each category. You would probably set up the table with salary grades in the first column. Quartiles 1 to 4 would constitute the next four columns. Each quartile position on the table would display either the number of people or the percentage of people from that category whose salary fell into that position. For you to know whether or not the resulting distribution profile is discriminatory, you would have to do the same thing for the unaffected categories of employees. I am certain that you can appreciate the magnitude of the task.

A simpler way to obtain a sense of whether or not you had a problem would be to use average salaries for each group, as shown in Fig. 8.2. By using an average you eliminate the task of spreading individual salaries across a grade. This approach also allows you to display data on all categories on one page. When the table is filled in, you can scan it for any obvious or serious disparities. This is the simplest way of doing the job, though you could convert actual salaries into percentiles. I do not see the value of the extra labor, however. Many people have difficulty dealing with percentiles, and actual average salaries don't really need any interpretation.

There is a hidden danger in dealing with averages. Averages lump together all salaries and in the process ignore the differences among them. As a result, the average may look fine, but you may have within

Salary grade	EEO category							
	B	H	O	I	F	A	H	Others
10	980	978	1018	950	985	1040	964	1000
20	1085	1077	1139	1078	1085	1159	1090	1110
30	1235	1237	1270	1238	1356	1301	1229	1280

Figure 8.2. Patterns of Average Monthly Salaries by Employee Group

that a few people who are a long way from the mean. A standard deviation tells you how wide a spread there is between individual salaries and the average salary. While the average salary across groups may be similar, the standard deviations may indicate quite a difference. Many hand-held calculators are capable of running a standard deviation.

Distribution studies can be made for a variety of issues. Besides affected categories, you could look at pay patterns across departments, locations, or any other classification that you thought might be hiding or breeding a problem. Compensation managers are responsible for monitoring the system that they design. They owe it to their organizations to be a watchdog on issues of pay. Conducting a distribution study once a year goes a long way toward ensuring that no one can ever bring a successful class-action pay suit against you.

Cost Analysis

In most organizations the payroll costs are the largest or the second largest single expense item. The two most common calculations are total cost of payroll and average salary cost per employee. There is no mystery to the whys and hows of these. However, some other variations on these basic measures are useful.

An often overlooked cost item is payroll taxes. An organization not only pays its employees an hourly rate or a monthly salary, it also pays a significant amount of money to the government. These funds go for Social Security, income taxes, unemployment insurance, and in some states disability insurance. To appreciate how much this could amount to, you can compute a payroll tax factor, as shown in Formula C-4.

Payroll Tax Factor

$$PTF = \frac{PT}{C} \qquad (C-4)$$

where   PTF = portion of total salary or wages (including bonus and incentive pay) absorbed by payroll taxes

PT = sum of payroll tax deductions for Social Security (FICA), federal and state income taxes, unemployment insurance, and state disability where applicable (figures will vary by state and by income level)

C = Total compensation (i.e., salary, bonus and/or commission)

EXAMPLE

$$PTF = \frac{FICA + FIT + SIT + UI + SDI}{salary/wages \ (+ \ bonus \ and \ incentives)}$$

Both the magnitude and the rate of growth of this expense item have become critical operating concerns for management. I believe that compensation departments should keep total dollars as well as percentages in front of management. The executives who run organizations owe it to their stockholders and employees to be cognizant of this cost and to be active in dealing with the various governmental bodies, to slow the inexorable rise in these job-killing taxes.

Management Reporting

Management's attention should be focused on strategic, macro level data. Rather than filling your report with counts of jobs leveled and salary actions processed, you should show how pay relates to other expenses, as well as to sales, number of employees and benefits. These variables are basics of a business whether it be profit or not-for-profit. One matchup that many firms monitor is employees and revenues. By dividing total revenue by total employees they obtain a number that they track as one mark of efficiency. If revenues equaled $200 million and there were 1,400 employees, the ratio would be $142,857:1 (employee). If this number improved significantly, it would be a sign that gross productivity was increasing. The improvement was not necessarily all in factory productivity. It might have been that salespeople were becoming more efficient or that engineering had simplified a design or that manufacturing had automated a procedure. The reason was not necessarily obvious, but the result was clearly positive. Of course, a decrease in the number would indicate a deterioration in performance somewhere. In a service business, higher productivity usually means that the organization is able to serve an increasing number of customers without adding to staff.

A similar efficiency measure is the average hourly rate. It is calculated as shown in Formula C-5.

Average Hourly Rate

$$R/h = \frac{P}{EHW} \qquad \text{(C-5)}$$

where   R/h = average hourly wage or salary paid
         P = total wages and salaries paid (e.g., \$57,017,000)
      EHW = Total annual employee hours worked times number
              of employees (e.g., 2,080 × 1,400)

EXAMPLE

$$R/h = \frac{\$57,017,000}{2,080 \times 1,400}$$

$$= \frac{\$57,017,000}{2,912,000}$$

$$= \$19.51$$

By adding the "hours worked" variable we have refined a gross compensation number into an hourly one. This is more workable. It is difficult for a person to deal with an eight-digit number. The figure \$57,017,000 is useful to rally support for an efficiency or productivity drive, but \$19.51 is a human-scale number. Employees can say to themselves, "If I can find a way to save just 10 cents an hour in labor cost, that will save the company almost \$300,000!" It is this type of micro-thinking that contributed to Japan's strong position in the world market. Most people can think of ways to save a dime, but they do not deal with \$500,000 often enough to know where to start.

We have looked at cost from several perspectives. The last one was the cost of function. The work force can be divided into many groups, such as level, job group, department, and location. One other function is supervision and management. Few people consider what it costs an organization to manage itself. Consider the portion of your organization that is populated by supervisors and managers. This category includes everyone from first line supervisor to the chief executive officer. All of these people exist in the organization, yet they are not producers. Their job is to manage the work of others. The question is, how much does it cost you for that service? The simplest way to find out is to compute a cost to supervise factor. See Formula C-6.

Cost to Supervise

$$SC = \frac{TSS}{TS} \qquad \text{(C-6)}$$

where   SC = supervision cost
      TSS = total salaries paid to supervisors and above (e.g.,
          $19,760,000)
      TS = total wages and salaries paid (e.g., $57,017,000)

EXAMPLE

$$SC = \frac{\$19,760,000}{\$57,017,000}$$
$$= 34\%$$

Beyond all that we have talked about, there are still some questions that compensation might be able to address. Remember, we made a case early on for the interrelated nature of human resources functions. By looking at hiring and employee relations issues we can find evidence of compensation program effectiveness. Where there is effect we might be able to identify cause. Here are a couple of questions that could be asked of other human resources sections:

1. Are we able to consistently hire below midpoint? The answer to this tells us if our structures are staying competitive. New hire records will show starting salaries.

2. Are people leaving for the same level job and getting substantially more money? This is another approach to the competitive structure question. The answer to this one can be found in exit interviews.

3. If there are incentive programs, such as piece rates and bonuses, do the people feel that they are challenging and fair? Surveys and interviews will provide the answers to this question.

4. Do supervisors and managers find the system easy to understand and, more important, explain to their staffs? Again, surveys and interviews will tell the story.

There are many more questions like these that can be asked about the system. In every case answers are available. When these are put into the mix with the more quantitative issues, a well-rounded evaluation of the compensation function emerges.

Employee Pay Attitudes

Tangential to the pay system and its utilization is the reaction of employees to their pay. Some short-sighted managers claim that in a tight job market it doesn't matter so much about people's pay attitudes because there are few other jobs for them to go to. But people aren't stupid and they get angry when they feel they're being screwed. They will find ways to obtain equity for themselves even when they have to stay in a low-paying job. Since our behavior is largely based on our perceptions of our environment, and since pay is part of our perceptual field, it follows that employees' view of their pay must correlate with some aspects of work behavior. What is not yet proved is exactly how, when, and how much attitudes impact behavior on the job. If you want your compensation department to be effective in terms of optimizing the organization's return on its salary dollars, pay attitudes have to be addressed. Lawler[1] has reviewed the research on the importance of pay and concludes this:

> Most of the research is fragmented, noncumulative, and poorly designed. Most of the forty-nine studies (reviewed by Lawler) that have tried to determine how important pay is represents a great expenditure of effort that contributes virtually nothing to our understanding. By selectively using the data from these studies, one can argue any position...

Smith and Wakeley[2] pointed out that pay has been viewed from several standpoints by theorists

1. Money is a general means to satisfying needs.
2. Money is a basic incentive.
3. Money may be an anxiety reducer.
4. Money keeps workers from being dissatisfied but does not motivate.
5. Money is an instrument to attaining a valued goal.

No matter which view you subscribe to, you would probably agree that pay is an important issue in the minds of your work force.

I believe that people fundamentally ask themselves two questions about their pay. First, am I paid fairly? Is the amount of money I make appropriate for the effort and responsibility I put into the job? Second, does the ratio of my input to my outcome compare favorably with the same ratio for other workers in my company, locale, and industry?

Since pay is important to your employees, you will want to know as much about their attitudes toward your system and its utilization as you can. The most common ways of obtaining that information are through interviews, focus groups, and surveys. Structured and unstructured interviews at orientation, during a person's employment, or at the time of termination can elicit a good deal of useful information. Surveys are much more complicated and time-consuming. They also can cause more harm than good if they are not administered properly or if the findings are not responded to. There are many surveys available commercially. Some offer extensive computer-based analysis as well as national and regional norms. It is not the purpose of this chapter to review them. My objective in mentioning surveys is simply to point out that they are probably necessary in some form if you want to find out how effective your pay program is in the eyes of the recipients. Also, I want to caution those who have not used surveys extensively that they are not as straightforward as they appear. I firmly believe that surveys should never be conducted with large groups of employees without professional assistance. My observation is that a very significant percentage of surveys backfire on the user due to lack of knowledge about how to design or conduct them, rash judgment of the results, or inappropriate or nonexistent follow-up with those surveyed. My conclusion is that it is important to know how your employees perceive their pay, and the only way to obtain those perceptions is through some formal structured interview or survey. However, be careful how you go about it. Pay may or may not be the most important issue on the minds of employees, but few issues are more sensitive.

The Strategic View

The focus up till now has been principally on administrative or micromanagement issues. The compensation group needs this type of data to monitor the performance of the system. The other side of the coin is the macro or strategic perspective.

Top management is not interested in the arcane technology of compensation administration. The senior team views compensation as an expense that, they hope, retains and incents the work force to perform at high levels. We never know how much of a person's performance is influenced by monetary rewards. Nevertheless, management accepts the premise that pay can be a stimulant. Compensation managers should point their management reports toward two issues: expense trends and correlations to performance.

Figure 8.3 is an illustration of a simple yet powerful display that can be presented to management. It shows the trend over time of payroll and benefit costs as a percentage of operating expense. These are two of the items tracked in the annual SHRM/SI HRE report. By comparing your data to other companies of your size, type, or region you can establish an ongoing competitive analysis.

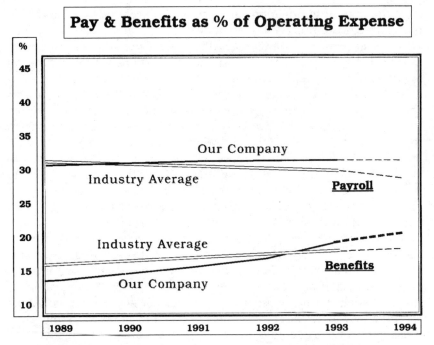

Figure 8.3. Labor Cost Trends

This is the level at which top management can and should usefully focus their attention. Presenting this type of data on a regular basis causes the compensation manager to be viewed as someone who transcends administration. The compensation manager becomes part of the executive team that manages the cost effectiveness of the human asset. Other types of ratios and costs that compensation can monitor are as follows:

Compensation and benefit costs as a percentage of revenue

Percentage of compensation that is "at risk"

Cost of overtime as a percentage of total pay

The second strategic compensation issue is the return on investment of incentive plans. Sales personnel have long worked on incentives. When used judiciously, incentives can be very powerful. There is a small but growing trend to put more pay at risk for positions other than sales. This can be very difficult to administer if there no sound individual and group performance measurement system is in place.

Incentive plans are only as good as the performance measures on which they are based. If you want to introduce pay at risk or other incentive programs you must first design and install a system to objectively measure and report performance. Most importantly, the work force must be able to understand it and believe it is fair. Incentives can be very immediate, as with weekly or monthly payouts. Or they can be longer term, with quarterly or annual rewards. You can pay for individual or team performance. Payouts can be based on productivity, quality, service, or sales targets using cost, time, quantity, quality, or human reaction indices. Long-term plans are often based on profit goals. There are so many variations that one could write a separate book on the pros and cons of each. For our purposes the issue is that performance measures are the foundation.

The best pay for performance system I have seen starts by focusing everyone's attention on the four strategic imperatives of that organization: quality, customer service, employee relations, and financial responsibility. Then, each person develops a set of objectives within the four imperative categories. The performance levels are all described in quantitative terms. There are both individual and team objectives, and pay is based evenly on individual and team performance. In addition, the company recently introduced an annual corporate profitability target with monetary rewards tied to it. The program was developed participatively with the supervisors and managers of the company. It was launched in 1992, and the impact on operating effectiveness and morale has been outstanding.

The experience of working with this company reinforced my belief that the key to top performance is to be able to connect an individual's or group's actions with a desired result. If you refer to the value chain in Chapter 4 it will give you an idea of how to apply the logic to trace action to value added.

    GEM #10   *We get exactly what we pay for.*

Summary

Although the compensation function deals mainly with quantitative issues, there are relatively few measures of the compensation group's efficiency and productivity. Staffing lends itself more to that type of evaluation because it is basically project work. Each opening is like a project, with a beginning and an end. Compensation is more like a process. It is a continuous flow with few clear checkpoints. It is very difficult to identify cause-and-effect relationships. Compensation has maintenance tasks whose efficient accomplishment can be evaluated. However, the results are of interest only to the compensation and human resources management.

To grasp the full value of the compensation function we have to study it more from a strategic effectiveness perspective. Many different indices can be gathered and viewed as a composite picture. In the end we make a judgment that goes something like this: The compensation system has a purpose that is quite far-reaching, important, and complex. To achieve its mission it must establish and maintain a structure, and we can audit how well it is attending to that responsibility. Another task for compensation is to service the needs of the organization with a minimum of exceptions to the system. We can track system utilization to see how well it is operating against preset standards and goals. Since creation of pay equity is a fundamental mission, we can look at the results of the use of the system to determine if pay is being properly distributed across all groups. We can also measure the cost of wages and salaries and check to see if it is within acceptable ranges. Third, we can measure employee attitudes toward the pay and performance appraisal system. Behavior will probably correlate with those attitudes. Finally, we must deal with strategic issues of expense management and return on investment of base pay and incentive programs. This is where top management should focus its attention. Played at this level, compensation shifts from an administrative function to a strategic partnership.

By evaluating how well the organization is doing across this wide range of indices, we can make a judgment as to the effectiveness of the compensation department. Compensation designs and develops systems. Wage and salary actions take place endlessly. The sheer volume of pay actions make it nearly impossible to prove individual causal connections between compensation staff activities and unit outcomes. Nevertheless, overall the department should be able to show it has strongly influenced the utilization practices and the cost outcomes of the system, as well as the employees' satisfaction with their pay. In addition, if compensation data is presented to management and moves them to make effective strategic decisions, the compensation department can put together a strong case for its having contributed to lowering turnover, increasing morale, and affecting operating ratios in productivity, quality, service, and sales.

9

Benefits

Managing the Trend

In 1940 the cost of the typical benefit program was approximately 5 percent of payroll. It wasn't until after World War II that "fringe" benefits became common. Between 1969 and 1980 a U.S. Chamber of Commerce survey showed that the average cost per employee for benefits had risen by 297 percent. During the same period average weekly earnings had risen by 223 percent. According to the Chamber, in the past ten years the cost of benefits has continued to rise. This has been driven by a combination of accelerating health care costs and a widening of the list of social welfare benefits provided by organizations. The annual SHRM/SI HRE report shows that benefits commonly amount to 30 to 40 percent of salary, depending on the industry. The good news is that the upward trend has slowed in the past two years (1992-1993). This is a direct result of the attention paid to it by benefits professionals and, most importantly, top management.

Over the decades from the 1950s on employees clearly have developed an expectation that the organization must do more than pay a them a salary. It must:

- Provide a financial and emotional security blanket in the form of health and life insurance

- Establish some sort of retirement security, given that the Social Security system is hemorrhaging

- Pay tuition so that an employee can continue to learn and build skills

In the past few years the organization has been handed the responsibility by the employees to provide some sort of assistance with child and elder care plus recreational and fitness facilities and programs. In short, the employer is being called on to play a multifaceted role in the life of the employee, somewhat akin to what the government used to do and is increasingly less able to perform or provide. With two-parent families no longer the predominant form, with the dissolution of extended families and community and church support organizations, and with local and national governments cracking under the strain of years of deficit spending, it appears that employers' involvement in the lives of their employees can only grow.

The purpose of the benefit program is to augment the salary program in its attempt to attract, retain, and incent employees. The question for us is, how do we tell if the benefits department is operating efficiently and effectively? By their nature, benefits probably help to attract and retain, but I do not think they stimulate. Benefits play a background role. They are there when an employee needs them, and when they are not in use they tend to be forgotten. In one sense they are like lifeboats on an ocean liner. You may notice them when you come aboard, but they are ignored until they are needed. The job of benefits is to make sure that when employees need to use a benefit they find it readily accessible and able to provide a satisfactory solution to their problem. How well the benefits department accomplishes this objective is the subject of this chapter.

Costing and Communicating Benefits

Cost is the most commonly discussed aspect of benefits. Premium costs, administrative costs, and staff costs are parts of the total cost of benefits. However, if we want to consider also return on investment, benefits probably impact the organization's effort to attract and retain. The question is, how do we know which benefits do that most effectively? One way to answer that is to survey the employees. Another, less obtrusive, method is to study employees' participation and usage patterns. It seems logical that a program that addresses the needs of many employees much of the time will receive heavy usage. Another issue in our examination of the benefit staff's efficiency lies in the management of mandatory benefits and required filings. Plan maintenance is an unavoidable responsibility, and the timeliness of this activity can be tracked. Since benefits quickly fade into the recesses of the average employee's mind, communication programs are important. We will look at what and how benefits communications might take place. Finally, cost containment is one of the more unequivocal measures of department effectiveness. Given the ever-increasing cost of benefits, cost control has become a primary aspect of the benefit manager's job.

Everyone who works on benefits programs can tell you what percentage of payroll these programs represent. It is important to keep that number visible because of its magnitude. No one can say what the number ought to be. It is a direct reflection of the employer's perception of its relationship with the employees, as well as the ability of the employer to purchase the benefit for the employees. There are two primary benefit cost measures from which all others emerge. They are the total cost and the support cost.

Total Cost

Most of the time when I ask someone what benefits cost their company, they give me a number that represents the direct expenses associated with their various plans and programs. These are insurance premiums; vacation, holiday, and sick leave pay; tuition reimbursement; profit sharing; thrift and pension plans; and recreation programs. Those people who are meticulous will include legally mandated programs, such as FICA, unemployment insurance, workers' compensation, and short-term disability. In addition, they will list discounts on employer goods or services; separation pay and moving expenses; paid breaks; jury duty, voting, and bereavement time; service and suggestion awards; and other programs peculiar to their organization.

When both sets of numbers are combined the sum can be quite impressive, yet, we still have only part of the expenses associated with benefits. The missing piece is the staff costs, overhead costs, and computer costs necessary to maintain the programs. When insurance claims are outsourced, the cost of that processing is included. But bring the work in-house, hire a staff, and give them space and equipment to do it, and it is forgotten. If the benefits program were shut down, people, space, and equipment costs would be eliminated immediately. By the same logic, so long as the program exists the support costs should be included.

Based on the foregoing, the computation for total benefit costs is illustrated in Formula C-7.

Total Benefits Cost

$$TBC = ST + OH + PC + PP + Misc \qquad (C\text{-}7)$$

where   TBC = total costs of benefits
ST = staff time, staff hours spent on benefit planning and administration multiplied by salary and benefit hourly rates (e.g., $148,000)
OH = overhead expenses for space, furniture, equipment, etc. (e.g., $22,000)
PC = processing costs associated with benefit program administration (e.g., $184,000)
PP = plan payments, insurance and retirement and payments for government-mandated programs—including charges by external plan administrators, trustees, etc. (e.g., $19,810,000)
Misc = vacation, holiday, sick leave, education, recreation, etc. (e.g., $9,047,000)

EXAMPLE

TBC = $148,000 + $22,000 + $184,000 + $19,810,000 + $9,047,000
= $29,221,000

Two quick calculations from this number produce the two most commonly discussed numbers: cost per employee and percentage of payroll; C-8 and C-9.

Cost per Employee

$$BC/E = \frac{TBC}{e} \tag{C-8}$$

where   BC/E = benefit cost per employee
TBC = total cost of benefits (e.g., $29,221,000)
e = average number of employees (e.g., 3,922)

EXAMPLE

$$BC/E = \frac{\$29,221,000}{3,922}$$
$$= \$7,450$$

Benefit to Payroll Ratio

$$B/P = \frac{TBC}{TSC} \tag{C-9}$$

where   B/P = benefit to payroll ratio
TBC = total cost of benefits
TSC = total payroll cost (e.g., $78,142,000)

EXAMPLE

$$B/P = \frac{\$29,221,000}{\$78,142,000}$$
$$= 33.2\%$$

Participation Patterns

Most benefit packages include some choices for the employee. In fact, there is a definite trend toward more flexibility in plans. Employees today are generally better educated and better informed than they were in the 1930s, when benefit plans were still in their infancy. They are better equipped to make their own decisions about which benefits they want and need, so plans with options for the employee to choose are common. Most are designed to provide a security core of health and life insurance while leaving many other options to the employees' choice. With the passage of legislation and pressure from unions and other outside social responsibility groups, many new optional plans are now available. In recent years, child and elder care have become popular benefits. Savings and profit-sharing plans, employee stock purchase plans, sabbatical, leaves and educational reimbursements are others.

The benefits section can study which programs are desired by employees by watching what the usage rates are for basic plans (health and life insurances), as well as who participates in which optional programs. Periodically, the percentage of participation or usage can be computed for a given benefit across different groups of employees. For example, you could look at the selection and usage of a particular benefit, such as an employee stock purchase plan, by exempt versus nonexempt employees. Or you could calculate usage by department or division. Age, sex, race, occupational groups, and other cuts are also possible. This type of analysis yields patterns that could help you design or redesign your benefit package into a more cost-effective system. Knowing usage patterns also helps you decide where to put your money when you decide it is time to change your package.

One note about overreliance on participation patterns needs to be made. If a company does an ineffective job of communicating a benefit, employees may not be using it because they do not comprehend its purpose or value. A focus group session with a representative group of employees will show why they misunderstood the program. Then a new communication can be planned with a subsequent pattern audit and feedback session.

Some companies add benefits that are current fads without taking the time to find out what the current needs of their employees are. An additional benefit that comes from studying participation patterns is the creation of an early warning system. Some legislation-based programs require a broad usage of a plan by people at all levels across the organization. If you do not watch that, your organization may be rudely reminded of it by an auditing agency. This not only causes embarrassment for you and the company, but people in some contributory programs, such as income deferral plans, may find that their tax deferrals did not turn out to be what you told them to expect in the beginning. Effective benefits managers require use and participation studies before they recommend changes or additions to the current package and to make sure that everything is running the way it should.

> **GEM #11**   *We learn more from watching what people do than from listening to what they say they want.*

Maintenance

As benefits have become more complex, support activity has become not only more time-consuming but also more important. Local and federal governments require a plethora of periodic reports. Both welfare and retirement plans must have reports prepared and mailed out to regulatory bodies. In the case of ERISA plans, account status updates must be sent out to plan participants. Recent FASB rulings have dramatically changed the way companies account for retiree benefits.

All of these types of reporting have explicit deadlines associated with them. Government agencies require that your reports be mailed to them on time, whether or not anyone will review them at the agency on a timely basis. I have found the best way to ensure that the myriad of reports are filed on time is to develop a master calendar. Each filing would be listed on the calendar by title and receiving agency on the date it is due to be mailed. By referring to this tickler each week, my benefits manager could see what was due for preparation and mailing. If you are tightly staffed, everyone has a constant batch of brush fires to deal with and it is very easy to miss a filing date. With a reminder system the chances of that happening are greatly reduced.

Maintenance is an important activity for benefit systems. The manner and timeliness with which it is handled is an indication of your staff's efficiency.

Employee Communications

Another important and often underplayed activity is the employee benefits communication program, the aim of which is to improve your return on investment (ROI) for benefits. I use the term ROI because of the passive nature of benefits. I noted at the beginning of this chapter that benefits very quickly become background. People are always aware how much their salary is and know exactly when they are due for their next increase, but they usually forget about their benefit package until they need to use part of it. As a result, the organization does not receive a very healthy return from its considerable investment in benefits. In order to improve that situation, the benefits manager needs to develop an active communications program.

There are many opportunities to communicate with employees. Here are some methods that are commonly used.

1. Orientation of new hires is your first opportunity to explain the package in detail.

2. Handbooks can be given out at orientation and updated as needed.

3. Brochures can be used in a variety of ways to describe individual plans or to present an overview.

4. Summary plan descriptions, which are mandated, provide the nuts and bolts of the various plans.

5. Posters and bulletin board announcements are very visible means of keeping employees aware of their many benefits.

6. Articles or a benefit column can be written for the employee newspaper.

7. Paycheck stuffers can be included in pay envelopes to remind employees about something that is timely.

8. Letters about issues such as changing coinsurance provisions can be mailed home where the spouse will see them.

9. Benefit bulletins and newsletters can be composed and distributed periodically.

10. Refresher/information meetings, during which employees can ask questions or receive updates, can be held at convenient times and places.

11. All-employee meetings can be scheduled to announce major changes and improvements.

12. Social Security inquiry cards can be distributed to those who want to check the status of their account.

13. Open enrollment periods provide natural opportunities to review plan provisions or highlights.

14. Benefit fairs can be set up in cafeterias or meeting rooms where it is convenient for employees to inquire about a benefit or to browse to refresh their memory of what is available.

15. The annual benefit statement is considered by most people to be the most powerful communicative tool.

16. Videotapes can be produced and run during lunch periods in the corner of the cafeteria or in a conference room for employees who care to watch on their own.

One company profiled in our 1992 Best-In-America report[1] uses screen savers on employees' networked computers to carry benefits and other messages. It's cheap, easy to do, and quick to update.

The list is not all-inclusive. There are other things that can be done. The question is, how many are you doing now? If you are not doing at least ten, you probably are not operating an effective communications program.

Gaining Control

From the end of World War II until the mid-1980s there was an uninterrupted growth in benefit programs. I can remember operating under the mandate from management that we would improve our benefit package in some way at least once each year. With the slowdown starting in the early 1980s and the realization of how expensive the benefit package had become, many organizations halted the 30-year trend and began to look seriously for ways to cut back plans or save money through administrative changes. With the low growth and profitability of the first half of the 1990s, benefit reduction efforts continued. There are four general opportunities for organizations to reduce benefit costs. They are found in

• Plan design
• Plan administration
• Plan communication
• Plan financing

Before you launch into any major changes in the design, administration, or communication of your benefit program it would be wise to consider what you are trying to achieve with benefits. Some companies have benefits simply because their competitors have them. Others know precisely why they have a certain mix of programs. It might save a lot of grief later if you can get management to sit down with you to reconsider their rationale for benefits. Once you all know why you have certain things and what you hope to achieve by spending more or less money on one program versus another, you and your staff will know where to look for reductions, eliminations, modifications, or even enhancements. It always pays to know where you are headed before you take off. As a wise armchair philosopher once asked, "If you don't know where you're going, how're you going to know if you're there when you get there?"

Plan Design

Practically speaking, it is very difficult to eliminate a long-standing benefit completely. Union contracts notwithstanding, employees come to expect a benefit as their right after it has been offered for a while. Although it is not impossible to drop a benefit, you usually have to come up with something to offset it or face a morale problem that could cost you more in lost productivity than the expense of the benefit. The other side of the issue is, what do you do when the company is running consistently in the red? There are some ways that you can directly reduce the cost of a benefit. First, you can introduce employee cost-sharing. On medical plans you can increase the employee's share of dependent coverage. You might be able to show employees that in order to maintain the same level of coverage as in the past they will have to contribute a couple of dollars for their own coverage this year. Legislation has come along in Sections 125 and 401(k) of the IRS code that permits employees to convert their sharing to pretax dollars. This makes it somewhat more attractive or at least acceptable to them.

So-called cafeteria approaches have added flexibility to benefit plan design. You can offer choices of two or more types of medical plans. HMOs and PPOs serve the needs of different populations by offering the best ratio of care to cost based on individual need. If your plans are experience-rated, the result should be stabilized or the cost lowered.

Wellness plans have been introduced in some organizations whereby employees who do not use their medical benefit can get a refund of some of the cost. These plans come in several variations and are being attempted in corporations, with differing degrees of success. The main concern with them is that people might not go to the doctor when they should. The result could be a severe problem later that might have been avoided if they had gone in the early stages of distress.

Another way to reduce cost and discourage unnecessary use of benefits is to tie the whole health-vacation-sick leave program together and cost it out to a total that is acceptable. If people use less than that total, they can get some form of reward. However, this is a sensitive matter, and a good deal of thought would need to go into the design of such a program.

The bottom line is that there is a strong trend toward individualism in designing plans these days. No longer do you have to have a benefits package that is a mirror image of some other organization's package. This calls for a new level of creativity, but it also offers another opportunity to demonstrate effective management of the benefits program.

Plan Administration

Chapter 10 will discuss administrative issues, which deal with both efficiency and effectiveness. Beyond bookkeeping tasks there are other ways that you can assess your administration from the standpoint of cost containment.

When processing a coordination of benefits (COB) claim filed by the working spouse of one of your employees, the "carve out" rule may pertain. Typically, your plan would pay only the difference between the benefit it would have provided and the benefit provided by the other employer. For example, if the spouse's plan covered $1200 of a $1500 claim and your plan would have done the same, in the past you would pick up the $300 difference. With a carve out rule, you pick up any uncovered amount up to your $1200 limit. However, as we go to press, this rule is changing and affecting your costs.

You can reduce or eliminate the ongoing expense of carrying retired or terminated employees who have very small balances in pension, profit-sharing, or thrift plans. For qualified plans, the law allows for speedy distribution of small balances through lump-sum payouts. A benefit consultant can help you set this procedure up. You can further reduce administrative expenses by reducing the number of choices in profit-sharing and thrift plans. Finally, you can limit the number of withdrawals or transfers during this year. All of these procedures take time and have little actual payoff for the company.

Probably one of the most effective activities you can get involved with is an employer group that acts to lobby and negotiate down the cost of health care. Hospitals and clinics need to control costs, too. If you can find ways of working with them to provide health care at lower costs to everyone, they are usually receptive. They know they cannot go on escalating the cost of medical services. In 1984 I predicted that "if they (the medical profession) do not find ways to contain expenses, there will be a successful move by Congress to set up a national health plan" (p. 132, *How to Measure Human Resource Management*). As I review this chapter in mid-1994, we are waiting for President Clinton's or someone else's health care program to work its way through Congress. It is certain that there will be some type of national health plan. Once again, we have evidence that when industry does not take care of its problems, government comes in—usually with a solution that business doesn't like.

Plan Communication

In the preceding section, I pointed out the many vehicles you can use to communicate benefits to your employees. By continually talking to and with employees about their benefits, you involve them in the program. It becomes something they participate in, not something that is handed to them without consideration for their perceived needs or interests. Besides informing them, the communication program should educate them. You can teach them something about how to deal with health care providers. Most people are intimidated by hospitals and doctors. Plan a "Health Day." Bring in health care professionals to teach employees how to ask questions and give them the confidence of knowing that they have a right to the answers. You can also train supervisors on some of the rudiments of benefits. By having supervisors answer basic questions on the line, you save staff time and employee time. Also, the employee-supervisor bond improves and you increase organizational productivity.

As I noted earlier, the best practice companies in our Best-in-America program use screen savers to communicate with employees. Everyone who is hooked into the network periodically finds a screen saver on their PC or workstation that talks about some aspect of the benefit program. It can be a reminder of open enrollment time, notice of a change in the plan, a call for feedback, or any other message that needs to be transmitted. There are lots of ways to communicate benefits beyond the traditional. Take a page from Einstein who is reputed to have said, "Imagination is more important than knowledge."

There is a trend toward health education in many organizations. Physical fitness programs, smoking cessation, first aid, CPR, nutrition, and stress reduction are now part of the employee health program in many organizations. But I cannot resist pointing out the paradox that exists in companies that spend time and money on stress-management programs and then send employees back into units where the organizational philosophy and operating practices create unnecessary physical and emotional stress. It is somewhat akin to giving people snakebite kits before throwing them into a pit full of rattlesnakes.

Plan Financing

Alternative plan financing offers many opportunities to quickly and directly reduce benefits costs. Not too long ago, almost all organizations carried standard full-cost insurance programs for health, disability, workers' compensation, and life coverage for their employees. They paid their premiums faithfully and hoped that experience would keep the rates from rising too much. In the late 1970s, more companies started to experiment with alternative financing arrangements. Minimum premium contracts, administrative-services-only contracts (ASOs) and self-insured plans became more widespread. In almost all cases these procedures for funding insurance programs have proved to be money savers. They eliminate prefunding of reserves for claims. Self-insured plans and ASOs eliminate state premium taxes as well as the risk and reserve charges of the carrier. In the early years, only the larger companies tried these options. Lately, I have talked with people in organizations with less than 200 employees who are taking advantage of them. The risks of self-insuring can be covered by an inexpensive stop-loss policy that covers you in case of extraordinary claims. Because of this growing trend, insurance carriers are not nearly as arbitrary as they were up to about 1975. They are vulnerable and they know it. If you do your homework and negotiate strongly, you can usually find ways to get the benefits you want at something less than the "sticker price."

In many companies, the cost of pension plans has become a burden. There are several ways you can reduce that burden for your organization. Here again is a case where good benefits consultants earn their fees by helping management choose among funding methods. Depending on the growth profile of your company, funding alternatives can save you a lot of money now and in the future.

There are many ways to manipulate the financing of your various plans. New approaches come to the market continuously. Choosing the alternatives that best suit your current and future needs can significantly impact the organization's bottom line profits. With changes in retirement plan funding you have a chance to significantly manipulate the cash flow of your organization. Today, there is no question that benefits management is a core issue within organizational profitability.

Summary

Organizations spend a great deal of money on benefits. Management finds itself pulled in two opposing directions at once. On one side is a strong push to continually expand the private sector's involvement in benefits. It will probably happen even more as the federal government finds itself less able to provide services without additional deficit spending. The impetus behind the national health program movement predicts that some type of plan will certainly arrive soon. It behooves benefits managers to prepare alternatives for dealing with it. On the opposite side is the drive to control costs in order to stay competitive in the world market. It is incumbent on benefits managers to be cost-effective directors of the program. Beyond just controlling cost there is an even more important issue. That is to show the top executives how the organization can improve its ROI in benefits. If you use your imagination and let your mind run a little, you will probably find new ways to make benefits benefit the organization as well as the employees.

The real effectiveness of benefits management won't be found in efficiency ratios. Although that helps, the important values are found among benefits strategy and macro-level management reports. Top executives need to see benefits data that will help them use a benefit as a lever in attracting and retaining key employees. The twenty first century is going to open on a dearth of technically skilled people in the new technologies. Benefit packages that are flexible and go beyond health and life insurance can give you an edge in recruiting that scarce talent.

10
Processing Records and Claims

Processing lends itself to measurement. Quality programs are focused on process improvement. Paper and electronic document processing is a very visible activity wherein items flow along a predictable path toward a predetermined destination. They usually pause at certain points in the journey for someone to treat them. The treatments may mean adding data, extracting information for another use, or modifying or deleting data. The document might reach a decision point where someone decides that, in whole or in part, it should either continue in its current direction, go off into another process chain, or dump its data and be discarded. Eventually documents conclude their journey in a file cabinet, a wastebasket, a computer file, or the hands of the customer. All of these actions can be measured in terms of quantity, time, cost, quality, and customer satisfaction. These facts apply whether one considers accounting, purchasing, personnel records, benefits claims, or any other business processing. Measures of quality, productivity, and service can be designed. Quality covers the cycle time of the process and its error or defect ratios. Productivity refers to unit cost and quantity. Service is measured in terms of customer satisfaction.

Counting Volume

A natural place to start measuring a process is volume count. This quantity indicator tells you how much is being handled. It can be expressed in several ways. You can count number of documents (paper or electronic) handled or number of entries made. If you were looking at insurance claims, you might count number of claims processed. You could differentiate claims by type, since some are more complicated than others. For example, coinsurance claims take more time than standard one-carrier claims. If you were looking at employee records, you might want to count the number of records created and changed.

A records clerk will sometimes make several additions or changes to a record at one sitting. Frequently, an employee may transfer between departments and be promoted at the same time. This requires a new department number, job title, salary, and performance review date. Since this case is clearly more complex than a simple address change, it makes sense to count the number of entries or changes rather than the number of files processed. By tracking how many transactions an efficient records clerk or claims administrator can handle daily, weekly, or monthly, it is possible to set the optimum staffing level for a given volume of work.

You can also project the number of processors required if you look at past history. If experience shows that you generally have 0.25 record changes per employee per month, you can predict your future workload by examining the projected employee level in future months. For example, using the 0.25 factor, the addition of 100 employees in the organization means 25 extra changes to handle. Formula C-10 shows the computation for volume processing.

Volume Processing

$$CPR = \frac{R}{S} \tag{C-10}$$

where   CPR = claims processing rate
         R   = total records processed (e.g., 850)
         S   = average number of staff processors (e.g., 3)

EXAMPLE

$$CPR = \frac{850}{3}$$
$$= 283.3$$

There is a handy format for keeping track of claim processing volume. Figure 10.1 shows the amount of activity by type each month and a running year-to-date (YTD) total. Through observation of past efficiency levels you have determined that a processor can handle a certain number of transactions per month (283). When your workload reaches or exceeds that level, you know automatically that it is time to consider an addition to staff in records.

Month		New hires	Term	Prom	Trans	Salary increase	Employee changes	Totals
Jan		98	80	52	87	208	88	613
	YTD*	98	80	52	87	208	88	613
Feb		63	51	69	29	214	36	462
	YTD	161	131	121	110	422	124	1075
Mar		54	75	84	55	254	40	562
	YTD	215	206	205	165	676	164	1637
Apr		119	70	164	78	281	55	767
	YTD	334	276	369	243	957	219	2404
May		96	62	104	70	217	89	638
	YTD	430	338	473	313	1174	308	3042
Jun		136	70	93	73	411	66	849
	YTD	566	408	566	386	1585	374	3891
Jul		174	75	82	61	398	64	854
	YTD	740	483	648	447	1983	438	4745
Aug		182	77	171	67	377	65	939
	YTD	922	560	819	514	2360	503	5684
Sep		144	88	88	181	194	118	813
	YTD	1066	648	907	695	2554	621	6497
Oct		152	90	90	80	310	78	811
	YTD	1218	738	997	775	2864	699	7298
Nov		160	92	91	78	389	81	891
	YTD	1378	830	1088	853	3253	780	8189
Dec		165	95	103	84	302	88	837
1992 TOTALS		1543	925	1191	937	3555	868	9026

* Year to date.

Figure 10.1. Record Processing Table

A number of clients have adopted this method. It is composed of five steps.

1. Develop standard processing times and acceptable error levels.
2. Monitor volume and staff levels.
3. As volume changes, compute the effect this will have on staff workload.

4. If the change will drive the acceptable processing performance beyond a tolerable range, it is time to act.

5. You can do one or more of the following:

   a. Starting with benchmarking you can compare your performance to others in similar situations to find the gaps in performance

   b. Either outsource the process or engage in a process improvement program using either reengineering of quality techniques.

   c. Once the process has been cleaned up, consider automating it.

   d. As a last resort, add staff.

Use of performance yardsticks takes the guesswork out of staffing. Most organizations are reluctant to add employees in staff departments, but this approach helps you justify, without argument, the proposed change.

In the insurance claim area, another way of looking at efficiency is the amount of time that elapses from the day that a claim is filed until a check is received by the employee. This is the cycle time of claim processing. It is, in part, also a way to increase or maintain positive employee attitudes toward the insurance program. Long delays in payment generate morale problems.

In this case the measurement, shown in Formula C-11, is a simple subtraction problem.

$$T = DP - DR \qquad (C\text{-}11)$$

where T = turnaround time
DP = date claim paid (e.g., September 20)
DR = date claim received (filed) (e.g., September 10)

EXAMPLE

$$T = 20 - 10$$
$$= 10 \text{ days}$$

Whenever contracts are being let with insurance carriers or claims administrators, an agreement should be reached on turnaround time. It should either be written into the contract or be put into an agreement letter. Any reputable administrator is willing to stipulate that, 95 percent of the time, standard one-carrier claims will be paid within X days. If you do partial processing of claims in your benefit office before forwarding them to the administrator, you should set your internal processing standard as well.

Errors

A final efficiency measure that has a qualitative aspect is error rate. The ratio of errors to total claims processed should be extremely low. The consequence of an error is more than the cost and disruption of rework: It usually causes a morale problem. Employees whose claims are short-changed, or even overpaid, quickly lose respect for the competence of the benefits staff. Formula C-12 gives the calculation for error rate.

$$ER = \frac{RC}{P} \qquad\qquad (C\text{-}12)$$

where   ER = error rate
        RC = rejected claims (e.g., 5)
        CP = total claims processed (e.g., 650)

EXAMPLE

$$ER = \frac{5}{650}$$
$$= 0.007\%$$

Computing Costs

Cost can be viewed from one perspective, the initial question being unit cost. What does it cost to process one claim or make one change to a document, such as an employee record? Since transactions vary in complexity, you will have to develop an average unit cost. The first step is to observe the operation and record how long, on the average, it takes to complete whatever the task is. This can be done by a supervisor, an industrial engineer, or the operator performing the task. There are obvious pros and cons for each approach. As manager, the decision is yours. If an operator is doing nothing but processing, you can count the hours spent at the job and divide by the number of transactions completed. This results in an average transaction time. However, if the operator also answers phones or is interrupted by other people or other tasks, then an individual transaction time log must be kept. Whichever system you use, in order to obtain a truly representative time you will have to collect data at different times of the day, week, and month. Fluctuations due to workload, fatigue, interruptions, or other variables have to be normalized. After you have dealt with all these issues you will be rewarded with a solid, dependable, average transaction time measure. All that remains is to apply cost variables to it.

Costs are essentially those expenses associated with staff time and overhead. For example, the hourly numbers might be

Average operator's salary	= $11.00
Average operator's benefits	= 3.85
Overhead	= 1.25
Materials and postage	= 1.50
Cost of supervision per operator (supervisor salary divided by number supervised)	= 2.10
Hourly cost of processing	= 19.70

Given that you can compute the average cost per document processed, as shown in Formula C-13.

$$PC/T = \frac{ST + OH + MP + MT}{P/h} \qquad (C\text{-}13)$$

where PC/T = processing cost per transaction
       ST = staff time, salary, and benefits (e.g., $14.85)
       OH = overhead (e.g., $1.25)
       MP = materials and postage (e.g., 1.50)
       MT = management time, cost of supervision (e.g., $2.10)
       P/h = number of items processed per hour (e.g., 8)

EXAMPLE

$$PC/T = \frac{\$14.85 + \$1.25 + \$1.50 + \$2.10}{8}$$

$$= \$2.46$$

Knowing the cost of processing is important from a managerial standpoint. A basic question for benefit managers is, "Should we process insurance claims ourselves, or should we contract that out to an insurance company or claims administration company?" In order to make that decision it is necessary to know what it costs to process employee insurance claims internally. In this example the processing clerk is making eight changes to the records per hour. If we were looking at insurance claims instead, we might find a much slower pace throughout, since claims are more complicated than records. Therefore, a rate of three or four per hour might be satisfactory. The setting of performance standards is a local issue. The rate will depend on the forms used, the amount of automation involved, the total range of tasks to be performed, and extraneous matters such as interruptions.

There are other issues, such as turnaround time, employee relations, and control, that are part of the decision. It may even be decided that cost is less important than employee relations or timeliness. Nevertheless, an appropriate choice is hard to make without all the facts, and cost is an essential variable in the mix.

Records Cost

Until recently, the cost of maintaining organizational records was seldom discussed. It was assumed to be a necessary and unavoidable part of doing business, and in fact it is. Yet, with today's concern for cost control, it deserves a review.

Management wants to know what it costs the organization to maintain records. If the cost seems excessive, outsourcing may be a solution. My experience is that the number is sufficiently large to deserve attention. It is often large enough to become a target for a cost-reduction project. Outsourcing is clearly an attractive alternative. If costs are equal, it removes the need for constant supervisory attention. This, in itself, might be justification enough to outsource record keeping. The counter issue is service. Will your employees and management be served fast enough with an off-site provider?

In most cases we have looked at activities from the standard input/output ratio. Here we are interested in what it is costing us to maintain records. The answer is simple. Our cost inputs are staff, equipment (computers, microfiche, etc.), supplies, and facilities. Facility costs for space, heat, light, and so on, may be considered a given and not included—that is a matter of choice. The percentage of total department costs that record-keeping costs represent is shown in Formula C-14.

Record-Keeping Costs

$$RC = \frac{ST + EC + S + OH}{DC} \qquad \text{(C-14)}$$

where RC = record-keeping costs
      ST = staff time, salary, benefits, and miscellaneous expenses
          (e.g., $85,200)
      EC = equivalent costs, purchase, depreciation, and operating
          costs for machines, desks, file cabinets, etc. (e.g.,
          $32,500)
       S = supplies (e.g., $23,800)
    OH = overhead (e.g., $14,650)
    DC = total department expenses (e.g., $1,200,000)

EXAMPLE

$$RC = \frac{\$85{,}200 + \$32{,}500 + \$23{,}800 + \$14{,}650}{\$1{,}200{,}000}$$

$$= \frac{\$156{,}150}{\$1{,}200{,}000}$$

$$= 13.0\%$$

Once you have all the numbers together, opportunities for cost reduction and better utilization of resources may become apparent. Even if the first result is satisfactory and offers little room for improvement, by tracking this percentage annually you will be able to maintain it within an acceptable range.

Satisfaction Factor

The final, and in some ways one of the most important, measure in the processing business is employee satisfaction. Prompt attention, rapid turnaround, and accurate processing are all expected, whether it be an insurance claim or a change to an employee record. Usually there is no question about employee or managerial satisfaction. If your benefits staff is not operating at peak efficiency, you will probably hear about it. Satisfaction can be calculated as a ratio of complaints to volume, as shown in Formula C-15.

Claims Satisfaction

$$CS = \frac{C}{P} \tag{C-15}$$

where CS = degree of employee satisfaction with settlement of
          their claims
       C = total claims contested (e.g., 8)
       P = total claims processed (e.g., 650)

EXAMPLE

$$CS = \frac{8}{650}$$
$$= 1.2\%$$

There is no norm to which you can compare your experience. One contested claim is too much, yet it seems inevitable that a very small percentage will be contested. Prompt, fair, and full treatment of the contested claim is the best that you can do.

Auditing Administration

No administrative system or staff is perfect. An administrative audit usually turns up procedural errors or omissions that can be corrected to save time and money. We have talked about errors and satisfaction. Tightening up on lax procedures reduces errors and increases employee satisfaction. You might find small savings coming from arithmetic errors. You might also find that a clerk is not well-trained and is paying for services not covered in the plan or paying more than is allowed. It is possible that ineligible people are being covered. An employee who does not have dependent coverage may be having child or spouse claims paid because no one checked the record. If you have a claim processing system where employees file directly with the carrier or service company, you could learn that terminated people are still filing and getting paid. Organizations that are very large or spread out across several states often find that changes in coverage and eligibility have not kept up or have never been made. Normally, administrative errors such as these do not cost a significant amount of money. Nevertheless, administrative procedures and records should be audited periodically just to keep the system operating smoothly. You want the organization to have confidence in your administrative system. Judiciously applied audits will help develop and maintain that confidence.

GEM #12 *You are wonderful, but there's always room for improvement.*

Summary

Whether you think of processing from the viewpoint of claims or records, the measures are similar. The only significant differences will be the results. Since claims are more complex, they take longer to process and are usually susceptible to higher error rates. The main point is that standards of performance can be set by which your staff's output can be evaluated. Performance targets also challenge them to find better ways to process.

Process work may not be the most exciting task in an organization, but it can be very satisfying. Making a large, complex process function efficiently and error-free is quite an accomplishment. Today, the administrator has a number of improvement tools to work with. The more successful ones learn what TQM, benchmarking, and reengineering can do and apply them where appropriate.

It must be acknowledged that outsourcing is increasingly appealing to top management. I believe that by the early twenty-first century, very few companies of medium or large size will maintain internal claims or record processing units. If it were as efficient to do it internally as to outsource it, logic says that upon outsourcing the vendor should need all your people (or an equal number) to provide the service from their site. I have never seen a case where the vendor employed as many people to do the job as did the employer. When an organization spends its resources doing what it does best, it is probably more efficient than one that engages in peripheral activities. If you plan a career in administrative work, I suggest you prepare to work in a service company that processes other people's records or claims.

11
Human Resource Information Systems (HRIS)

The Birth of HRIS: The 1970s

By now you have pored over a couple dozen formulas and could use a break. I think it would be useful to trace the evolution of computerized information systems in order to better understand the measurement methods we use today.

Automation came over the horizon of the then personnel function in the late 1960s. Manufacturing, sales, and accounting had already installed computer systems. The introduction of the fabulously successful IBM 360 series in the middle of that decade launched automation in a big way. Visions of faster, cheaper minicomputers were beginning to form in the imaginations of a few visionaries. However, personal computers were still fifteen years away. By 1970, mainframe systems were still the primary game in town. They were expensive, not easy to program, and largely incomprehensible for the lay person. I recall going to a personnel system seminar presented by one of the few personnel system vendors in about 1971. My impression was that although this was a very complicated idea requiring error-free human performance, it was clearly going to be the tool of the future.

If you had the dubious pleasure of working with early attempts at automation you would have been as skeptical as most people. I still remember the games people played when a client record system was being automated in my company in 1966. All account executives, who had maintained control over their own records, were required to submit data to the central data processing (DP) department located in the basement of our building. There, thousands of punched cards with their upper-right-hand corner sawed off sat in bundles. Periodically someone would grab a batch and try to run a report. More often than not, one or more cards would be incorrectly punched and either the program would stop or an incorrect report would emerge. The account executives swore at those %#@#$%& s in the basement who struggled mightily to make the system work. And the dp folks in the basement tried in vain to explain requirements to people who didn't want to understand and to produce reports that others felt they could produce better. If you missed it, be thankful.

The first automated personnel systems were designed for record keeping and reporting. They were useful, despite the problems, in large companies that had large numbers of employees. The sheer volume of data developed in creating a new employee file, making changes to employee records and maintaining employee history, benefits administration, and pay programs cried out for a better way. With the passage of Title VII of the Civil Rights Act of 1964, organizations had to develop record-keeping systems covering data on minority hiring and representation within the work force. Given the required cross sorting of minority classifications by job level, pay, and promotion history, automation was the only practical method. I recall a statistic someone published that claimed that without automation there would not be enough clerical personnel in the United States within twenty years to manually process the data that business and government would need.

Computers were sold on the premise that they would increase productivity and decrease the number of clerical personnel needed. This appealed to top level executives because they could envision replacing some hard-to-manage people with obedient machines. As it turned out, the salespeople's promise to improve productivity eventually did come true. However, in no case that I ever saw or heard of was the clerical staff substantially put out of their jobs. This concern for job displacement was an echo of the same fear that arose with the introduction of labor-saving machinery in the early factories. Then, the fear was so great that industrial sabotage was carried out by the workers in the early 1800s who feared for their jobs. The term *sabotage* came from Europe where workers sometimes threw their *sabots*, their wooden shoes, into the gears to cause machinery breakdowns. So far as I know, no one ever tried to stuff a shoe between the tape drives of a mainframe computer. What some did do was not cooperate with programmers so that programs and reports weren't useful.

Early Problems

In their eagerness to be useful and to win over skeptical, and sometimes hostile, future customers, the management information services (MIS) group would overpromise and underdeliver. Although their intentions were good, they courted failure by ignoring the low odds for success at that time. Their successes were offset by the memory of past failures. They won their spurs very grudgingly from reluctant clients. Although top management wanted their large investment to pay off, the people in the trenches had different agendas. Justified or not, they often excused themselves with the phrase "computer failure" as the reason for substandard performance. It's still being used today, isn't it?

Besides the feelings surrounding the introduction of the new machine, there were communication problems. On the lay side we certainly didn't understand what the techies were talking about. Quite often the MIS staff used jargon to hide behind or obfuscate their explanations. Users typed their precious data onto cards or forms and consigned them each night to the black hole called the data center. This was called "batch processing." What happened there no one really knew. As a result, as recently as the late 1970s the DP function was accepted as a mysterious labyrinth through which only the incumbents could possibly lead the way. This communications gap bred still more distrust of MIS staff. The combination of distrust, misunderstanding, obfuscation, and loss of control drove many people to maintain their own backup data set using their old reliable manual methods.

The final phase of the exclusive mainframe franchise was marked by the growing cost of DP operations. Mainframe computers were extremely expensive in terms of cost per data point processed. After a decade of large investments, top management began to look for lower-cost solutions. They couldn't drop automation, but they needed alternatives. Fortunately, about this time technology came to the rescue with the development of minicomputers. These smaller, cheaper machines could be scattered throughout the organization and assigned the job of processing local data. They could be hooked to the mainframe for access to certain centralized data. At night the local data could be sent to the mainframe records for updating. This arrangement gave the local staff real time access to their data and a lower cost per data point. The only piece missing was report generation. Most reports still had to be hard-coded or put through a report generator, usually by a programmer in MIS. This kept the staff users at the mercy of the central function. Personnel packages began to be written for use on minis and gradually the personnel department, now called human resources (HR), was gaining more control over their data.

Current Status

In the ten years since the first edition of this book the human resources profession has taken to computers with a high degree of interest and energy. As recently as the early 1990s, however, a large number of HR departments were still in the semi-automation age. Many still had few, if any, computers in their department. Those who did often received little or no training in how to use them. I was in the office of an HR section manager who had a beautiful computer hutch with an IBM-PC and boxes of software. When I asked him to boot it up so we could look at something he said, "I don't even know how to turn the darn thing on."

Some HR departments gave their people dumb terminals. This meant that they could sit in front of a monitor, view, and type in data. But they couldn't do anything with the data except send it off into the invisible world of the data center. Reports still had to be produced by someone in the MIS function on request from HR. This was a time-consuming, inflexible method, and caused long delays in bringing on even simple enhancements. Until technology advanced, HR could not effectively respond to requests for information.

Gradually, HR got on-line, which meant that they could actually interact with their database in real time. Today, most HR functions have packages designed for human resources work. They have PCs or workstations and are able to work their data with ease and generate reports of their own design and making. But believe it or not, quite a few HR departments still have only the meagerest of computer support. Even with the low cost of PCs and powerful database and HRIS software packages, a surprisingly large number of HR people don't have direct access to their own PC or workstation.

Despite the advances in hardware and software, the next step of converting data into strategic and tactical management tools has largely evaded the vast majority of HR staffs. Some have developed succession planning systems and a very few (probably less than 10%) have career planning systems. Applicant-tracking packages are prevalent in many employment functions, and training is applying registration and scheduling software to manage large-scale training curricula.

The Missing Piece

The missing piece is performance management packages. There is very little application of operating data in making employee related decisions. Figure 11.1 shows a simple example of how having operating data could affect today's drive to reduce operating costs. Typically top management says to the HR director, "Cut $x out of your operating budget next year." Because most HR departments do not have good data on their operating costs at the activity level, they are left with only one alternative: cut staff! However, when HR knows its operating costs, it has alternatives to laying off staff and in the process reducing its ability to provide responsive, high quality service. Figure 11.1 shows that nearly 60 percent of the cost of hiring is taken up with relocations. With a simple change of policy, the operating cost of the hiring function could be dramatically slashed. This is an example of the next step in the evolution of HR data system capability.

It is no secret that HR staffs usually have poor quantitative skills. Some even openly oppose the use of hard data, preferring to work on intuition, experience, and guesswork. Even after nearly twenty years of preaching data management to HR people I continue to be amazed at why so many steadfastly refuse to move into the modern era of management. It is the classic example of cutting off your nose to spite your face. HRIS as a function has a powerful key for repositioning HR as a value-adding operation. The HRIS group has the tools to provide both HR and its organizational customers with data that they can use to improve the quality, productivity, and service of their units. Without this data, HR managers and so-called professionals are working with only half their brain. They are also ignoring one of their responsibilities to their internal customers, which is to help them improve their quality, productivity, and service.

EXEMPT COST PER HIRE

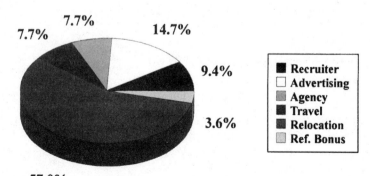

Figure 11.1. Exempt Cost Per Hire

Beyond Record Automation: HRIS in the Twenty-First Century

This book is about the use of quantitative data in management of the human resources function, as well as in interactions with HR's customers. Collectively, I call it human asset management. This chapter will provide examples of how the HRIS function can contribute to the operating efficiency of the HR function and the strategic imperatives of the organization. It will also display and explain ways to measure the internal efficiency of the HRIS function itself and the value added by its services.

The major challenge as I see it is for HRIS and HR management to collaborate on developing value adding and predictive data. The great majority of the data in HR information systems is employee records. This covers everything from hiring and career experience to EEO and benefits administration. What it doesn't contain enough of is first, the operating data mentioned earlier and second, any predictive or projective capability. More than knowing what happened yesterday, managers across the organization need to have some glimmer of what is coming over tomorrow's horizon. What good would the marketing function be if it could not see what the competition was planning or how the customer's tastes were changing? Similarly, what good is the HR department if it can only tell us what happened yesterday, not what might be coming up tomorrow? When the HRIS section collects and maintains operating and market data, and the HR managers monitor cost, time, quantity, quality, and human results, the two can work together and begin to describe what the organization has to prepare for tomorrow. When they do that they become business partners rather than simply vendors of services.

> **GEM #13** *We don't need more data, we need to understand how to use the data we have.*

Internal Measures of HRIS: #1 = Cost

By now you know that the variable that attracts the most interest from management most of the time is cost. For a very long time top management has been frustrated by the ratio of the amount of their investment in automation and the visible return from it. The following are some measures of cost:

Cost per programming job: Job Cost (JC)
Cost per report: Report Cost (RC)
Cost of staff training: Training Cost (TC)
Budget: Operating Cost (OC)

Cost per Program

Programming assignments vary by degree of difficulty, size of program, language used, etc. Any systems manager knows how, or should know how, to differentiate and classify programming assignments. By categorizing them into A, B, C jobs or other defined groupings the manager can begin to monitor performance of the programmers. The formula is simple. See C-16.

Job Cost

$$JC = P \times H + M + E + O \qquad \text{(C-16)}$$

where   JC   = job cost
          P   = programmer hourly rate pay and benefits (e.g., $35)
          H   = hours worked on the program (e.g., 70)
         M   = material cost (e.g., $15)
          E   = equipment cost (e.g.,$700)
         O   = overhead factor (e.g., $375)

EXAMPLE

$$JC = \$35 \times 70 + \$15 + \$700 + \$375$$
$$= \$3540$$

This calculation can be made by job type. It tells which programmers are ready for which level of work based on how long it takes them to produce error-free program code.

An even simpler way to calculate the programmer's cost is to load in an overhead factor to the hourly rate. This saves one extra calculation.

Report Cost

The cost of report generation is a function of time plus material, equipment usage and overhead. For the purists among us, the cost of capital can be subsumed in these costs. This formula, C-17, is very similar to the previous job cost calculation.

Report Cost

$$RC = H \times P + E + M + O \qquad \text{(C-17)}$$

where   RC   = report cost
        H   = programmer hours worked (e.g., 20)
        P   = programmer hourly rate (e.g., $35}
        E   = equipment cost (e.g., $200)
        M   = material cost (e.g., $5)
        O   = overhead factor (e.g., $170)

EXAMPLE

$$RC = 20 \times \$35 + \$200 + \$5 + \$170$$
$$= \$1075$$

This is the same calculation as is done in manufacturing. In both cases, a product is being produced. The question of how technical, complex, or sophisticated the product is will be answered in the resulting cost. Issues of research and development costs are relevant if we are running an in-depth analysis of the long-term cost per unit produced. That is usually not applicable to report costs in HRIS.

Staff Training Cost

This cost can be a very simple or a very complex task. The simplest way to compute it is to take the direct cost for the training (i.e., seminar cost, plus travel and lodging). A more complex and accurate way is to include the lost productivity of the programmer while traveling and in class. Lost productivity can be computed in two ways as follows:

1. Average percentage of time the programmer spends in production (programming). Time spent on miscellaneous work (i.e., meetings) is not counted.

2. Return on investment of programmer production time. This can be obtained by tracking the value of the programmer's work. The simplest way is to take samples of work over, say, a six-month period and go to the customer's management. Ask them what the value of the programs were in terms of improving their productivity, quality, or service. Did the programs save them time, cut down on inherent errors, or allow them to respond to customers more effectively? If so, what was that worth?

On-the-job training takes place all the time through conversations with peers and supervisors. This is very difficult to locate and frankly, it isn't worth the effort in most cases.

For a full exposition of training cost calculation see Chapter 16, "Management Development." Formulas D-1 and D-2 provide two ways of calculating training costs: cost per trainee and cost per trainee hour.

Budget

The operating cost of the HRIS is often a significant number. It is the number that top management usually looks at and acts on. This not necessarily the best way to manage. Nevertheless, it is the prevailing method. A better way to set budgets is to look from the outside in. What are the HRIS customers' objectives? How can HRIS help in their achievement? What does that suggest in terms of program and report development and delivery? Therefore, what should be the budget of HRIS? This is a variation on the zero-base budgeting method.

Suggestions that information services should be a certain percentage of operating expense are ridiculous. Those types of ratios are an admission that we don't know how to find the value of a function or that we don't have the energy necessary to truly manage this function. For every percentage anyone can offer there are a list of exceptions, to the point where the exception becomes the rule. The operating effectiveness of any function is obviously something to be managed—not only from a cost standpoint, but from a value standpoint. The question is not only, what does it cost? The seminal issue is, what is its value added? When we begin to think that way we will be more competitive in the world market.

Time Responsiveness

Time and cost are parallel measures. Time drives cost. The more time spent doing something, the more it costs. Of course, the extra time may be worth the higher cost in terms of quality. A handmade watch may cost many hundreds of times more than one that is mass produced. A plastic model running on a microchip can be had for $20 or less. A Piaget™ Oval or a Rolex™ Oyster costs several thousand dollars. But the difference in quality, style, dependability, and useful life makes it worthwhile for some buyers. The question then is, how much time can we afford to spend doing something? The answer is the ratio of cost to value. There are four common time measures:

Response Time (RT): How long it takes to start the job after the request is received

Time to Repair (TR): How long it takes to complete the job from start to finish

Turnaround Time (TT): The total elapsed time from the receipt of the request to completion of the job

Overtime Hours (OH): Number of overtime hours paid during the reporting period

There are many ways to count time, but these four pretty much cover the time management needs of the HRIS manager.

Response Time

From the customer's viewpoint, response time is often critical. The quality movement has made time a popular issue. Total Quality Management (TQM) programs deal with cycle time. This is the time from the beginning to the end of a process. Response time is the first submeasure of cycle time, C-18. It is the elapsed time from the point at which a request for service is received until someone starts working on the request. It is not the same as time to deliver or time to complete. That represents the total time of the cycle.

Response Time

$$RT = ST - RR \qquad (C\text{-}18)$$

where RT = response time
       ST = time at which action starts in response to the request (e.g., February 10)
       RR = time at which the request is received (e.g., February 7)

EXAMPLE

$$RT = 10 - 7$$
$$= 3 \text{ days}$$

Time to Repair

Another type of time is time to repair (TR). This is the segment of time from the minute the technician or programmer from HRIS arrives on site to effect a repair of a software or hardware problem until that person has fixed the problem. Time to repair can be as short a time as a minute to as long as weeks. It is usually an hour or less. The HRIS manager can require a repair report from the staff each time there is a request for assistance. This is a common practice among technicians and systems engineers who service requests from outside customers.

The calculation would be exactly the same as for response time. Take the point at which the repair person starts on the job and the time he or she finishes it. As I said earlier, this may be only minutes, so you might want to set up the metric on a quarter-hour basis.

Turnaround Time

This is a measure of the total cycle time from the time a request for service is received until the finished product or service is delivered, C-19. It includes response time as well as any other time segments within the total process. It is calculated the same way as the two previous time measures. This measure is important because it is the one that the customer is most interested in. Of course, you have to respond relatively quickly, but if you never complete the job or take too long to finish it, the customer is going to be unhappy.

Remember: When you develop your performance measurement system you need some metrics to tell you how your processes are running. You also need numbers that are important to your customers; namely, the results of your attempt to service their needs. You can win all the process awards and still be seen as a failure. The key success indicator is customer satisfaction.

Turnaround Time

$$TT = RR - RC \qquad\qquad (C\text{-}19)$$

where TT = turnaround time
         RC = time at which the request is completed (e.g., February 14)
         RR = time at which the request is received (e.g., February 7)

EXAMPLE

$$TT = 14 - 7$$
$$= 7 \text{ days}$$

Overtime Hours

One of the more neglected managerial performance metrics is overtime. Since accounting systems are normally not set up to roll out the overtime pay each month, few managers know how much overtime they are paying for. Only when the budget starts to be overrun do most of them learn the overtime cost.

There is no formula as such for this measure. Simply call payroll and ask them how many overtime hours they paid your people this period.

Of course, you want to know the total dollars spent as well as the number of hours paid.

Quantity: Frequency and Volume

This set of metrics focuses on volume, although frequency can also be computed if there is a need. Quantity, size, or amount of something are easy to calculate. It is simple to track the volume or frequency of some action. It is only a matter of recording the number of times or things that happen in a given period. The most common quantity metric of information systems is report or job volume. Whichever you choose to call it, the process is the same.

Report Volume

This can be viewed either as the number of reports produced (not the best measure) or as the number of lines or pages produced, the number of calculations made, or any other volume indicator you feel is most useful.

Counting on the number of reports produced says nothing of their size or complexity. Number of pages is more specific, although it doesn't account for partial pages (a minor matter). The best is the number of lines and/or the number of calculations. The reason for having the printer count lines is obvious. If you want to be very specific, the number of calculations is best. This last measure says something about the complexity of the work being produced.

Backlog

The number of backlogged jobs or the number of backlog hours of work is a common measure in systems departments. The reason for monitoring this is obvious. It tells you how close you are to promptly responding to your customers requests. It is not uncommon for systems departments to have six months or more of backlogged jobs. This does not mean that everyone has to wait six months to have their job attended to. Priorities are given to different types of jobs. Some are turned around in a matter of hours. Others may never work their way to the top of the programmers' work pile. HRIS managers can estimate the number of hours in each job received and add that to the backlog. When the job is started, it comes off the backlog list and moves to the current project list. When it is completed, the number of hours spent should be recorded and compared to the estimated hours. If the HRIS were a freestanding company selling its services on the market, it would have to know how much time, and therefore money, it was spending on each job. With outsourcing of IS functions coming into vogue, it would seem to me to be a good survival strategy.

A large backlog can be very stressful to both the professional staff and to management. Knowing that you have a megapile of work staring over your shoulder can be very disconcerting. It takes away from the sense of accomplishment we all need in our work. In those situations people never feel closure despite the fact that they may be turning out a mountain of very fine work. On the other side of the equation, when management has to look at a monthly backlog report and never sees the volume come down they get upset.

There is a way to handle a monster backlog. I suggest that all jobs that are not going to be attempted within the coming quarter be removed from the backlog report and sent back to the requester. This serves two purposes. First, it takes a load off the mind of the programmers. Second, it tells the requesting department that honestly you are not going to get to their work in the foreseeable future.

Quality: Errors and Availability

Quality is the most volatile issue in information systems. Since customers don't always know how to explain their needs providers of information services sometimes misdeliver through no fault of their own. Quality is always defined by the customer. Many times the customer is willing to accept a product that you are not too proud of. But the customers' needs are paramount. If they are willing to take something "as is" because it fulfills their requirement at the moment, that is their choice.

Inside the department there are measures of process quality that have nothing to do with your customer. As a manager or professional you want to have your operation run efficiently. Repeated errors cut into productivity and efficiency because you have to spend time fixing them. There are a set of error measures from which you can choose.

Programming Errors

Program errors are often called "bugs." I doubt that a program was ever written that didn't have a bug in it. Even with the latest programming tools and fourth generation languages, programming is a complex art. Nevertheless, error rates are one of the ways that we differentiate between good and not-so-good-programmers. There are three metrics that can be used to get a handle on errors:

Program error rate

Compiler rerun rate

Product error rate

All three deal with the number of errors that show up in a program when the program is being compiled or when products such as reports are subsequently produced. In the case of program errors you could set some type of standard that says for a given type of program more than x number of bugs on the first presentation of the program is unacceptable. It is a little harder to check compiler rerun rates unless you have very good control of equipment usage. The issue is, how many times does the programmer have to recompile before getting the program to run all the way through without error messages? The final error check is in the finished product. If a program is written to produce a report does the report have any program (not data) errors? If the program is something like a screen layout for data entry, are all the sequences and defaults correct? It is simple to set some type of expectation of error-free work for your programmers. If you don't, they may think it isn't important to do quality work. Remember the golden rule of business: You get what you measure. If you require that people perform to a quantitative standard that is fair, you will find that most of them will meet or exceed your standard.

Uptime Percentage

A quality measure that is important to the customer is the amount of time that the information system is up and running. If people can't access your system, they can't do their work. This tends to make them cranky. Therefore, it is a good idea to keep the system up as close to 100 percent of the workday as possible. Now, with people telecommuting and accessing the system at any time of the day or night from their home, uptime is critical. If a user gets a bright idea, or even just can't sleep, he or she might want to dial in and access the system. When it isn't available—other than for scheduled maintenance or upgrading—you might have an irate message on your E-mail the next morning.

Uptime percentage is easy to track. For every hour that the system is supposed to be working, how many minutes is it up? Secondarily, of the total number of hours available in a day (24), month (729.6), quarter (2188.8), or year (8760), how many hours was the system up? I prefer to talk about uptime rather than downtime. It is a more positive way of looking at what you have accomplished. Hopefully it will be around 99 percent. That will be a more impressive number than 1 percent downtime.

Human–Staff Reactions

We don't want to forget the staff. Human measures can include morale and attitude scores on some type of survey. There are a plethora of attitude surveys on the market. You have only to choose one with which you feel comfortable. They all provide scaled scores. Most of them have norms to which you can compare yourself. This way, you can monitor not only your progress internally against your last score, but how you match up with other groups that are important to you. On this point, please note that a gross score for anything is usually pretty useless. You want norms for your industry, region, type of company, or some other demographic that means something to you. What difference does it make if the norm for large bank HRIS staff attitudes is x.x, if you aren't a large bank? Your trade association might be able to provide norms or at least send you to a firm that can do the job for you. As of this point, mid-1994, the Human Resource Systems Professionals association is looking into the development of norms for HRIS operations.

A secondary human measure for HRIS staffs is stress. Although it isn't practical to run some type of stress survey or test, there are ways to find out how your staff is feeling the pressure. One of the best methods is to track negative acts. These include unscheduled absences. People often take more time off when they are stressed. It is a way to break away and make some space to breathe. You can also keep an eye out for other indices. What is the level of cooperation? Are people smiling? Are they going to lunch with each other or have they started to avoid casual contact? You don't have to put a number to these incidences of behavior change. Just stay alert.

External Measures: Value Added

The basic question in every operation, at all times, under all conditions, is, *what value is being generated?* This holds as true for HRIS as it does for the factory floor or the sales staff.

When your programmers turn in a completed project, there is some specific, identifiable product. A customer is going to pick up that product and put it to use. The point is, what difference does it make? If the customer now has a report, what good is it? How does its use affect anything? Kind of an interesting question, isn't it? Have you ever wondered as a provider of a data service what good the user finds in it? Some examples are programming of a data entry screen. Are the data entry clerks making fewer errors and finishing their work units faster? In the case of reports, what is the user doing with the report you programmed or produced for him or her?

Ultimately, all work can be measured against standards of quality, productivity, or service in the customer's area. Your work may be traceable through changes in the customer's operating costs, time, quantity, quality, or human factors. There is value for both the customer and your staff to know the effect of the work turned out by HRIS. If you were to check on the effects you might be pleasantly surprised to find how you were adding value. One thing we learned long ago was that when the staff got feedback on their work they found much more satisfaction in it than when they didn't. It makes sense doesn't it? Whatever your hobby might be, from knitting to carpentry, if you never saw the result of your skill and effort what fun would there be in doing it? That is one of the reasons we keep score. Remember what Robert Galvin of Motorola said, "If you don't measure it, you're just practicing." In addition to job satisfaction, there is another pragmatic reason for tracking the value of your work. The next time you go to management for additional resources you will have some justification for them.

GEM #14   *If it doesn't add value, it is expense, and we have enough of that.*

Summary

For decades people claimed that data processing and programming were too complex to be subjected to any form of measurement. That is categorically untrue here, just as it is in every other type of work. In the early days of automation, when only systems people were allowed to play with the machines in the data center, some believed that electronic data processing was truly a mystical art form. However, in recent years, with the arrival of PCs and computer training becoming a part of the curricula even of grade schools, the mystique is gone. We know that all jobs exist because they add value. It wouldn't make any sense to create a job that was a waste of time and money. So, how have we found value in all jobs?

The answer to that question is simple. What is the purpose of this piece of work? What do we expect it to yield? What difference would it make if the end product came out late versus on time? What difference would it make if it had lots of errors or no errors in it? What difference would it make if it cost ten times as much as it does?

You see the point. What are we doing? Why are we doing it? If we do it right, what will we expect to see? If we do it less well or flat-out wrong, what do we expect the effect will be? The difference between these two outcomes is the impact. This difference, this impact, is measurable in cost, time, quantity, quality, and/or human terms. When impact is converted to money, it shows the value added. It works for programmers just as much as for assembly line workers. The logic is the same; only the terms, complexity, and potential value differ.

SECTION D

Supporting the Human Asset: How to Measure Employee and Labor Relations

12
Orientation and Counseling

The employee relations (ER) function has always suffered from an identity crisis. The view has seemed to be that if we didn't know what to do with a certain task, it was given to the ER folks. After all, they didn't hire, pay, or train people. They didn't process benefits or negotiate labor contracts and grievances. They were the ultimate people people. The annual Society for Human Resource Management-Bureau of National Affairs (SHRM-BNA) survey of personnel activities, budgets, and staffs lists about fifty activities for which the HR department has all or some responsibility. Nearly 30 percent of these are usually handled by employee relations. As if that were not enough, the range of activities covers such dissimilar tasks as new hire orientation, unemployment compensation administration, recreation and social programs, counseling, employee communications, suggestion systems, and food service management. This heterogeneous mix gets in the way of clearly describing what the function is all about. The diversity of jobs demands a range of skills unequaled by any other function in the organization. On the one hand, it is the most "touchy-feely" of all functions. On the other, it can be the most hardnosed area. The department can justifiably be described as a catch-all. Given its scope, it is difficult to know where to start and what to include. It is impractical to attempt the measurement of more than half a dozen different tasks. Clearly, we must be selective. We must pick those activities we believe are the more important ones and focus our efforts on them. I have chosen to look at five issues: new hire orientation, counseling, absence, turnover or retention management, and unemployment compensation administration. Then, I will introduce the idea of customer satisfaction surveying. This is a task that ER might handle well, since it has the broadest range of contacts across the organization. Labor relations is usually a separate function. However, rather than create a section devoted solely to labor relations, I have chosen to include it with employee relations in this section.

Getting Started

New hire orientation is an activity that is seldom subjected to measurement. One of the reasons is the objectives of orientation are often not clear. Generally speaking, we assume that we orient new employees to speed their integration into the organization. That is a rather difficult result to isolate and evaluate. Most managers now realize that the time spent in orientation is worthwhile. It helps to shorten the acclimitization period of the new employee. Today, most companies require a new hire to attend some type of formal orientation program shortly after they report for work. In the hurry-up decades of the 1970s and 1980s, that was not universally true.

In most companies new hire orientation is now an act of faith. As such, it is almost impossible to assess its effectiveness. If measurement is desired, then some sort of cost and impact goals must be specified beforehand. Given a set of desired outcomes, a program or quiz can be designed to evaluate whether or not the goals were achieved.

Most new employees arrive at work the first day in a positive frame of mind, highly motivated to work, and somewhat confused by the new setting. During the first few hours on the job, some are intimidated by the strange environment. A new hire orientation program is an excellent way to deal with this problem. When employees are put at ease and helped to be mentally alert yet relaxed, they learn faster, make fewer mistakes, and generally develop on-the-job confidence.

One major electronics company has a secondary orientation that takes place on the job. It goes beyond the general program, which is designed to communicate information needed by all employees. This departmental orientation covers issues indigenous to the department. Five subjects are discussed:

1. *Jargon.* New hires are taught the company's and the department's language. Every industry and every organization has a language of its own. New employees are often confused, embarrassed, and make mistakes simply because they do not understand the language.

2. *People.* The orientation discusses the kinds of people with whom the new employee must deal. Idiosyncracies, styles, and personalities are covered so that the person knows what to expect and can figure out how to work effectively with new co-workers.

3. *Resources.* The new employee is shown where to find the tools and supplies needed to do the job. Information is also provided on the administrative procedures that need to be followed in order to obtain these items.

4. *Problems.* Every organization has problems. This company tells people what kinds of problems they can expect to encounter. It also teaches them acceptable ways to handle the resulting frustrations.

5. *Priorities.* Last, and probably most important, the goals of the work group and the company are explained. The purpose is to let the employee know where to focus his or her energies in both the short and the long run.

All this is part of acculturation. Many companies have adopted corporate visions, which they share with the new hire at the time of orientation. This helps the person learn quickly what is expected and accepted, what is celebrated, and what is not allowed.

Orientation Cost

Since orientation is a discrete, identifiable event, it is relatively easy to measure. Cost can be measured at three levels: cost per employee, cost per department, and cost of staff time to orient. The first measure is cost per employee, as shown in Formula ER-1.

Orientation Cost per Employee

$$OC/E = \frac{[T \times (R/h \times E)] + DC}{E} \qquad \text{(ER-1)}$$

where OC/E = average cost to orient an employee
   T = time spent in orientation (e.g., 4 hours)
   R/h = average hourly pay rate of attending employees (e.g., $10.25)*
   DC = HR department cost per employee (e.g., $195)
   E = total number of employees oriented (e.g., 20)

*Pay rates should include benefits also.

EXAMPLE

$$OC/E = \frac{[4 \times (\$10.25 \times 20)] + \$195}{20}$$

$$= \frac{\$1015}{20}$$

$$= \$57.50$$

This basic ratio can be computed either by using actual hourly rates of each new hire or, more easily, by using an average hourly rate for each job group represented in the orientation. If this task were done on the job by the local supervisor, it would cost more and would be less effective. Supervisors and managers do not know corporate policies as well as the employee relations staff and therefore cannot give the same quality of information in the same time frame. Orientation cost is part of the cost of turnover. It goes into the indirect cost line on the turnover cost estimator (to be discussed later in this section).

The second cost measure, cost per department, deals with the lost productivity a department suffers when the new hire is in orientation. Since this is a total cost and not a ratio, the calculation, as shown in Formula ER-2, is a straight multiplication problem.

Departmental Orientation Cost

$$OC/D = TO \times R/h \times N \qquad (ER-2)$$

where   OC/D = orientation cost per department
         TO   = time spent in orientation
         R/h = average hourly rate (e.g., $10.25)
         N   = number of new hires in orientation from a given department (e.g., 5)

EXAMPLE

$$OC/D = 4 \times \$10.25 \times 5$$
$$= \$205$$

This formula can be extended to the total organization. If the orientation were taking place within the department, the cost of lost supervisor time would have to be added in. So, although at first glance it may seem that a significant amount of wage and salary time is being lost by production to orientation, when the cost of many supervisors' time is added in, it is clear that handling the process in the HR department is more efficient. The third cost measure, cost of staff time (as shown in Formula ER-3), makes this point clear.

HR Department Orientation Expense

$$\frac{SOC/H = T \times R/h}{N} \qquad \text{(ER-3)}$$

where   SOC/H = staff orientation cost per new hire
            T = ER staff time spent preparing and conducting orientation (e.g., 16 hours)
         R/h = average hourly rate of employee relations staff, including benefits (e.g., $16.20)
            N = number of new hires oriented (e.g., 20)

EXAMPLE

$$SOC = \frac{16 \times \$16.20}{20}$$

$$= \frac{\$259.20}{20}$$

$$= \$12.96$$

Clearly, a supervisor cannot orient a new hire for something close to $13.00 That is less than one hour's pay for the average supervisor. The issue of quality of the orientation does not even have to be discussed when the cost disparity is as great as it obviously is here.

Evaluating the Impact

As in most cases, the result is more important an issue than is the cost of an activity. When I was an HR director, I always wanted to know the new hires' reactions to our orientation program. I suspect that you do, too. An easy way to learn that is through a simple quiz or survey. A sample of a survey is shown in Fig. 12.1. These are some of the basic questions to which a recent hire can respond accurately and without any fear. By making the name optional, you will probably get the most truthful results. As long as you have a job title and department number, you can trace back any problems that may show up.

In my opinion the most valuable question is number 4. We both know that there are supervisors and managers in every company who believe that they are the sole authority on everything in their department. If they are administering policy and procedures in a manner contrary to company intent, you will want to know about it. You have probably experienced supervisors who take a new employee under their wing on the first day and say something like, "I know what they told you in orientation, but let me show you how things really work out here." If that is going on, you might find out about it through a survey.

To assist us in evaluating our New Employee Orientation Program, please complete the questions below and return to Personnel. You need not sign your name, but please indicate your job title, department, and the requested dates.

Instructions: Circle the number that best describes your feelings about each statement below. For instance, if you strongly agree with the statement, circle number 6; if you mildly disagree with the statement, circle number 3; etc.

	Strongly disagree	Disagree	Mildly disagree	Mildly agree	Agree	Strongly agree
1. I felt very welcome and at home after my orientation.	1	2	3	4	5	6
2. The information I needed to know on the following subjects was clearly provided:						
(a) Insurance and benefits	1	2	3	4	5	6
(b) Familiarity with the facility	1	2	3	4	5	6
(c) Policies and rules	1	2	3	4	5	6
(d) Affirmative action plan	1	2	3	4	5	6
(e) Safety/security	1	2	3	4	5	6
(f) Forms and records	1	2	3	4	5	6
3. The orientation leader was well informed and answered my questions.	1	2	3	4	5	6
4. What I was told at orientation proved to be accurate in my daily work.	1	2	3	4	5	6
5. I learned in orientation where to find the additional information I might need.	1	2	3	4	5	6

Comments or suggestions: _____

_____

_____

_____

Name (optional)	Job title	Dept. #

Date of orientation	Date questionnaire returned

Figure 12.1. Orientation Survey

Counseling: the Early Warning System

Counseling of employees, supervisors, and managers has no beginning and no end. It is a continuous process that can and does take place anywhere at any time. The counseling staff cannot go a day without someone stopping them somewhere for information or advice. No place is sacred, no place secure from the person who needs counseling or who wants to lodge a complaint (nor should it be). The counselor has to deal with employees in the office, the hallway, the shop floor, the cafeteria, the parking lot, and even sometimes in the restroom. We don't realize what a valuable, indispensable role ER people play until we walk down the hall with them and see how often they are stopped by an employee with a question or a problem. In effect, ER staff act like a safety value, always on hand to release some of the pressure that naturally builds up from friction within an organization. When I was an HR director I thought of my staff as the lubricant of the company. They helped the parts work together with less friction and heat.

Situations like this impede most attempts at measurement. They make data collection a complex problem. The nature of a great deal of counseling rules out the usual forms of effectiveness evaluation. The only practical way to deal with this dynamic, amorphous phenomenon is to start at the beginning.

Since counseling does take place everywhere at any time, data collection is difficult. If counselors counseled only in their offices, it would be relatively easy to keep track of the number, type, and time of counseling sessions. Since much counseling is unplanned and away from the office, it is believed that precise records cannot be kept. That is true, in part. The standard method of record keeping on counseling is to create a simple manual log or electronic spreadsheet that has columns for name, department, type of counseling (the topic), time spent, action taken, and whatever else might be desired.

If this is a paper logging system, it is inconvenient for the counselors to carry a heavy book everywhere they go. As counselors walk about the organization, they may counsel with several people on different subjects for different periods of time before they return to their office. When they return, they may get involved in other duties and forget to log the talks. Therefore, there will always be some margin of error. But valuable record keeping of counseling sessions is not as difficult as people might think. There is a simple way they can log all pertinent data as they go: keep a small pad in their pocket, purse, or briefcase. After each conversation, they can step aside for a moment and make a note of the person, department, topic, and time. When they get back to their desk, they can take another minute to log the record into their permanent system. The problem with data collection is not the inconvenience, but that the counselors don't like to do it.

Have you ever noticed how well a professional athlete remembers minute details of the sporting event just completed? A golfer can tell you exactly where every shot in the past round landed, what club was used, which way the wind was blowing, and so on. A baseball player can talk you through an entire game, recounting what each batter did. This memory skill is not confined to athletes. The same applies to bridge and chess players, as well as people who are intensely devoted to any hobby. At work, anyone who is concentrating on their job can demonstrate amazing recall. After several years of observing and checking with employee counselors, we estimated that they were about 95 percent accurate in their recall of all sessions. They almost always remembered who they talked to, what departments the employees were from, and what the subject was. They were about 90 percent accurate in recalling the amount of time spent per session. These people were just as professional in their work as any athlete. Their dedication to their job and their interest in maintaining the system was such that they were able to keep very accurate information on counseling. When they knew they needed to remember, they did.

Before you are misled into believing it is no problem at all, let me confess that it took some time for the counselors in my department to reach acceptable levels of precision, but it wasn't because they didn't know how to keep records. In the beginning they openly opposed the idea, and the excuses they used were numerous as well as highly imaginative. Once I gave them the "or else" option they fell into line. After all, democracy only goes so far, and then a manager has to give orders. The turning point came when they began to believe in the value of keeping the data. Shortly after the counselors started turning in their monthly consolidated report, they saw the benefit to themselves and to the department. They could see just how much they had accomplished the previous month. They began to see trends, which we all used to head off problems before they became unmanageable. The longer this went on, the more value they found in the reports. As they came to realize the benefit, they sharpened up their memories. Within just a few months they stopped talking about the extra work involved. They gave up the belief that the data would be inaccurate. Their skepticism, and sometimes fear, about how the information would be used disappeared. From then on we never worried about the validity and reliability of the counseling report. The key here, as in all other attempts to persuade people to do something, is to lead them to see the benefit in doing it. Reasonable people will respond when they are shown the payoff.

As I mentioned earlier, the best way to run a measurement system is to have everyone collect as much of their own data as possible. At the end of a reporting period the data can be picked up by one person and put into a consolidated report. One of the most comprehensive report forms in the system is the employee relations counseling summary shown in Fig. 12.2. Basically it is a spreadsheet adapted to this use. The counseling summary contains four categories of information. First, across the top it lists the types of counseling subjects covered. This list is based on experience. If you keep track of your counseling by subject matter for a month or two, you will be able to consolidate it into a manageable number of categories. Down the left side you put in the departments, job groups, levels, or other classifications of employees who used the service. The most common way to do this is to list departments. If your system is computerized, you could sort your list by as many categories as you have identified in the computer. The

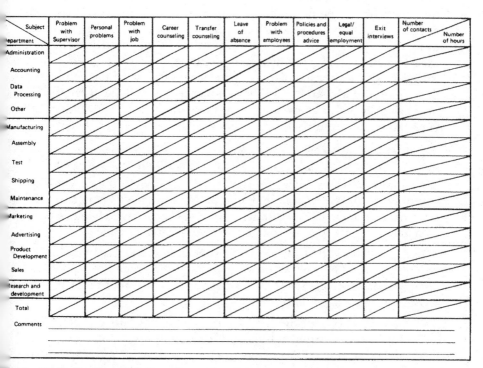

Subject Department	Problem with Supervisor	Personal problems	Problem with job	Career counseling	Transfer counseling	Leave of absence	Problem with employees	Policies and procedures advice	Legal/ equal employment	Exit interviews	Number of contacts	Number of hours
Administration												
Accounting												
Data Processing												
Other												
Manufacturing												
Assembly												
Test												
Shipping												
Maintenance												
Marketing												
Advertising												
Product Development												
Sales												
Research and development												
Total												
Comments												

Figure 12.2. Employee Relations Counseling Summary

greater the number of sorts, the greater the value of the information. Looking inside the cells, you see they are divided. The subdivisions are for the number of contacts made per subject and the number of hours spent discussing the subject. The far right column is a total contacts and hours summary by classification.

When this report is filled out for all counseling conducted during the month, you may find that there are a few blank cells. That is all right, because problems tend to run in cycles, and from time to time a particular issue is not a question or a problem for some departments. Overall, the filled-in form has an overwhelming amount of data. Careful reading will disclose a richness of information that will point the manager directly toward the most pressing issues of the day. Ultimately, the purpose of this data collection is to provide you with an early warning system that keeps the company out of trouble. By seeing trends early you can react before there is a major problem.

Analysis Calculations

You can do an eyeball analysis of the data on the summary form and pick up most of the pertinent information. However, if you have the data in an electronic spreadsheet, you can run a few other computations that will add to your understanding of the environment. My experience has shown me that an in-depth analysis of counseling data is a much more accurate display of the state of mind of the employees than is an attitude survey. Without going into this issue at length, let me just make some points about attitude surveys. First, attitudes surveys suffer from a number of inherent weaknesses. Here are a few:

1. Unless you have norms against which to measure the results, they are of little value. Numbers are relative, which means that you need comparative numbers from repeated surveying. But, if you survey only every two years, your population may have changed by 25 percent or more. The remaining employees may have changed their idea of what is acceptable, so they are also different people.

2. A corollary is that surveys are a snapshot of one day in the life of an employee. Many extraneous issues may influence the responses. Something as unrelated as a fight with a spouse that morning can turn an otherwise satisfied employee into a complainer.

3. Surveys supplied by outside companies may offer regional or national norms against which you can compare your responses. Interesting, but limited. You have to go beyond that. No other compa-

ny has the same mix of people, products, objectives, philosophy, style, etc., as yours.

4. Unless your responses have an importance scale built in, it is hard to tell whether or not you need to respond to a low score. Maybe employees do not like something, and maybe they do not even care.

5. All survey methods suffer from weaknesses of validity and reliability because they survey human beings. People are mercurial. They change. Some are even too frightened or too paranoid to give honest responses.

6. Finally, after decades of research that has resulted in a great deal of ambiguity about attitudes, Fishbein and Ajzen[1] tell it like it is:

> Unfortunately, despite the vast amount of research and publication on the topic, there is little agreement about what an attitude is, how it is formed or changed, and what role, if any, it plays in influencing or determining behavior.

The use of attitude surveys in industry, in most cases, is an example of how "pop psychology" has been introduced by people who do not have the knowledge or experience to practice the science. It seems to me that until the day comes when companies are committed enough to hire professionals and to support valid research projects, we are better off dealing with what employees do than with what they think.

Formulas ER-4 through ER-6 provide examples of the several perspectives used in analyzing counseling. Formula ER-4 takes department population into consideration. In effect, it weights the volume of counseling by department size so that each department can be viewed relative to other departments.

Departmental Counseling Factor

$$DCF = \frac{SD}{DP} \tag{ER-4}$$

where   DCF = departmental counseling factor
  SD = sessions per department (e.g., 80)
  DP = department population (e.g., 360)

<u>EXAMPLE</u>

$$DCF = \frac{80}{360}$$
$$= 22\%$$

This measure allows two types of analysis. First, how much counseling is taking place relative to other departments? Second, is the trend increasing or decreasing overall? It is a volume analysis and does not segregate sessions by type as does Formula ER-5.

Counseling Topic Factor

$$TP = \frac{T}{SD} \qquad \text{(ER-5)}$$

where   TP = percentage of each topic discussed
        T = number of sessions on that topic (e.g., 20)
        SD = total sessions for the department (e.g., 140)

EXAMPLE

$$TP = \frac{20}{140}$$

$$= 14.2\%$$

This measure will reveal the topic that comes up the most. When tracked from month to month, it will show any trends in counseling topics. It can also be compared across departments to see if a topic is a concern for the whole organization or only for isolated departments.

Another issue besides number of contacts is the amount of time being spent by topic and in total. Time is probably the more important issue, since it usually indicates the severity of the concern. We found that the relationship of contacts to time also was interesting to watch. If you look at the average time per topic over several reporting periods, you may find it increasing or decreasing at a significant rate. These early warning signs are most valuable for the employee relations manager who is trying to be proactive.

Counseling Topic Time

$$CTT = \frac{ST}{N} \qquad \text{(ER-6)}$$

where   CTT = average time per topic
        TT = total session time per topic (e.g., 15 hours)
        N   = number of sessions per topic (e.g., 25 sessions)

EXAMPLE

$$CTT = \frac{15 \text{ hours}}{25 \text{ sessions}}$$

$$= 0.60 \text{ hours per session (36 minutes)}$$

This same formula can be used in aggregate to measure the average session time for all sessions. This gives you an overall feeling of the level of intensity. However, the most useful application was just shown.

These measures can be used for classifications other than departments. As long as you have the capability to do multiple sortings of the data, you can apply these measures to levels (exempt and nonexempt), job groups (programmers, assemblers, accountants, etc.), or EEO-affected categories. The more sortings you can compute, the more data you have to manage the problems.

At the beginning of this section you saw a summary table of counseling data that presented a great deal of information. Its only weakness is that it shows only one month's activity. Some other formats also provide a full breakdown and have the bonus of showing more than one month at a time. Figure 12.3 is a bar graph that gives you a three-month perspective. Each month you drop off the oldest month and add in the newest one. Segmented bar graphs offer the advantage of being able to show trends across several topics simultaneously. In Figure 12.3 you can see that problems with employees and exit interviews have both risen dramatically over the three months displayed. Conversely, policy and procedures questions have fallen from 37.4 hours to 9.4 in three months.

Given the first issue of rising rates, you could go to the employee relations staff and ask them what is happening. They can check their logs and usually pinpoint the sources. They may say that the problems are spread across the organization, or they may say that they are pretty much confined to a given department or group of people. Once they isolate the source, you can usually do something to fix the problem or to have someone else fix it.

When you do solve a problem, you see the results in examples such as the policy and procedures trend. For instance, if you hire a large number of new employees and supervisors over a short period of time, you may find them besieging your staff with policy questions. Then it is a simple matter to run a training program for supervisors and watch the volume go down. By calculating the time, and thus the dollars, wasted in October versus December, you can show a quick cost-benefit analysis of your training class. And remember, it takes two to talk. The 37.4 hours in October only covers the person with the problem. While they were off the job talking with your staff, your people were also precluded from doing something else productive. Hence, the production time lost was really at least 37.4 × 2, or 74.8 hours because more than one person may come in on a contact. Time is money, and by multiplying 74.8 by the salary rates of your people and the com-

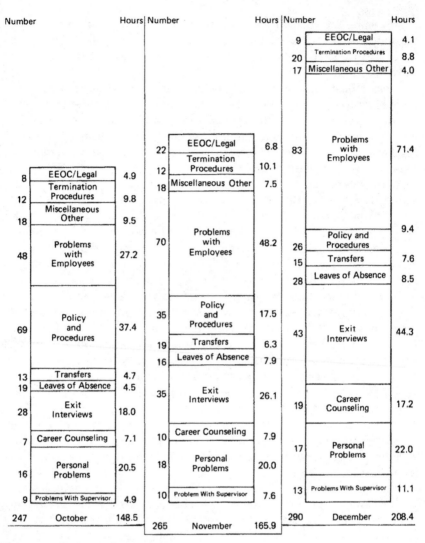

Figure 12.3. Counseling Trends

plainants you have the cost of the counseling. Then, when you multi-ply the December rate of 9.4 × 2 times the salaries involved, you have the difference that the training made. It is a simple method that will not stun your audience with its impact, but it will show that you are making a contribution and that you are bottom-line oriented.

There is one note of caution with this bar graph or with any calcula-tion of counseling time. Although you may see counseling employees as serving a useful purpose, some managers view it as wasted time.

They see it as an excuse for an employee to take some time off the job and shoot the breeze with your staff. You must be able to assure them that this is worthwhile time and that your staff does not conduct coffee klatches to keep the employees amused. The question is, what is the value of counseling?

You can point out that if your staff were not dealing with issues that the supervisors obviously cannot deal with, the problems would remain unresolved. They might seem to disappear, but actually they go underground if they are not addressed properly. So, instead of one employee being off the job talking about a concern and getting professional help, there would be two or more employees off-line probably making a molehill into a mountain.

It is a great temptation, once you have your system up and running, to go skipping up to the boss's office and declare how well the system is operating. Just remember, the boss has a different perspective. What you might think is a vindication of your program, your boss might see as a job that does not necessarily need to get done. The point is be prepared with evidence that there was some tangible value.

GEM #15   *Success is defined by results, not activity.*

The Value Question: Was the Problem Solved?

It is possible to calculate a percentage of counseling effectiveness by dividing the number of satisfactory resolutions by the total number of counseling sessions, but that probably isn't the most useful or moving statistic you could establish. Besides, there may be a problem in reaching agreement on what is a satisfactory resolution. Follow-up cannot be done on many issues because of their sensitive personal nature. For instance, you probably don't want to ask employees if they are still snorting coke.

However, some cases are a little more obvious. Very often there is simply a question to be answered. Sometimes you can see for sure that you prevented an unwanted termination. If a conflict has been resolved, that can be shown. When unproductive employees have their concerns taken care of and their productivity goes up, that is a measurable payoff. A rehabilitated alcoholic is an obvious result of professional help. The policy and procedures training program mentioned before is a very visible example. There are some instances where you can show unequivocally that counseling paid off. Reductions in turnover and absenteeism or increases in productivity are measurable results.

In the absence chapter you will see an example of the effects of counseling on absenteeism on a hospital staff. Much of the work of a counselor will have to be assessed by word-of-mouth reports, which is all right. If you can show that you have had a number of success stories, you do not have to quantitatively evaluate everything you did in employee relations. It all comes down to what difference it made. What was the problem or purpose behind the counseling? Was it merely general advice? Was it a specific, visible event such as employee or supervisor behavior? Was there a unsatisfactory work or personal result that someone wanted counsel on? This might be a quality, productivity, service, or interpersonal relations problem. To measure the result of any action, whether it be producing a widget on an assembly line or counseling a confused or troubled human being, you have to decide what the purpose is behind the action. If you know that and can put it into visible rather than feeling terms, then you can measure it.

In the case of counseling, you might be trying initially to reduce the emotional or psychological stress the individual is feeling. That's fine, but if you want to find some tangible value ask yourself what difference it makes when the person is not stressed. Are they more productive? Do they make fewer errors. Do they treat customers better? These are the productivity, quality, and service improvements that can come from counseling or advising an employee.

GEM #16   *When you are stuck trying to locate value ask what difference your action or the outcome will make; keep asking until a visible result appears.*

A Quarterly View

Financial reporting is typified by reports of earnings for the present quarter versus the same quarter a year previous. The reason that this method is widely used in businesses is that it shows trend. That is what management wants to see: Are we getting better or worse?

This approach can be applied in human resources reporting as well. It works just as well with counseling as it does with financial reporting. Figure 12.4 shows a quarter by quarter comparison of counseling by topic, giving both the number of contacts and the total time. The example shown would be a year-end review. From it, one could look for seasonal trends that predict probable occurrences. In the sample, the third quarter appears to be a time when there are fewer problems than other periods. This may mean a slackening of the workload and a time when other types of activities might be planned.

	Q1 1992 #/hr	Q1 1993 #/hr	Q2 1992 #/hr	Q2 1993 #/hr	Q3 1992 #/hr	Q3 1993 #/hr	Q4 1992 #/hr	Q4 1993 #/hr
Policies and procedures	186/34	114/46.5	158/48.9	129/39.6	145/36.9	66/17.1	186/37.3	89/31.3
Employee performance problems	179/62	105/53.1	138/48.2	144/61.5	120/40	113/41.1	143/58	135/62.8
Personal problems	68/39.2	186/78.8	192/56.2	84/58.8	81/52.3	72/28.2	114/49	114/61.6
Job performance problems	68/31.2	99/51.6	149/64	63/42	116/43	84/28.4	111/46.1	92/48.5
Salary administration	44/24	0	37/15.1	0	33/14.8	1/0.3	38/17.9	4/2.5
EEO matters	4/1	21/24.9	5/2.6	3/1.5	22/12.9	6/2	10/5.5	4/2.3
Exit interviews	114/44.6	81/32.4	134/56	91/32.1	118/58.6	186/41	122/53	64/29.3
Career opportunities program	17/5.9	284/71.1	33/10.8	258/94.8	15/5.1	217/53.1	21/7.3	136/69.6
Career pathing	26/15.9	42/22.5	18/3.3	15/12	6/2	35/16	14/7	118/55
Management training	0	27/21	0	291/219	0	57/39.4	0	0
Employee training	0	12/12	0	45/72	0	6/3.8	0	13/26.8
Termination procedure	68/11.1	0	58/20.6	0	61/19.2	0	62/16.9	0
Total	758/268	813/406	906/318	1116/633	717/285	764/270	741/290	761/390

Figure 12.4. Counseling Quarterly Report (Headquarters)

The point of this kind of reporting is that it helps the employee relations manager plan and organize the staff for maximum performance. Good managers plan ahead, but that is hard to do when you have only a hazy notion of what to expect. A detailed knowledge of what has gone before along with the direction and strength of the trends is invaluable for planning the future.

Customer Satisfaction

Customer satisfaction is a subjective and personal rather than an absolute or concrete phenomenon. Whereas you can measure the time, cost, quality, and quantity of something against a known standard, customer satisfaction is nothing more than a perceptual teeter-totter. On one end of the seesaw you find customer fulfillment; on the other you find customer expectation. If fulfillment is at least as great as expectation, you have satisfaction or equilibrium. With so much being written and spoken about customer service these days, some people have sought a niche by talking about customer elation—going beyond satisfaction. Frankly, the first task is to continuously achieve satisfaction. Later you can talk about nirvana. The problem with satisfaction is that quite often the provider does not know the customer's expectation. I had a case recently with a client where the provider didn't even want to ask the question. Instead they wanted to present their products and ask the customers how satisfied they were with the current offering. This is an invitation to extinction, otherwise known as termination or outsourcing. To further complicate the matter, sometimes expectations are even unknown by the customer. Have you ever been shopping with someone, asked them just what type of garment they are looking for, and heard them tell you, "I can't describe it, but I'll know it when I see it."? That is what customer satisfaction is like, sometimes.

So often the staff provider is more interested in surveying satisfaction levels related to current products than to expected service. The reason for this is that those people don't understand the customer provider relationship. As Peter Drucker told us, the purpose of a business is not determined by its products but by the needs the customers satisfy when they buy the product or service. We often have to refocus staff people on service delivery as a key issue. Although we include a section on the staff department's products and ask the customers how important each is, attention must also be given to the six service delivery factors described in Zeithaml's research covered in Chapter 4. The staff erroneously thinks that they have to sell their products with the survey. In actuality, the customer is just as interested in how reliable, responsive, and knowledgeable the staff is as what their products are like. The key to always remember is that the customer does not want our products. The customer wants his or her need satisfied.

Summary

Whenever I bring up the topic of measuring the effectiveness of counseling, I am confronted with the question of how you measure the results of people talking to each other on such a wide variety of topics in so many different settings. The answer is to define what you are trying to measure. What are the people talking about? That is the topic category. How often do they talk about it? How much time is spent on it? And most important, why are they talking to you about it? What is the *result* they want to achieve? Any or all of these can be monitored and measured to one degree or another.

The monitoring system described in this chapter is a great early warning device. It can tell you about simmering problems that you can jump on before they boil over. The most important issue is, is there a connection between the topic and some organizational phenomenon such as absence, turnover, loss of productivity, quality problems, or something else you can identify? Did your counseling affect that? In Chapter 13 I will show an example of how counseling affected absenteeism and saved a company well over $60,000 in one year. I've seen many cases where the availability of an employee relations professional has obviously affected absence rates, turnover, formal complaints to regulatory agencies, and so on. The before and after record of these types of occurrences is so strikingly different that no one has to prove that an employee relations person made the difference.

The point is to systematically and regularly gather data on the work of the ER staff. Then trace connections between their activities and some specific or general outcomes. When you pull all that together and apply your experience and intuition, you will be surprised at how much you will learn, and how you will be able to show value added from employee relations work.

13
The Hidden Costs of Lost Time

How Absence Correlates With Turnover

Employee absence is a costly nuisance. If left unattended, absence can become a significant expense. It is becoming more difficult to track absence, at least among exempt-level personnel. Many companies abandoned absence monitoring of professionals and managers some time ago. They also instituted an overall pay-for-time-not-worked system wherein they lumped all absence. This includes a set number of holidays, vacation days, and absent or "personal" days.

There are many reasons for an employee to be absent from work. Some are legitimate. Sickness, family emergencies, or some personal business that can be dealt with only during working hours are absences for which an employee reasonably takes some time off. However, there are other more capricious sources of absence, many of which can be prevented. Research has shown a correlation between absence and dissatisfaction with pay. It is the employee's way of "getting even." The rationale used is, "You won't pay me what I am worth so I'll just take a day off and let you give me sick pay instead." Excessive absenteeism is a sign of turnover to come. Other sources of irritation and stress can also prompt an absence. Poor supervisory practices most often correlate with turnover, but they may also foster absence. Excessive workloads for a long period of time can cause psychological or physical overloads, resulting in taking a couple of days off. In the worst cases, high stress can cause permanent problems. However the absence comes about, there are several ways to measure its rate of occurrence and its cost to the organization.

The basic absence rate calculation used in most national surveys, such as the SHRM-BNA, is shown in Formula ER-7.

Absence Rate

$$AR = \frac{WDL}{e \times WD} \qquad \text{(ER-7)}$$

where   AR   = absence rate (monthly)
       WDL = worker days lost through absence (e.g., 320)
          e = average employee population (e.g., 550)
        WD = number of work days available per employee per month (e.g., 22)

EXAMPLE

$$AR = \frac{320}{550 \times 22}$$

$$= \frac{320}{12{,}100}$$

$$= 2.6\%$$

As with most other ratios, this one can be computed by department to find locations where absence levels are relatively high. It can also be applied to job groups to search out types of employees who are exceedingly absent. In order for an absence control program to work there are two prerequisites: accurate employee time records and a standard acceptable absence rate.

Knowing the amount of time lost through absence is the starting point. The other issue is the hidden cost of absence. Kuzmits[1] provided the basis for a formula that is still usable to measure absenteeism costs, as shown in Formula ER-8.

Absenteeism Cost

$$AC/E = \frac{ML(Wh + EBC) + S(R/h + SBC) + Misc}{E} \qquad \text{(ER-8)}$$

where   AC/E = absence cost per employee
         ML   = total work hours lost for all reasons except holidays and vacations (e.g., 78,336)
         Wh   = weighted average hourly pay level for groups (e.g., 85% of hourly absences at $8.25 = $7.01; 13% of nonexempt absences at $9.80 = $1.27; 2% of exempt absences at $16.15 = $0.03; total = $8.31)
        EBC   = cost of employee benefits (e.g., 35% of pay: $7.01 × 35% = $2.45)

S = supervisory hours lost due to employee absence, based on sampling to estimate average hours per day spent dealing with problems resulting from absences: production rescheduling, instructing replacements, counseling and disciplining absentees (e.g., $\frac{1}{2}$ hour per day = 3,840)

R/h = average hourly pay for supervisors (e.g., $13.20)

SBC = cost of supervisor's benefits (e.g., 35% of $13.20 = $4.62)

Misc = other costs, temporary help, overtime, production losses, machine downtime, quality problems (e.g., $38,500)

E = total employees (e.g., 1,200)

EXAMPLE
$$AC = \frac{(78,336 \times \$10.76) + (3,840 \times \$17.82) + \$38,500}{1,200}$$

$$= \frac{\$842,895 + \$68,429 + \$38,500}{1,200}$$

$$= \frac{\$949,824}{1,200}$$

$$= \$791.52$$

Measuring this quantity brings home to supervisors and managers that absence carries with it a high hidden cost. The peripheral costs of supervisory time, temporary help, poor quality work, and so on, add significantly to the loss.

One manufacturing company in the midwest reduced absenteeism in the factory and saved over one million dollars annually in pay for time not worked. Still another way of viewing absence is from the standpoint of its effect on labor utilization. This can be seen in the two-step process of Formula ER-9.

Effect of Absenteeism on Labor Utilization

$$U = \frac{Nh}{h} \qquad \text{(ER-9)}$$

where   U = labor utilization percentage

Nh = nonproductive hours: absence, breaks, downtime, prep time, rework (e.g., 380 hours)

h = work hours available (e.g., 10 employees $\times$ 40 hours $\times$ 4 weeks = 1600 hours)

EXAMPLE

$$U = \frac{380}{1600}$$

$$= 24\% \text{ (utilization} = 76\%)$$

To show the effect of absenteeism, subtract absent hours (e.g., 80) from Nh and recompute.

EXAMPLE

$$U = \frac{380 - 80}{1600}$$

$$= \frac{300}{1600}$$

$$= 19\% \text{ (utilization} = 81\%)$$

Utilization would have been 5 percent higher if no employees had been absent. In today's marketplace that could contribute significantly to competitive advantage.

Absence is an insidious type of problem because it is, by definition, invisible. It is not so obviously a matter of something going wrong as it is a case of something that should occur not occurring. The missing occurrence is the arrival of the scheduled employee at work. When that does not happen, it sets in motion a chain of other events that negatively impact hard measures such as quality and productivity as well as human stress imposed on other employees by the absence.

Value of Absence Control

Absenteeism may also affect things such as morale for the employees who come to work every day. It can create other types of dissatisfaction among employees in a work group, who may have to take time to indoctrinate temporary employees filling in for those who are frequently absent. By maintaining current data on absence and showing its negative effects, you may cause management to step up to an issue they would rather ignore. If they do, you will have helped them save the company money and improve morale.

Most surveys have shown that Pareto's law applies to absences; that is, approximately 20 percent of the employees account for 80 percent of the absences. If we were to divide all absence into three types we could label them capricious, personal business, and problem. The first category I mentioned before. It covers the days off people take because they are angry with the company or are not motivated to work that day. The first sunny day in spring, the opening of hunting season, or the morn-

Category	Number of employees	Average days lost previous	Total days lost	Total estimated cost, in dollars
Alcohol	25	20	500	34,545
Drugs	8	28	224	15,746
Family	21	15	315	21,763
Mental	6	24	144	9,948
Other	9	12	108	7,461
Total	69	19.8	1291	89,193

Figure 13.1. Frequency of Absence by Category

ing-after blues are examples of no work motivation. Personal business is just what it implies. Sometimes a person has to take care of family matters and can do that only during working hours. Going to a lawyer, closing the sale or purchase of a house, picking up grandma at the airport, and taking a child to the doctor or on a special shopping trip are a few of the many responsibilities we all have. Employees figure that if they have a lot of sick leave earned, they may as well use some of that rather than take a vacation day. The last category, problem, covers the gut-wrenching matters of alcohol and drug abuse, and mental health and family problems. Sooner or later, these issues show up at the employee relations office. We have even created a special service to help employees deal with these concerns. We call them employee assistance programs (EAPs). If you check the work records of employees who utilize the EAP services, you will probably find that they have higher than average rates of absenteeism. Figure 13.1 shows a typical example.

By computing the lost time costs, you can find the effect of absenteeism on your organization's profit and loss statement. If you are able to "solve" some of these problems through your EAP service, you can track the effect that it has on absenteeism. If it reduces absences, which it will, calculate the cost saving to the company. This can be expressed in terms of productive days gained and the dollar value of that gain. You may find that the EA program more than pays for itself in direct benefits. The rehabilitation of a sick employee or the rescue of a troubled family is an added incalculable payoff.

Sample of Counseling's Effect on Absenteeism

Table 13.1 shows an example from a case in a large hospital where counseling had a profound effect on staff absence. What was clear to management at the hospital was that employees who come for counseling typically have excessive absenteeism. That makes sense. The

Table 13.1. Payoffs of Counseling

		#1 The Problem		
		Days Lost		**Cost to the**
Counseling Topic	**Number of Employees**	**Avg. Past 12 Months**	**Cumulative Total**	**Company (Avg. Pay)**
A	30 x	20 =	600	$ 41,400
B	4 x	30 =	120	8,280
C	11 x	28 =	308	21,252
D	16 x	25 =	400	27,600
E	11 x	19 =	209	14,421
Total	72	24	1637	$112,953
		#2 The Payoff		
Employee Status	**Number of Employees**	**Absence Rate**	**Productive Days Gained**	**$ Value @ $18K per Year**
Back at Work	51	4.4%	915	$ 63,135
Terminated	12	-	-	-
On Leave	9	-	-	-
Total Cost of Counseling = $31,600 >	>	>	>	ROI = 200%

categories of counseling topics are depicted as A through E. They were largely personal issues: problems with families, substance abuse, financial difficulties, and so on. In the top half of the exhibit you see the history of absenteeism. In the bottom half you see the results a year later after professional counseling was applied. Not only did the counseling pay off on a two for one basis in dollars through reduced absence, it positively affected the lives of the 51 families.

In conclusion, absence affects both the hard data issues of productivity and human issues such as morale. Excessively absent workers impact the morale of the employees who come to work every day and can create other types of dissatisfaction among their co-workers. By maintaining current data on absence and showing its negative effects, you may cause management to step up to an issue they sometimes ignore. If they do, you will have helped them save the company money and improve morale.

Clarifying the Concept of Turnover

Movement of employees into and out of organizations, commonly called *turnover*, is one of the more heavily studied organizational phenomena. The U.S. Bureau of Labor Statistics uses the terms *accessions* and *separations* to describe movements across organizational boundaries. Transfers and promotions are not considered part of turnover because they do not involve movement across the membership boundary of an organization. Accessions are generally *new hires*. Separations are subdivided into *quits, layoffs,* and *discharges.* Turnover is further typed as *voluntary* and *involuntary.* Quits (resignations) are the normal label for voluntary departures. Involuntary examples are dismissals (firings), layoffs, retirements, and death. Under normal business conditions, voluntary turnover is greater than involuntary. Voluntary turnover is more often studied by management, which desires to reduce it or maintain it at an acceptable level.

The extensive and repeated downsizings that began in the late 1980s and threaten never to stop combine a variety of methods of terminating people. Some are straightforward layoffs. Many also include so-called early retirement programs that have confused the distinctions between voluntary and involuntary. The underlying question is, when is early retirement voluntary and when is it the only real choice? There is no standard answer to that. Each case must be examined by the people on site, and their determination must rule.

Zero turnover is not desirable for several reasons. First, long-tenured employees generally have higher salaries. This is one of the unspoken plays of those "retirement" programs. Companies traded off years of experience and skill for lower salaries. If all employees stay and the organization grows at a normal rate, most employees eventually will be at or near the top of their pay ranges and total salary expense will be very high. Second, new employees bring new ideas. A number of stagnant organizations have become inbred and are no longer in touch with their constituency. The automobile industry lost touch with its public in the 1960s and allowed foreign car manufacturers to take as much as 50 percent of some U.S. car markets. Labor unions have, in some cases, failed to develop new leadership from the rank and file. In the 1970s they awakened to find that the membership had developed new needs and new values, many of which the leadership was not aware of. Any organization must continually renew itself with fresh ideas from new members. Therefore, a small amount of turnover is healthy.

Rather than focus on the causes of turnover, we will concentrate on methods of analysis. The question, "What is the turnover percentage in your organization?" is too simplistic. A single number tells little. Even if the number compares favorably with a previous period, it is not very helpful. One number does not tell who is leaving or for what reasons. As with most variables we have discussed, the data has to be cut into smaller, more discrete clusters if it is to yield true understanding of the phenomena at work.

The two basic calculations from which all subdivisions are made are the accession rate and the separation rate. They are shown in Formulas ER-10 and ER-11.

Accession Rate

$$AR = \frac{H}{e} \qquad\qquad \text{(ER-10)}$$

Separation Rate

$$SR = \frac{NT}{e} \qquad\qquad \text{(ER-11)}$$

where AR = accession rate
  SR = separation rate
  H = number hired during the period (e.g., 725)
  NT = number terminated during the period (e.g., 656)
  e = average employee population (e.g., 3097)

EXAMPLE

$$AR = \frac{725}{3097} \qquad SR = \frac{656}{3097}$$
$$= 23.4\% \qquad = 21.2\%$$

For many years there was little agreement on the employee population figure that should be used. Some practitioners used beginning of period population and others used average or end of period population as the divisor. Finally, *average population* has won out and become the standard figure. This factors out most of the effects of heavy hiring or terminating.

Subdividing for Understanding

There is practically no end to the ways in which turnover data can be cut. Some common categories are

- Length of service of current employees
- Length of service of terminating employees
- Stability (instability) factor of a given population
- Survival (loss) rate of new hires
- Termination rate by organizational unit (department, headquarters, division)

- Termination rate by demographic group (age, race, sex, education, grade, performance level, job classification)
- Termination rate by reason for leaving

The formulas are all quite similar. Except for length of service, it is only a matter of dividing the number of employees in the referent group by the average population. The first example, tenure or length of service, is computed in Formulas ER-12 and ER-13.

Average Tenure—Current Employees

$$SS = \frac{TSS}{E} \qquad \text{(ER-12)}$$

Former Employees' Average Service Period

$$SL = \frac{TSL}{E} \qquad \text{(ER-13)}$$

where   SS = average length of service of current employees—stayers
TSS = total sum of years of service of all staying employees (e.g., 112,025)
SL = average length of service of departed employees—leavers
TSL = total sum of years of service of all departed employees (e.g., 16,589)
E   = total number of employees in that group (e.g., stayers = 2041; leavers = 1056)

EXAMPLE

$$SS = \frac{112,025}{2041} \qquad SL = \frac{16,589}{1056}$$
$$= 5.5 \text{ years} \qquad = 1.6 \text{ years}$$

This calculation suggests that most employees who leave have relatively short tenure with the organization. We know from experience that the longer employees stay with an organization, the more likely they are to continue to stay. Another way to put it is that most of the voluntary turnover comes in the first two years of service.

When I was with a west coast bank, in the course of checking turnover patterns by length of service we discovered an abnormally high rate for people with two to three years of service. By digging into the records of all those who left we discovered that the management trainees from a certain mountain state college were leaving shortly after completing their training. Apparently, the word had gotten around this B-school that we had an excellent training program. After finishing their training and getting six months or so of branch experience, they went back home where they wanted to live all along.

Stability calculations tell you whether or not the turnover rate for a given population, i.e., employees with over five years of service, is changing. It answers questions such as, "Are our older employees leaving at the same rate as we would expect them to?" You can calculate it from either side, stability or instability, as shown in Formulas ER-14 and ER-15.

Stability Factor

$$SF = \frac{OS}{E} \tag{ER-14}$$

Instability Factor

$$IF = \frac{OL}{E} \tag{ER-15}$$

where   SF = stability factor of an existing population
        OS = original employees who remain for the period, for example, 1 year (e.g., 832)
        IF = instability factor of an existing population
        OL = original employees who left during the period (e.g., 80)
        E = employee population at the beginning of the period (e.g., 912)

EXAMPLE

$$SF = \frac{832}{912} \qquad IF = \frac{80}{912}$$
$$= 91.2\% \qquad = 8.8\%$$

Obviously, SF and IF are reciprocals. In this case, 91.2 percent of the employees with over five years of service stayed and 8.8 percent left during the past year. That can be compared with previous experience, and a value judgment can be made.

Survival or loss rate of new hires is conceptually identical to stability factor, only here the base population is new hires and not existing employee groups. A time period, say a month or a quarter, is defined, and all hires during that period are counted. At some point in the future, perhaps six months or one year later, all hires from the base period are traced and counted, either as stayers or as leavers. The computation is shown in Formulas ER-16 and ER-17.

Survivor Rate

$$SR = \frac{HS}{H}$$ (ER-16)

Loss Rate

$$LR = \frac{HL}{H}$$ (ER-17)

where   SR   = survival rate of new hires
         HS   = number of new hires from the period who are still employed, stayers (e.g., 209)
         LR   = wastage or loss rate
         HL   = number of new hires who left, leavers (e.g., 79)
         H   = total number of new hires during the period (e.g., 288)

EXAMPLE

$$SR = \frac{209}{288} \qquad LR = \frac{79}{288}$$
$$= 72.6\% \qquad\quad = 27.4\%$$

This measure can be used as part of the recruiter effectiveness composite. However, since a new hire's survival is out of the hands of the recruiter, remember to use this indicator with great caution.

Multidimensional Analysis

It is often enlightening to look at turnover from more than one perspective at a time. For instance, you could correlate voluntary turnover data by age and level of performance. First, you could compute the percentage of turnover for age groups (e.g., 20 to 24, 26 to 29, 30 to 34, etc.). Then, you could do the same for levels of performance. There are two ways to look at performance, as shown in Formula ER-18.

Turnover/Performance Relationships

$$PT = \frac{R}{L} \qquad PT = \frac{R}{TR}$$ (ER-18)

where   PT   = percent terminating at each performance level
         R   = number rated at each level
         L   = total number terminating
         TR   = total rated at a given level

EXAMPLES

$$PT = \frac{27}{225} = 12.0\% \qquad or \qquad \frac{27}{79} = 34.2\% \qquad \text{performance level 6}$$

$$= \frac{79}{225} = 35.1\% \qquad or \qquad \frac{79}{365} = 21.6\% \qquad \text{performance level 5}$$

$$= \frac{63}{225} = 28.0\% \qquad or \qquad \frac{63}{593} = 10.6\% \qquad \text{performance level 4}$$

$$= \frac{42}{225} = 18.7\% \qquad or \qquad \frac{42}{53} = 79.2\% \qquad \text{performance level 3}$$

$$= \frac{8}{225}* = 3.6\% \qquad or \qquad \frac{8}{10}* = 80.0\% \qquad \text{performance level 2}$$

In the sample, 225 employees terminated voluntarily. Twenty-seven were rated 6, or the highest level in their performance. In the total organization, 79 were rated 6. Thus, while 12 percent of the terminations came from level 6, 34.2 percent of the organization's highest performers left. An additional measure that can be obtained is the performance level of the average terminee. This can be obtained through a weighted average calculation of the left column. The answer in this sample is 4.27. In order to correlate age, performance, and turnover you need to have both the age and performance rating of each terminee.

When you have the three types of data, you can plot them all on a line chart. In the sample in Fig. 13.2 we are interested only in high performers who left voluntarily. They are defined here as employees with performance ratings of 5 or 6 on the 6-point scale. Employees with ratings of 1 to 4 are not included.

This example shows an organization with some problems. You can no doubt see that turnover is highest from about age 27 to 38, which is also the age group that has a large percentage of high performers. In addition, as age increases the percentage who are high performers decreases. The age profile shows a very large group in the 45 to 54 range. If you put some of these findings together, you can see that there is reason for concern across all three dimensions. Multidimensional analysis is the best way to get inside the numbers to find correlations that point to otherwise invisible organizational phenomena.

GEM #17   *Understanding relationships among data opens the door to improvement.*

*Column adds to 219 + 6 who did not get rated.

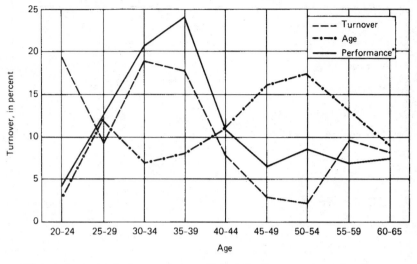

*High performers only: i.e., employees with 5 or 6 ratings on a 6-point scale.

Figure 13.2. Age-Performance-Turnover Relationship

Before we leave this area, a word needs to be said about looking at
the reason for leaving. Most organizations collect data at termination
time regarding the reason for the termination. If a good job is done,
the data can be considered reliable. This information can be displayed
very effectively in a multilevel bar chart similar to the one used in the
counseling area. It can also be displayed in a bar chart with an individual bar for each reason. All the other formulas we have looked at tell
us who is leaving—this tells us why. Unless you know the why you
cannot do much about the who. After you know why, you can figure
out what to do and where to do it. That kind of analysis and action is
bound to produce positive results.

Turnover Cost

Everyone knows that turnover is costly. Just how much it costs
depends on what you include. Expenses generally fall into categories:
recruitment costs, orientation and training costs, and lost productivity
or opportunity costs. It is impossible to calculate exactly what all that
amounts to, but it is substantial. Figure 13.3 lays out all standard types
of costs. To keep the job simple, you can develop some standard costs
for different categories of jobs. The most formidable issue seems to be
calculating lost productivity. I suggest you pull together a task force of

Direct Hiring Costs

New Hires

1. Advertising $ _____

2. Agency and search fees   _____

3. Internal referral bonuses   _____

4. Applicant expenses   _____

5. Relocation expenses   _____

6. Salary and benefits of staff   _____

7. Employment office overhead   _____

8. Recruiter's expenses   _____

9. Total direct hiring costs   _____

10. Divide line 9 by number hired. Cost per hire   _____

Indirect Hiring Costs

11. Management time per hire   _____

12. Supervisor/lead time per hire   _____

13. Orientation and training per hire   _____

14. Learning curve productivity loss or
    opportunity loss per hire   _____

15. Total indirect hiring costs per hire   _____

16. Total hiring costs per hire   _____

17. Multiply line 16 by number hired
    Total hiring costs ₁   _____

Direct Internal Replacement Costs

Replacements

18. Applicant expenses $ _____

19. Relocation expenses   _____

Direct Internal Replacement Costs (Continued)

Replacements (continued)

20. Salaries and benefits of staff $ _____

21. Employment office overhead   _____

22. Total direct replacement costs   _____

23. Divide line 22 by number placed.
    Direct costs per placement   _____

Indirect Internal Replacement Costs

24. Management/time per hire   _____

25. Supervisor/lead interview time per hire   _____

26. Training time per hire   _____

27. Learning curve productivity loss or
    opportunity loss per hire   _____

28. Total indirect replacement costs
    per placement $ _____

29. Add lines 23 and 28. Total cost
    per placement   _____

30. Multiply line 29 by number placed
    Total internal replacement costs   _____

31. Total turnover costs   _____

32. Target percentage reduction   _____%

33. Potential savings $ _____

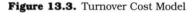

Figure 13.3. Turnover Cost Model

managers from each function for an hour or two. In the space of a couple of hours you will reach a consensus on a standard cost by level or type of job. From then on you simply plug these into an equation and multiply the answer by the number of terminations in that group. This gives you a workable, if not precise, figure for trend analysis and problem identification.

Unemployment Claims Control

An important but seldom seen activity is supervision of the unemployment insurance claim process. In many states, when an applicant's claim for unemployment benefits is denied, this reflects favorably on the employer's experience rating. Accordingly, it behooves the company to contest all claims from former employees that it believes are unfounded. Often this task is the responsibility of the employee relations group. A simple but effective way to report the results of that cost containment effort is shown in Fig. 13.4.

Note first that the savings from the two previous years is shown in the upper right corner. This serves two purposes: One is public relations and the other is motivational. First, assuming this is a report that is updated monthly and distributed outside your department, the report continually reminds the executive reader that you are cognizant of the value of cost containment. It does not take long using this reporting philosophy to convince line management that you are an integral part of the profit team and not a cost center. Second, keeping past performance visible for your employee relations staff helps to stimulate them to do better. I remember vividly how a determined employee relations manager reacted when I told her that I thought we

1991 Year-end total						68,835.00
1992 Year-end total						128,227.60

1993	New claims contested	Determinations		Appeals		Pending	Potential savings, in dollars
		Won	Lost	Won	Lost		
Jan	15	3	0	0	0	12	4,873.00
Feb	16	2	5	1	0	21	4,680.00
Mar	15	2	5	0	0	29	4,810.00
Apr	10	1	1	0	0	37	2,912.00
May	20	2	0	0	0	55	4,602.00
Jun	18	12	7	0	1	54	32,162.00
Jul	9	5	1	1	0	57	13,754.00
Aug	16	6	2	1	1	65	17,030.00
Sep	15	6	3	1	0	71	20,020.00
Oct	19	7	6	2	0	77	20,098.00
Nov	10	4	6	0	0	77	9,906.00
Dec	8	10	5	2	0	70	26,314.00
1993 Totals	171	60	41	8	2	70	163,161.00

Figure 13.4. Unemployment Insurance Record

could save an additional 25 percent in the coming year. I thought it was a formidable goal, one that I would have trouble selling to her. She looked at the report and saw how well she had done for the past two years. Then she looked down the savings column for the current year, month by month. For a long minute she sat there, and I could see the wheels turning in her head. Finally, she looked up and said, "We can do it!" She knew from looking at her past performance, exceptional as it already was, that she could try new or better techniques and meet the objective. I am convinced that without the past record of success to convince her, she would have been reluctant to commit herself.

One of the great unseen benefits of measurement is motivation. When your people see that they can do something and do it well, they are motivated to surpass themselves. There is a cycle to high performance that is based on the principles inherent in self-esteem. In order for people to build and maintain high self-esteem, they must be successful. By starting with reasonable, attainable goals and achieving them, a person feels a sense of increased self-esteem. This motivates him or her to try for a higher goal. If that is challenging but possible, the chances are that it will be reached. Success once again increases self-confidence and self-esteem, and the upward spiral continues. Everyone wins, the person grows, the department succeeds, and the organization prospers.

Workers' Compensation Management

The same principles that were applied to unemployment insurance can be employed in managing workers' compensation claims. In essence each is a case to be managed. Although the details are different, the dynamics are similar. You can contest a workers' comp claim. If you win, chalk it up as an implied saving. For example, if you fight an alleged back injury and show it wasn't caused by work, you save what the average back injury case costs. Even when you have a legitimate claim, you can manage it to keep the costs to a minimum. Your workers' compensation carrier should be working those cases as a matter of routine service. When you manage a case effectively, you will see the dollar difference it makes.

Summary

Absenteeism, turnover, unemployment, and workers' compensation claims offer the human resources professional an excellent arena in which to exercise analytic and creative skills to obtain visible, quantifiable results. Everyone can appreciate the value of reduced absence and turnover, and controlled claim costs. Best of all, from your standpoint, the results are very quantifiable. You will be able to show management exactly how you are contributing to the bottom line. In addition, line supervisors universally are annoyed by these lost time and turnover cases. By working closely with them you will show them that you are truly a problem-solving business partner of theirs.

The cost of these events are very significant in an era when operating expense is under great pressure. Savings in excess of $1 million per annum are commonplace. Absence and turnover also increase stress for co-workers and supervisors. Somehow the absentee's work must get done, and usually co-workers absorb some of it. Even if they don't, an absence may impede their work.

Separation rates have been skewed by ongoing massive layoff programs. Old patterns have been destroyed. Nevertheless, unwanted turnover creates problems and demands attention. Turnover needs to be subdivided into categories for better understanding. Then, its cost should be calculated and presented to management. There are many remedies for excessive turnover, but first you need to isolate where and why it is happening. Then, show the cost to get management's attention and support for attacking the problem.

Unemployment and workers' compensation cases are annoying as well as costly. There is a good payoff for your efforts in managing these issues. Even medium-size companies can save hundreds of thousands of dollars by vigorously managing these phenomena.

14
Labor Relations

In the 50 years since the end of World War II the American labor movement has suffered huge losses of membership in private industry. If it were not for the government, workers' unions would represent less than 10 percent of American workers. The reason for this is that management finally got smart or less greedy, depending on whose view you subscribe to. Historically, unions came into being to serve a very real and important purpose. The early leaders of the industrial revolution generally treated the working man, woman, and child very badly. When it became clear that only a show of unity would transfer some of the power balance toward the workers, they organized themselves. Eventually, due to cruel reactionary tactics on the part of some of the owners, the federal government stepped in and provided additional protection. In the period between the two World Wars, union membership grew until approximately 40 percent of the direct labor force in American industry was represented by one union or another.

After the World War II, management began to provide better working conditions, greater safety, and improved health and welfare benefit programs. Whether the motivation was altruism or expediency is debatable. In either case, management began to take some of the power out of the unions' traditional demands. Gradually, the unions were co-opted out of their main bargaining tools. In addition, social factors such as a better educated work force and improved technology, made workplaces somewhat safer and cleaner. All this has resulted in a 75 percent reduction in union membership since 1950. The net effect is that unions and management are finding more common ground. In many cases the century-old adversarial relationship is softening. Despite this general trend, unions are still a factor in some industries, so labor relations staffs are not about to be out of work.

Measuring Effectiveness

The effort of the labor relations staff doesn't lend itself readily to ratios and formulas. Their work can be viewed in two ways. One is a confirmation of "system" maintenance such as the benefits of keeping in touch with the employees and union officials. The other is "project" or situational responses such as grievance handling and contract negotiations.

In the first case you are involved with what might be described as preventive maintenance. Keeping the system clean and well-oiled (friction at a minimum) means there will be few breakdowns. When employees feel that they are being treated fairly and are being listened and responded to, there is no need to file a grievance. So, it makes sense for labor relations specialists to work with first line supervisors, foremen, and leads to avoid problems. In the second case, any analysis of legitimate grievances often shows they could have been prevented with some astute handling when they first appeared as irritations. It takes a lot less time, money, and effort to keep problems from occurring than it does to deal with an arbitration or a strike. Therefore, evaluation of labor relations work follows a combination path of prevention, resolution, and negotiation, not necessarily in that order.

Level One Prevention

The first level to look at is the incidence of problems or grievances. What is the rate of questions, problems, and grievances occurring during this period versus the last? Differentiate between a question, a problem, and a grievance. What is the topic in each case? How often does each topic come up? In which business unit is it occurring? Tracking frequency by topic and unit tells you how successful your preventive maintenance program is. We'll get to resolution in a minute. If the system is running comparatively smoothly, your rate of occurrence will be low. If it rises in one unit or on one topic, that is a sign that more maintenance is called for.

The next question is, how do you put a value on low occurrence or incident rates? This is the same question asked of any preventive program. Safety, security, and employee relations have the same question. The answer is simple. What is the cost of a typical incident? On average, how much resource does an incident take? Resources are time, money, and possibly equipment and materials. In the case of safety, there is lost time and sometimes material and equipment losses. (Not to mention possibly serious injuries.) In security breaches there is time and possibly facility damage and material loss. In labor relations, what happens when a question, problem or grievance occurs? At the least, time is spent on it. There may be direct costs as well. Play through several scenarios and see what truly happens. Then, you can attack an average cost to each type of issue. So, the answer is twofold. First, trace the number of incidents in this period versus the average period. If you are starting from scratch, you have to wait a few months until you have at least a couple of quarters behind you. Second, what is the typical or average cost per incident? This is like the standard cost in any other type of evaluation. The value of your work can then be calculated as the saving in cost or time or any other resource between the standard and your current level of performance. Figure 14.1 is a simple matrix that will help you calculate the cost of each type of issue.

You can put the matrix on a spreadsheet and see how the resources are expended for each type of issue. Probably more important than the immediate cost is the lesson that you can learn from each occurrence.

Learning Points

With everyone talking about companies becoming learning organizations, what can we learn from these labor spats? What clues do you get about what is wrong when you look at these experiences? What patterns, if any, are apparent? If you dig into the testimony of all sides, what do you think is going on? Are they all really random? What are the sources of the issues? Is it pay, working conditions, supervisory behavior, or something larger over which you have no control? If the company is in trouble, some people get very nervous and look for problems. Whenever there is a lot of publicity about some environmental issue, there are always people who will swear that your company is suffering from it no matter what evidence is presented.

Issue Cost	Question	Problem	Grievance	Arbitration	Total
Money					
Time					
Material					
Equipment					
Other					
Total					

Figure 14.1. Labor Relations Cost Matrix

Years ago at a company I worked in, there was a lot of external publicity about bad air and fumes in some buildings. Our building was less than five years old, and our operation was very clean. Yet, in one section of the office a few people complained long and hard about fumes. We brought in specialists and ran every test in the book to no avail. The air was literally clean enough to breathe. Still, a couple of employees claimed that they could smell the nonexistent fumes. Overly impressionable people are hard to convince.

Look for repeating data. Look by department; by level; by job type; by supervisor; by age, race, or sex; or by any other categories you can think of. You can make a big matrix and check every time there is an issue of a given type or in a certain place. There is usually some pattern, particularly if there are a large or a growing number of complaints. If you see a pattern emerging, you can often get to the source of the issue before it becomes a full-blown problem. Some of the most effective union avoidance programs use this type of tracking mechanism. An early warning is the best warning. In either case, you are able to identify and thereby measure a change.

Level Two: Resolution

As you know, grievances are the first formal level of labor action. Sooner or later, no matter how effective your preventive maintenance program is, you are going to have a formal grievance filed. It might be legitimate, or it might be a malcontent just stirring up some muck of his or her own making. In any case, you will respond. Measuring the effectiveness of grievance resolution is not as simple as an outsider might think.

Obviously, you can add up the time spent by all parties involved and what that cost directly and indirectly in terms of wages and lost productivity. If you are going to do that, I suggest you develop some standard costs per hour for different types of people so that you don't have to calculate it fresh every time. Then, you can add in the cost of any settlement. Eventually, you will have a total cost, which you can compare to average grievance cost. However, this is where the complexity comes in.

You can settle a grievance quickly by giving the complainant what he or she wants. In some cases it is the wise thing to do. Again, to the casual observer it might look like a low cost in terms of time. But what is the cost of giving in? In both the short and long term what will it cost the company? If you project the effect that the settlement might have not only on the plaintiff but on all employees affected by the settlement, the cost could be very great over a long time period. You may also be setting a precedent that will adversely affect your bargaining position in the future. It goes like this: Does allowing X imply that maybe Y and Z are also acceptable? Does allowing X under these conditions imply that it is also acceptable under other conditions? It is a tricky business, as labor relations people know.

Therefore, grievance resolution must be considered very carefully. We need to educate supervisors. Most companies do have training for first line supervisors regarding the terms of the contract and the implications thereof. My sense is that labor relations training is looked at only from a negative standpoint. The question in my mind has always been, "Is there some way to play a positive, proactive hand in this game?" Clearly, when we look at anything in our lives purely from a negative point of view, we can only expect to experience negative occurrences. Perhaps if we examined labor relations from an objective perspective we might obtain some new insights. I'll say more about that later.

Level Three: Negotiation

This level completes the circle and ties back to maintenance. Through better agreement or contract negotiations you set new levels of performance for the system. That may imply new, more, or different performance measurement activities. One of the first lessons of contract negotiations, as you may know and as I alluded to earlier, is, don't set up something you can't live with. This is what happened from 1950 to 1980. Management continuously gave away their rights to manage the human asset in exchange for labor peace. Eventually, it went so far in some industries that management didn't have any flexibility. It almost destroyed several major industries in the United States. Today, the vulnerability still exists in contracts where only a union member from Local X can turn a knob on a machine. People have to sit and wait for someone who isn't there to be found to come and perform a task that a two-year-old could do. It is embarrassing for the waiting employees, and the message it sends is that management is a bunch of dummies for letting this happen. It is stupidity beyond imagination. Ultimately, it does no one any good.

How do you describe the value or effectiveness of a negotiation? The simplest way is to ask how close the agreement came to the original goal. There is no absolute value. What were you willing to give and what did you want in return? What were the relative values of

each? Clearly, you can cost out a contract. That is the absolute cost—
but it is a relative value. The value is relative to the objective. What
did you get in return for what you gave? What is the economic value
of that? Did you give job security in return for flexibility? If so, what is
the net trade-off today, next year, and five years hence?

Performance measurement is all about tracking relative values as
they move through time. What is getting better, as you see it? And
what is getting worse, from your perspective? That is all management
is about as well. Monitoring progress toward specific goals. If you
know what you want from your labor relations, you can then measure
how successful you are at any point in time.

Why Labor Relations

If you just landed on earth from another planet and you began a study
of our institutions, you would eventually reach this topic. Naturally,
you would ask, "Why do you have labor contracts?" You would be
told the history of labor-management relations and how they had led
to the current point. Your next question might be, "Isn't there some
simpler way to insure labor stability for both sides?"

If you were starting American business from scratch, what would
you do to make sure that the employees didn't need to have an advo-
cate to stand up for their rights? Being a person of good will, you
probably would involve the employees more in the management of the
work. Notice I said the work. I didn't say the organization. I believe
that if people have some control over their work life they don't care
that much about how you manage other stakeholders, provided it
doesn't ruin the company. Being a person of good will, you would
probably establish a work environment wherein everyone could be as
comfortable as the task allowed. Being a person of good will, you
would treat the employees like friends and family members. You
would get to know them and something about their life outside of
work. You would take a genuine interest in their welfare both on and
off the job. You would defend them when that was required, and you
would run the company in a manner that would promote growth,
financial stability, and security. If you did that, there wouldn't be
much need for the employees to complain or to be fearful.

So, let's look in that direction. Isn't that what much of the latest self-
directed work teams are about? They give power to the employees not
only to regulate their work, but in some cases to make decisions about
hiring, firing, and paying team members. Motorola started an experi-
mental program to share salary increase power with the work teams.

At this point in time, mid-1994, only about 20 percent of the increase is voted on by the team, and some outside critics are saying it is a dangerous idea. But Motorola is a smart company usually found on the leading edge of management technology. Since the mid-1970s they have espoused participative management methods. Their employee relations have been exemplary over the past four decades. And today, they are one of the more prosperous and innovative companies in the world. Do you think there is a correlation?

Other companies such as Federal Express have built solid employee relations based on good will mixed with good business. You can't please everyone all the time. There are a lot of alienated people in the world and some work for your company. But they represent only about 1 percent of your workforce. So, instead of building labor relations programs aimed at controlling the 1 percent how about working for the benefit of the 99 percent?

> **GEM #18**   *There is ample evidence that a correlation exists between positive management attitudes and practices regarding employees and better productivity, quality, and customer service.*

Measuring the Upside

Typically, we think of performance measures as relating to problems. Let's turn that around and look at positive performance measures. The upside deals with improvements in the three basics of management: quality, productivity, and service. When these are well attended to, the result is almost always reflected in increased profits. There have been a number of studies confirming this. Schuster[1], Kravetz[2], and Huselid[3] have all conducted research and found evidence that supports correlations between so-called enlightened management practices and improved profitability.

Mark Huselid's work is the most recent. It takes some appreciation for statistics to grasp the full implications of his original research. Nevertheless, common sense and a little intuition show what he is trying to say.

Essentially, Huselid tested the link between HR management practices and objective measures of turnover, productivity, and financial performance. For the casual variable he used an index of HR management practice sophistication (HRSOPH) that had been developed in a Department of Labor study. That index measures the amount and quality of attention paid to personnel selection, performance appraisal, compensation, grievance procedures, information sharing, attitude assessment, and labor-management participation. HRSOPH has a range of zero to 100 with higher numbers indicating sophistication. Huselid contacted 3,400 firms having over 100 employees and $5 million in sales. He obtained data from 968 firms from 35 industries.

His first finding was that high HRSOPH was positively related to company size (number of employees), industry type, capital intensity, business planning sophistication, formal HR planning, and the number of years HR has been involved in the company's strategic business planning process. HRSOPH is negatively related to the extent of union coverage and the use of cost leadership as a competitive strategy.

His general findings were that larger firms and firms which spend more money on capital equipment also invest more in sophisticated HR practices. Firms with more sophisticated business planning see the value of more HR planning. Finally, large differences were found across industries.

It was acknowledged that employee behavior can not always affect financial performance (competitors, general economy, etc. have an effect). Therefore, the first payoff associated with the use of HRSOPH was sought in intermediate outcomes, such as turnover and productivity. In the first test Huselid found high HRSOPH associated with low turnover. His second test showed high HRSOPH positively impacting sales per employee (productivity).

Huselid went on to calculate the impact of increasing HRSOPH. He found the increase of one standard deviation (16 points on the index scale) from the average of 56 to 72 would raise net sales an average of $8,337 per employee per annum. Over a five year period, using an 8 percent discount rate, this translated into $33,287 per employee.

To link all this to firm financial performance (i.e. profitability), Huselid used both accounting profit calculations and economic profit calculations. He found that increasing HRSOPH one standard deviation produced a five year market value increase in profits of $7,868 per employee.

These remarkable results were confirmed across a wide range of industries and firm sizes. This general study supports the belief that when you invest in employee management you increase profitability.

Summary

Labor relations work can be viewed from three perspectives: prevention, resolution, and negotiation. The objective in each should be to find a position that creates the best win-win situation for both parties. The stance that labor and management are intrinsically enemies is an anachronism. It is too inefficient. Companies cannot compete, grow market share, and provide jobs if there is continual fighting between bosses and employees.

Try to think about labor relations activities from a positive place. Train supervisors to see that there is another way to look at their relationships with the employees. The Japanese supervisor is much closer to his or her employees than is the typical Western supervisor. That personal touch had a lot to do with the self-sacrificing attitude of Japanese workers over the past forty years. I'm not suggesting that Western management try to emulate Eastern methods. But inside those methods there is a kernel of human relations wisdom that we would all be wise to find.

SECTION E

Developing the Human Asset: How to Measure Training and Development

15

Career
Development

Employee Development
Reverses Its Field

Traditionally, employee development was approached as a duality: from the viewpoint of the job or organization and from the viewpoint of the employee. Either we tried to fit people to the job or the job to people, or both simultaneously. Each rationale had its purpose and value. First, we wanted to ensure that the organization's needs were being fulfilled. Second, we hoped to incent people to stay by giving them opportunities to learn, grow, and advance themselves.

However, in the past decade career development has been thrown a new challenge. As organizations reduced the number of levels and concurrently moved toward cross-functional and self-directed work teams, the question became, what do you prepare people for? The predictable, fixed, multilayered job hierarchy is fast disappearing in many organizations, and it is not likely to return, given the intensity of global competition and the need to control expenses. So it is logical to assume we need new methods or at least new thinking regarding what a "career" means and how we develop people.

I suggest that there are three issues. One is the need to understand the business processes of the organization. Whether one works for a bank, an airline, a petrochemical company, or a software developer, there are processes by which inputs come into the organization, are employed in the transformation or value-adding stage, and leave the organization bound for the customer. Employees obviously need to learn how to apply themselves in this endeavor. The second developmental requirement is interpersonal skills. As organizations move toward more team projects and processes, the ability to interact with peers and others becomes critical. Fewer and fewer will be able to work totally alone. And more people fail for interpersonal deficiencies than for lack of technical skills. The third issue focuses on analytic capability. It is a paradox that as information becomes ever more readily available people are not developing analytic skills simultaneously. We are literally drowning in data, yet most of it is wasted because we have not been trained to understand it. Peter Drucker was quoted by the *Wall Street Journal* as saying something to the effect that today's managers don't know what data they need, how to get it, or what to do with it when they have it. We have experienced this in extremis with HR staffs. They are either not interested, intimidated, or ignorant of the availability or use of data. This is a major weakness in the American work force, and one that training can easily solve.

General vs. Specific Development

In the 1960s the general attitude was that if you knew how to manage one situation you could manage any situation. This myopic notion came out of the arrogance of the B-school whiz kids who graduated in the 1950s. They thought they could run complex operations employing thousands of human beings by subjecting the system to some esoteric model developed by an academic who couldn't manage a two-car parade. It led to the growth of the conglomerates in the 1970s. Over time this belief was proven to be untrue as one after another stumbled, fell, and were dismembered. Talented people might be able to do several jobs well, but not every job. Practically speaking, we are all somewhat limited by our aptitudes. I know personally that there are a number of jobs that I can do, but there are a larger number that I cannot do well. I think this is true for most people. This leads to the conclusion that the most effective development approach probably combines elements of both the job perspective and the human perspective.

My experience with organizational training and development over more than 25 years leads me to state that it is more training than development. I see much professional and managerial training taking place in a partial vacuum. Much of it is program driven, rather than objective driven. By this I mean that many training programs are designed and conducted with no specific sort of long-term goal in view. Despite what trainers claim, I'm willing to bet that they can't connect more than a quarter of their programs to some organizational objective. In short, many are isolated educational or skill development efforts that don't necessarily lead to any visible purpose. There is a place for general education and training, but from a priority stand-point there are many more immediate specific needs. In the following pages I would like to suggest a methodology that is logical, specific, measurable in terms of results, and much more efficient than the current standard approach. It is the targeted approach.

A common stimulus for the creation of a training program is a needs analysis. These surveys ask people to give the training department information on the skills that are needed in the organization. The resulting data is generally a collection of unsubstantiated opinions about a broad range of issues that can be fitted into a formal, traditional, educational experience, i.e., a class. Based on this response, organizations will develop a curriculum often containing dozens of programs. These will subsequently be offered and conducted, and typically some self-report type of evaluation will be carried out. The cost of these procedures often runs into the millions of dollars, and when they are over no one asks what the return on that investment was. Without belaboring the unbusinesslike nature of this approach, let me point out that this may be training, or likely education, but it certainly can't be validly termed development. Let me suggest other approaches that may not be perfect, but are certainly more reasonable, and I guarantee it will pay dividends.

The Development Trend

There is a very definite shift toward self-development. Many development professionals tell me that they are trying to move the responsibility for career development away from the organization and toward the individual. At the least, development professionals are advising employees that they must take an active role in their own career growth. This is a far cry from the years between 1960 and 1985, when development was scripted by the organization and the individual went through the procedure step by step. We used to refer to it as "getting your ticket punched," meaning that you had fulfilled the requirements for promotion. This will not be the case in the future. Since events are so uncertain and change is so rampant, organizations don't know what to prepare people for. Because of that, I believe there are other paths that should be followed to give people the practical skills and knowledge most likely needed in the future.

The place to start with career development is with the creation of your development team. Even in an era of uncertainty direction has to be set by someone. Because employee development is a complex art, several disciplines must play a role. I believe there are at least six types of people who are needed. First, a line management representative must be included from the area you plan on servicing. After all, development of employees is a manager's job, and the training department is there just to support the effort. Next, you will need representation from human resources planning, staffing, and career development. The planners should have a unique perspective because they are closer to the corporate business plan than anyone within human resources development. Their job is to see that the business plan is translated into an HR department plan. Staffing is involved because normally they are the ones who have to find the people who will later be developed. Career development people are, in my scheme, the ones who design career path systems, do career counseling and assessment, and handle the job-posting program. I believe job posting is more effective when run as a career development system rather than as an adjunct to employment. Job posting, beyond just filling vacancies, should be used to develop people by moving them into jobs that they are interested in doing and that suit their aptitudes. The last groups to be involved on the development team are the trainers who will design and deliver, or broker, the training intervention part of the development system. Each of the functions represented on this team brings with it a unique viewpoint and a special set of skills and knowledge. Cumulatively, they should be able to select and design the most effective program in the most efficient manner.

Once the team is formed, a target development area is selected. This can be done in many ways, but usually it is driven by a functional point of view. For example, suppose it has been decided that one of the areas that most needs development is customer service. In order to match and develop people for jobs in customer service, we need to do two things. First, the duties, responsibilities, and requisite skills and knowledge have to be defined. Competencies, not jobs, are the foundations of career development.

Second, a model of effective customer service needs to be developed. There are many methods for doing this, examples of which can be found in career development textbooks. Fundamentally, the model describes the behavior and the results obtained by an effective customer service representative or manager. The data is drawn from records and interviews within the customer service department and from contacts with people who interface with the department—including customers, of course. The result of this two-pronged approach is a clear picture of what you are trying to find and develop in customer service staffs. There are selection methods, such as assessment programs and testing, that will surface the people who have the best aptitude and potential for being successful in customer service work.

These people should be the first to be developed. We are in the business of helping people grow and succeed, and this method offers them an excellent chance to do so. How well they do can be tracked and compared to the traditional hit-and-miss method. The results should show that the resources put to this program generated a favorable return on investment. The following case is an example.

One of our client companies was experiencing some market share erosion. In an effort to remain competitive, they began a cost-cutting program. Naturally, training came under the ax almost immediately, and someone decided, without recourse to evidence, that the entry-level customer service representative training could be cut from two weeks to one. This would yield a savings of several tens of thousands of dollars. When that change was made, our client contact person decided to study the effect. He found that the new reps who had only one week of training took longer to solve customer problems, made more errors and on every performance metric did not measure up to the reps trained on the two-week program. In fact, the performance of the new reps never reached the level of the old reps. The cost savings from cutting training by one week was eaten up within 45 days, and thereafter the company was losing every day. When this data was shown to management the course was reinstated as a two-week experience. Later, they even added a couple more days of training.

Another procedure targets current and foreseeable business problems and opportunities. This is looking at career development from the outside in. By quickly developing a training experience that upgrades specific critical skills, emerging quality, productivity, and service issues can be addressed and solved very cost-effectively. This puts your company on the front end of the competency curve. If you view your organization from the standpoint of the customer and the competition, you will find many places to apply training—counseling or on-the-job experiences. Given the new or enhanced knowledge or skills, people will perform better. This means the organization gains competitive advantage.

Job Posting As Career Development

Earlier I alluded to the idea that a posting system is a career development activity. Whether or not you agree with that, you can still measure the relationships of the job-posting system to the development of employees. As organizations flatten, lateral movement and building a broad range of experiences and skills is one of the best career moves a person can make.

Mechanically, the posting process works like the employment process. You produce applicants, make placements, and spend resources doing it. The first thing you can show management is the volume of applicants and placements handled each month. This type of data lends itself to bar charting. Each month you can draw in the bars representing the number of applicants and the number of placements. A quick visual survey tells the reader something about the trend in workloads as well as the results.

The second issue you can talk about is the cost per placement. Earlier in the book you were shown how to calculate the cost of hire and cost of replacement from internal sources. Using those two figures you can demonstrate how much you save the organization on the average every time you fill a job through the posting system. This number could be carried on one side of the monthly report. If it is shown on a cumulative cost savings bar, management can watch it grow each month. Figure 15.1 is an example of such a report. This data can be summarized on a quarterly basis, and year-to-year comparisons can be made. If you use common financial-style reporting (i.e., quarterlies with year-to-year comparisons) your documentation will begin to look more like standard business reports. This lends credibility to them and stimulates readership.

The third and probably the most important issue is retention. Using job posting along with other developmental experiences will improve

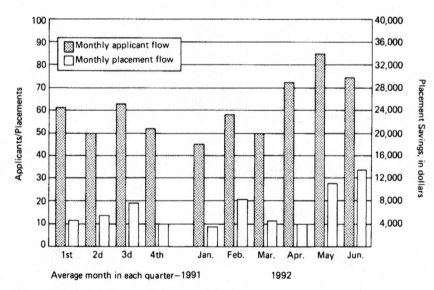

Figure 15.1. Job-Posting Volume and Savings

your organization's ability to retain the people it most needs and wants. When a person is placed through the posting system they should be talked to about how the organization sees this move as a good career step. Even if the person is only trying to escape an unpleasant situation, there is something to be learned from it. You know that personal attention is one of the most effective methods for generating loyalty. In today's fast-changing, highly confusing world, nothing is more desired than some personal attention and caring.

Summary

The central issue is development of individual competencies in concert with the needs of the organization. Training is one part of career development. Job posting is another. Personal counseling is also important. The purpose of all this attention is to retain good people and to help them grow as far as they can in ways that also help the organization achieve its goals.

Over the past decade there have been two significant changes in employee development thinking and systems. One is the move from a job to a competence focus. Jobs change too rapidly today. Older, rigid systems of jobs and pay no longer serve. We need to develop portable skills. The second change has been to shift responsibility for employee development from the organization to the individual.

Although development is a personal matter, risks are increasing and consequences of errors are more painful, so there is an increasing need to take a systematic approach. By involving people from both the line and staff sides, all perspectives and values can be considered. Optimum efficiency and effectiveness can be achieved if all processes work in concert toward a common purpose. Those who argue that things are too uncertain today to plan for anything are simply showing their ignorance regarding how to cope. Don't worry about them. They won't be around much longer. There is ample evidence among the best companies that they proceed from a programmatic style. While acknowledging that they don't know what is coming either, they attempt to at least improve the odds that they will have the right answer by working from a well thought out system rather than by trying to react after the fact.

16
Management Development

Education vs. Training

For people who are interested in measuring the results of their development programs there is a single driving question: "What is your overriding purpose?" Do you want to educate people or do you want to train them? Education is the presentation of concepts and information to people for the purpose of imparting knowledge. Usually, training is and should be more of an interactive exercise whose goal is to develop skills and competencies within the work force. It is one thing to know; it is something different to be able to do.

Ten years ago I estimated that about 75 percent of the supervisory and management programs were more educational than training. This is slowly changing. The shift, although glacial in its speed, is toward skill building. Still, much too much time is spent dealing with concepts of communication, motivation, leadership, and the like. The student-worker goes away better informed about these principles of management, but can seldom apply them. Even when programs appear to deal with specifics, they are still presented in an educational manner. A good example of this is a class in conflict resolution. These programs usually start by covering the research findings, which are the current theoretical basis of the topic. Then, they turn to a case study or a game simulation so that the subject can be viewed in some kind of context. It is hoped that this exposure will give the worker-student a thorough understanding that can later be transferred to the work place.

That method is perfectly satisfactory if the objective is to educate someone. However, it is impossible to measure the result of your development effort at a level beyond attitude or knowledge . It would be suspect, if not invalid, to infer that something happened in the workplace as a result of a "training" experience if the program was conducted as just described. We cannot claim to have made someone proficient at something if we have presented only concepts.

Proficient is defined with one word—*skilled*. In order to become skilled you must have more than knowledge, you need to apply that information. If you wait for the employees to apply it on the job after the class is over, then they have trained themselves. You have educated them. The bottom line is that cause-and-effect relationships cannot be proven in educational programs. In other words, if you educate, you cannot prove that your program was the causal force in the person's new behavior.

One of the latest and very expensive developmental fads is survival or outdoors team building programs. The assumption is that people learn teamwork from building rafts and climbing cliffs together. They probably do. I imagine it is a lot of fun for the fit and agony for the unfit, but in either event the vendors of such programs are enjoying a good income. The problem with this approach is that there is no conclusive, consistent data suggesting that these wilderness based team-building games carry back to the office or plant.

If you want to measure your results, you must provide skill training in the job context. The reason for this is that raft building doesn't have any of the risk factors in it that corporate performance does. In short, it is fun, but float or sink, you still have your job when you get back to the company. To build skills you have to start at the beginning. As Bob Mager[1] states,

> Before you prepare instruction, before you select procedures or subject matter or material, it is important to be able to state clearly just what you intend the results of that instruction to be.

Mager goes on to point out that your instructional objective should state:

1. What you want the learner to be able to do
2. Under what conditions you want the learner to be able to do it
3. How well it must be done

If you do that at the beginning, then all design and delivery decisions are made under those criteria. In the end it is relatively easy to test for acquired skills. In addition, it is usually possible to go into the organization later to find out if the skills were used and what impact they had. I'll show how to do this later in the chapter.

Three Basic Measures

When management takes an active interest in training, they usually look at cost first. They want to know how much was spent on training. The second and third questions are, how many people got training and what did we teach them? Implied in that is the assumption that they learned something useful. The fourth, and least considered, issue is, did anything happen in the organization as a result of the training? Fortunately, if you design training programs along the line that Mager suggests, you will be able to answer those questions.

The three general measures of training are cost, change, and impact.

* Cost—expense per unit of training delivered
* Change—gain in skill or knowledge or positive change in attitude by the trainee
* Impact—results or outcomes from the trainee's use of new skills, knowledge, or attitudes that are measurable in monetary terms

We will examine each of these measures by using different analytic models to illustrate the many ways in which training and development can be quantitatively evaluated. As always, the issue is not can it be done, but what is the better way to do it?

Cost

This is the easiest variable to measure. So long as accurate accounting is maintained, cost measurement is simple. The simplest calculation is a matter of adding up all expenses and dividing the total by the number of people trained. Expenditure variables will differ depending on the number of direct and indirect costs included. Samples of the most obvious, out-of-pocket, direct costs are

* Consultant fees
* Training room rental (if off-site)
* Supplies
* Refreshments
* Travel and lodging

Examples of indirect costs would be mostly overhead types of factors such as

- Trainer's salaries and benefits
- Trainee's salaries and benefits
- Department plant and equipment (overhead)

Hence, the calculation for cost per trainee would be as shown in Formula D-1.

Cost per Trainee*

$$C/T = \frac{CC + TR + S + RC + T\&L + TS + PS + OH}{PT} \qquad (D\text{-}1)$$

where C/T = cost per trainee
      CC = consultant costs (e.g., $2,000)
      TR = training facility rental (e.g., $350)
       S = supplies, workbooks, paper, and pencils (e.g., $1,100)
      RC = refreshments (e.g., $75)
    T&L = travel and lodging for trainees and trainers (e.g., $2,400)
      TS = trainers' salary and benefits (e.g., $250)
      PS = participants' salary and benefits (e.g., $4,300)
     OH = training department overhead (e.g., $500)
     PT = number of people trained (e.g., 40)

EXAMPLE

$$C/T = \frac{\$2{,}000 + 350 + 1{,}100 + 75 + 2{,}400 + 250 + 4{,}300 + 500}{40}$$

$$= \frac{\$10{,}975}{40}$$

$$= \$274.38$$

A Training Cost Spreadsheet

If you have an automated training registration and scheduling system, you can capture training costs easily. If you do it by hand, it is still a simple task. An example of the spreadsheet would be something like Table 16.1. As costs are accumulated they can be entered into the appropriate cell by line item number from your budgeting system. Thus, when you are finished with a course you can look at its costs compared to other courses. You can also match it against the budget for a Planned vs. Actual review.

---

*If you want to add in program development (PD) cost you would divide total PD cost by the number of people to be trained. Then add the pro rata result to the number in the example ($274.38).

Table 16.1. Training Cost Spreadsheet

Cost \ Phase	People	Material	Facilities	Equipment	Miscellaneous	Total
Diagnosis						
Design & Development						
Delivery						
Evaluation						
Total						

The basic training program cost report could include variables such as

- Total training costs
- Total hours of instruction
- Total number of trainees
- Cost per trainee
- Cost per trainee hour

Cost per trainee hour is a finer and more valuable measure than cost per trainee. The use of hours serves to normalize or standardize the denominator across programs of differing lengths. The calculation for cost per trainee hour is shown in Formula D-2.

Cost per Trainee Hour

$$C/Th = \frac{TC}{PT \times Th} \qquad \text{(D-2)}$$

where   C/Th = cost per trainee hour
        TC = total cost of training (e.g., $10,975)
        PT = number trained (e.g., 40)
        Th = hours of training (e.g., 16)

EXAMPLE

$$C/Th = \frac{\$10,975}{40 \times 16}$$

$$= \frac{10,975}{640}$$

$$= \$17.15$$

In addition to looking at the raw cost of a program, you can do some comparison costing. That can be a comparison of training expenditures among various groups. You could check to see the amount of money being spent on exempt versus nonexempt employees. You could look at it across departments, EEO categories, or job groups. The purpose would be to make sure that you are training everyone to the extent necessary.

You can also compare program costs between internal and external sources. You will almost always find that it is cheaper to bring a program in-house than it is to send people to it. That is fine if you want to show management which is the less costly approach. Be careful with this, however, because there is more to training than cost. You may not be able to provide the same level of quality if you do it in-house. You or your staff instructor may not be as expert in the subject as the outside presenter. That problem is solved if you can hire the outside expert as a consultant to conduct the program. Still, there are other benefits from outside programs that cannot be matched. The opportunity to associate with people from other companies is often very valuable. Your trainee has a chance to pick up knowledge beyond what the trainer offers. Some people are sent away to programs as a reward or to give them a break from work. People even get sent to off-site programs to give their supervisor a break from them. Whatever the reason, off-site training may be the appropriate choice. Networking is an effective training experience itself. However, if cost is the key consideration, you will always be able to show it is less expensive to do a program in-house. The main reason is that the fee per student will be lower if you have a group. Secondly, you won't have to spend as much for non training purposes such as travel, lodging, food, and sundry expenses.

The final cost issue that we will deal with before looking at one of the analytic models is the make versus buy decision. The number one cost question underlying training is, is it cheaper to train employees or to recruit them? By now you have seen how to calculate employment, turnover, and training expenses. You will often find that it costs more to recruit people with certain skills that it does to train the existing staff. Some managers don't want to wait. One benefit of training over recruiting is that your current employees are a known quantity. No matter how good the recruits look, they are a question mark. You do not know how new people will fit with your employee group, the organizational philosophy, or the operating style. If you know the relative costs of the make or buy choice, your information should add value to the decision process.

	Inputs, in dollars				
	People	Material	Equipment	Facilities	Total
Diagnosis					
Design					
Development					
Delivery					
Evaluation					
Total					

Figure 16.1. Training Input Analysis

Input Analysis

An input analysis approach is a systemic method of identifying and comparing the many costs involved in two or more training programs. It does this by breaking down the total training process into its main phases, which are then matrixed with the basic inputs. The matrix is shown in Figure 16.1. Each cell is filled in with the appropriate cost figure, and all phases and inputs are totaled. One matrix is completed for each program under consideration. The final set of matrices are compared for cost differences. This supplies the answer to which program is most cost-efficient, but it says nothing about which will be most effective. Whether or not a comparison is desired, every training program should be subjected to an input analysis.

Programs are the trainer's tool. You should know how much the tool is going to cost and how that cost breakdown looks before you start a program.

Change

Although it is important to know how much you are spending to train, how the money is being used, and who is getting the training, it is more important to know what the result or outcome is. Change can be measured at the individual level in terms of knowledge, skill, or attitude improvement. Comparisons can be made across groups as well.

There are several levels of sophistication in training evaluation. As the degree of sophistication goes up, the value tends to go up with it. Examples of before and after measures, which quantify the results of a training program, are presented in Formulas D-3 through D-6.

Knowledge Change

$$KC = \frac{K_A}{K_B}$$ (D-3)

where   KC = knowledge change
        K_A = knowledge level after training
        K_B = knowledge level before training

This information can be obtained by pre- and post-testing. Scores can be obtained before and after each class or before and after the total program. This not only serves to demonstrate that people are learning what you want them to learn (i.e., the objectives of the course), but test results point out specifically what is not being learned. By reviewing the tests in class, the trainer has an opportunity to reinforce the learning. Formula D-4 gives a similar calculation for skill changes. What it doesn't tell you is whether or not the training is impacting the organization.

Skill (Behavior) Change

$$SC = \frac{S_A}{S_B}$$ (D-4)

where   SC = observable change in skills as a result of training
        S_A = skill demonstrated after training by work output, critical incidents of interpersonal relations, or other observable phenomena
        S_B = skill level existing previous to the training using the same criteria as above

Data for this skill change ratio can be gathered through questionnaires, interviews, demonstrations, or observation with trainers, subordinates, peers, or supervisors. The key to obtaining something of value from any measure is in being specific in describing the skills or behaviors to be evaluated. You can't put a value on vague explanations, but if you see someone doing something you can measure and evaluate it.

Attitude Change

$$AC = \frac{A_A}{A_B}$$ (D-5)

where   AC = attitude change
        A_A = attitude after training
        A_B = attitude before training

If the objective is to go beyond knowledge or skill change to attitude change, the same pre- and post-testing method can be used. In this case, either a standard or a specially designed and validated attitude instrument would be used. Since attitudes are particularly vulnerable to influences in the environment, thought should be given to the timing of the post-test. Attitudes immediately after the training may be affected once the trainee reenters the work environment. The change may be either positive or negative, and in either case will confound the change attributable to the training. A test six months after the conclusion of training could tell how much change has been impacted by the environment.

If you find that the environment does not support the new attitudes, it does not make sense to continue to train. Unless you do post-testing, you will never know what happened. The most poignant example I ever saw of that was an ethnic awareness program that a company ran in the 1970s. In an effort to help everyone deal with the advent of Title VII of the Civil Rights Act, which covered equal opportunity, a large company on the West Coast put all supervisory personnel through a two-day program dealing with cultural aspects of the various minorities. It cost the company a lot of money. Through pre- and post-surveying they found that the course had had a negative effect. It had backfired because of the way it was conducted. If they hadn't checked and had carried it further through the employee population, it would have been at best a terrible waste.

Performance Change

$$PC = \frac{P_A}{P_B} \qquad \text{(D-6)}$$

where PC = change in work performance as measured by the organization's performance appraisal system

P_A = latest review score from a performance appraisal conducted at least 90 days after the training

P_B = performance review score from the performance appraisal conducted prior to the training

In this case, since performance appraisal scales are usually small (e.g., 1 through 5 or 1 through 6), the difference in a single point may appear dramatic in terms of percentage change. Caution should be exercised in discussing an individual's performance change lest you be accused of overstatement. This measure takes on more meaning when a large number of appraisals are compared and consistently positive results appear.

A final word of warning. There may be a halo effect. That is, the supervisor knows the employee went through training and expects improved performance. If the supervisor is not careful, something that is not there may be inferred.

Impact

The relationship between change and impact measurement is one of value. Whereas change and cost are two distinctly different variables, change and impact are sequential measures along a continuum. The following are two examples which may help to draw the distinction.

A machine operator, Debra, is taught to run a cutting machine. At the end of the program Debra's skill and knowledge can be tested by a performance test. Let us say that before the class she could cut 80 units per hour. After the class a test shows that she could cut 100 units per hour. Clearly, the level of skill and knowledge changed in a positive direction—Debra is more efficient as a result of the training. If she goes to work and consistently averages 100 cuts per hour, the impact of the training is felt in the cost of goods manufactured. Assuming the reject and scrap rate is the same as before, Debra is now 25 percent more productive. That is the amount of change. The component cost of labor as an input to the cutting cost is thus reduced by 25 percent. That is the impact. If you didn't measure on-the-job performance you would never know if the training is useful.

In a second example, a salesperson, Peter, is put through a sales training course. The purpose of the class is to teach salespeople how to close a sale. At the end of class, a test of knowledge of the principles can be given and a simulated sales call can be practiced. If Peter performs according to the model being taught, you can claim a gain in skill and knowledge compared to pre-course tests. The record of his subsequent customer calls and sales can be kept. If the ratio of sales to calls goes up or down, that is a change measure. In the up case, a cost-benefit analysis will show that as a result of the training, which cost X dollars, the company is now getting Y dollars of production from Peter. Presumably Y is greater than X and is also greater than it was before the training. That is the impact. When you convert the difference as show by the impact into money that is value added.

Most measurements of training are relatively simple. Except when you are running an experimental/control group comparison, you can get along without fancy statistics. The key factors are the discipline necessary to make sure all the details are attended to and the accuracy of the data. Cost-benefit analysis is common sense. Add in all the costs and measure it against the payoffs. The benefits may be both quantitative and qualitative. Productivity measurement is a matter of comparing the cost of specific inputs to specific outputs. It is an idea similar to cost-benefit analysis, but it is usually applied to issues that are very specific, narrow in scope, and quantitative in nature.

Some trainers still balk at measuring impact and value. This isn't because they're mean-spirited, it is because they don't know how. When you try to assess the value of training beyond sales, production, or service outcomes, you find it isn't easy. But it can be (and is being) done.

Levels of Evaluation

There are several levels of sophistication in training evaluation. As the degree of sophistication goes up, the value tends to increase with it.

The first, most used, and lowest-value method is the *trainee reaction survey*, also called the "smile sheet." The nickname comes from the notion that if the trainer smiles a lot, the trainee will give the program a good evaluation. Self-report data is very weak, yet it continues to be the most common method. The second and slightly more useful method is the knowledge test. This is usually a paper and pencil quiz that measures how much the trainee knows. It is given after the program, and there is no pretest against which to compare scores. Therefore, there is no proof that the trainee's knowledge level increased because of the program. The third level measures performance after the program. This is better than the second level because you look at the trainee's ability to perform, but still there is no comparative data. The fourth level measures performance before and after the program and includes a follow-up check some months later. This is a strong measure, and the first one in which you can infer causal relationships from the training. The fifth and top level is the same as the fourth, except the control group is compared to the trainee group. The control group is very similar to the trainee group except that it does not get trained. If the trainees' performance improves and the control group's does not, it is reasonable to claim that the training was the primary cause—provided there were no other identifiable intervening events. This last level is a time-consuming exercise and is not often done in industry.

Intervening Variables

The classic question in training evaluation is, how do you know that training caused the change? A counter question might be, how do you know that a salesperson is effective? The answer to both is, we don't know. In sales we assume that when a salesperson brings in an order he or she must be effective. The fact is that sales or purchases depend as much or more on extraneous factors as on sales ability. Timing, product quality and price, competitor's actions, the general economy, and a dozen other factors affect sales more than sales ability. Nevertheless, we pay salespeople on the basis of sales brought in no matter what caused them. So, why do we ask the causation question of trainers? I believe that trainers seldom have good relationships with their customers.

In the cases I've witnessed over the decades, the trainers who had established a partnering relationship their internal customers had no issue of causation. They had reached a point where they were trusted to deliver. This is how they earned that position.

They talk to the supervisors of the prospective trainees and discover what business problem the supervisor is expecting training to fix. If training is the appropriate solution, the trainers involve the customer in the design and planning. Then, the program is delivered. After the training is completed, the trainers go back to the source, the supervisor/customer/partner, and asks what happened. The customer knows that either nothing other than the training occured or that something else did. They know that the trainee's process was or wasn't changed. They know if a new incentive pay plan or automation was introduced. If the market or the environment is affecting outcomes, they know. If any major change occured, they will know it and be able to describe it. Then, the trainer and the customer discuss what influenced the change. They can estimate the relative effect of training and the other variables. Statistical proof isn't necessary—or possible. Solid, face value evidence almost always carries you through.

When you build a partnering relationship you no longer have to prove your worth. The projects you partner on become a joint game. You sink or swim together. You learn together. No reasonable person in business expects to bat a thousand. He or she just wants progress. If you don't know how to partner and develop face valid evidence of training's effectiveness, read on. If that still doesn't do it for you, call me. I'll run through it with you—no charge.

> **GEM #19** *Effective, credible trainers establish themselves first by building partnerships with their customers and second by delivering solutions to business problems.*

Two Training Evaluation Methods

Throughout the text I have repeatedly pointed out that effective evaluation can be carried out by using logical models. Training is a good example of that premise. More than any other function, training has control over its own environment. Trainers can close their doors and design their courses to fit the needs of the customer. Once they have the trainees in the classroom, the trainers are the boss. Trainers can set up any reasonable sequence of events and put the trainees through them. Given that type of power, it follows that trainers can make some very definitive statements about their work. And they can support their claims.

The first example is a straightforward model that I used when I was running training inside a computer company in the years about 1977 to 1982. Although today's environment is fast moving and changeable, so was the computer business then. The second example is the result of an experiment carried out by 26 companies under Saratoga Institute's direction in 1992 and 1993. It was detailed in *Training Magazine* in the summer of 1994.[2] Companies use this methodology to diagnose business problems, apply training as needed, measure and evaluate the training's effects, and share the data.

The first system provides the trainer with the data to carry out an evaluation on the fourth level described previously. By adding a control group to the process, an evaluation on the fifth level is possible.

The initial step is always to determine what the business problem or opportunity is. Training must never take place in a vacuum. Given that step, if training is part of the solution, then proceed.

1. Set behavioral objectives for the trainees. For each session (module) specify the desired behaviors, the conditions, and the criteria of performance.

2. Design the program to meet the objectives.

3. Collect baseline data from the trainee's department(s). The variables measured must be ones that relate to the upcoming training. (To have a fifth-level evaluation, select a control group at this point and collect the same data.)

4. Conduct the training. Give pre- and post-tests of skills and knowledge (or attitudes, if appropriate) at each session.

5. Approximately 60 to 90 days after the final session collect data comparable to step 3.

6. Compare the step 3 and step 5 data. This is the before and after course impact evaluation. It tells you if the class appeared to make a difference. Look for extraneous variables that may have affected the results. (Compare to the control group if you have one.)

7. Approximately six months after the last session have the trainees return for a refresher day. Give them a retention test before you start the review. This tests how much they remember six months after the event.

If you have carried out all the prescribed steps, I guarantee that you will be surprised at the results of steps 6 and 7. In six years of running this type of training in the computer company, the class average for the six-month retention test was never below 86 percent, and the standard deviations were extremely low. People will learn, they will use, and they will retain.

The second method is what we call SIIV. It stands for Situation–Intervention–Impact–Value. This is the process developed by the 26 companies. The basis for the success of the method is twofold. One is that it is conducted as a partnership with the management personnel who are interested in solving the problem. Two is that it is skill-focused.

Situation Analysis

1. Study the business problem or opportunity looking for its source and the factors and forces driving it.

2. Decide whether or not training might contribute to the resolution of the problem or the exploitation of the opportunity.

Note: This step looks deceptively simple and not new. Almost every trainer will tell you that he or she does this. The evidence is overwhelming that they do not do this well or completely. I can't state this strongly enough. And it is this failure to effectively and thoroughly analyze the true problem or opportunity that dooms evaluation. When we don't know what is causing something, it is not possible to effectively plan a solution, deliver it and draw a correlation between the supposed solution and the eventual outcome.

Intervention

3. If training is deemed to be part of the solution, design and deliver it in a skill (not theory) form that is visibly linked with the business problem.

4. Monitor performance on the job (usually through the supervisor of the trainee's unit) after the training. Identify any extraneous variables that may also have effected outcomes.

Impact

5. When the data on performance change is in and if it has been established that training was a force in that change measure the impact of the change, before and after the training intervention.

6. Effect or impact can be, and often is, attributed to factors other than training. The supervisor is the authority and can testify to these effects.

Value

7. Calculate the value of the impact in monetary and, if applicable, human terms.

It is not necessary to attempt a statistical analysis of the proportional value of the training intervention versus the extraneous variables. Management is not interested and tends to view such attempts as wasteful and self-serving. If the matter was entered into as a partnership, such an analysis is irrelevant. Your customer will gladly testify that the training had a substantial positive effect. In some cases training will be the principal and perhaps only visible factor. But whether it is or whether it has to share credit with other actions is frankly not important. If it has a positive effect, everyone involved will be able to see it.

Measures of Management

In about 1977 a nationally recognized training "expert" stood before the audience at a training conference and declared that supervisory and management development programs could not be measured for their effects. And he was right! He was correct within the context of training as he saw it. What he was talking about was education, not training. He was referring to theoretical classes on communication, motivation, and leadership. So long as he viewed training as the presentation of principles and concepts, he was 100 percent correct.

But you know different. You know you have to get off the abstract level and train managers how to do a number of tasks better. If you do that, you will be able to measure their performance as well as the impact of that performance. You see, management is a concept, an abstraction. No one has ever seen anyone "manage." It is not a concrete, observable, discrete act, and therein lies its mystery. Concepts cannot be measured because they exist only in the mind. Ergo, management cannot be measured, because measurement requires something visible and capable of specificity.

The solution is relatively simple and is to be found in the problem itself. If concepts cannot be measured because they are nonspecific and nonobservable, then the answer to the problem is to reduce them to their discrete, observable components. This is the methodology that physical and social scientists have always used. In order to understand the whole, one starts by learning as much as possible about the parts.

The same approach, much less demanding thankfully, can be used to understand more precisely what management is. Once we break down the process of management into a manager's many observable acts, the mystique disappears. Therefore, the real question is not, what is management? It is, what do managers do (effectively)? The answer to this tells us what we can train and what we can measure.

We can show that managers perform their tasks better after a training program. They interview more efficiently, and they handle performance reviews and administer salaries with fewer problems. They coach, counsel, and discipline better. However we define *better*, they can be seen to budget more accurately, write more effectively, and schedule more efficiently. In short, they do the multitude of trainable tasks better.

Helpful and enlightening as that may be, it is still only part of the picture. Ultimately, a manager is measured by the results of the department. Results are a reflection of the manager's ability to direct human, financial, and technological resources to achieve the department's objectives. If we can find connections between the tasks a manager performs and the output of the department, we can show that improved task performance relates to department results. The connections are these: The tasks are the contexts within which one communicates, motivates, and leads. It is by improving task performance—that is, gaining competency in relevant areas—that we can help managers become better communicators, motivators, and leaders. Then, we assume that effective managers are defined by good communicating, motivating, and leading behavior. This leads to the final step: Effective managers are people who get results through other people.

You can infer that your training programs make effective managers if you can prove that you have helped them to perform their tasks better, and you can prove that if you follow a training system similar to the ones outlined in this chapter.

Summary

If you want to measure the effects and value of training at any level, you can. You can even put a dollar value on the impact. The models described here are proof that no matter what type of training has been applied, from entry-level skills to executive development, it can be measured and evaluated. The only proviso is that you follow the principles and the steps described.

Trainers and managers get into trouble when they try to shortcut the systems. We can't jump from a situation analysis to value with any degree of certainty. In short, you're just guessing. To find value we have to follow every step, linking one to the other, until we reach the end of the value trail.

If it were easy to measure training effects, everyone would have been doing it decades ago. As a result, training departments and trainers would not be the early victims of every cutback. It is obvious that most executives still view training as a discretionary activity rather than a task as vital to success as production and sales. When you start to show management exactly how much value a program contributed, you will never again be viewed as administering a "nice to do" activity.

17
Organization Development

Organization Development: Past and Future

In the early 1980s I wondered if organization development (OD) would evolve from the touchy-feely, humanistic psychology, 1960s-1970s model to a more concrete, business-oriented modus operandi. With the massive restructuring of the 1990s, one would think that OD would be a key player. My experience is that OD is just beginning to learn how to play in this arena. The restructurings are being led directly by line management, with OD playing a supporting role. Socio-tech questions now are being considered by line managers. If this is the result of exposure to OD types, then we must say that OD has fulfilled its destiny. I'd like to give OD more credit, but I'm not sure that is the case.

Management is generally becoming more enlightened about the treatment of people. It is also becoming more demanding about the return on its investments. With markets becoming more competitive, managers everywhere have no choice but to become more productive and efficient if they want to survive. Organization development can not only make a contribution in today's market, it can prove its contribution; that is, it can evaluate its outcomes in quantitative as well as qualitative terms. The issue that has blocked measurement efforts up to now is not the mechanics of mathematics or experimentation, but an unwillingness to attempt measurement. Many OD professionals view themselves as being somehow related to the education and healing professions, and they simply cannot identify with quantitative analysis of their work. But to survive in this intensely competitive world, OD practitioners have to accept and internalize the fact that they are also part of commerce.

Organization Development and the Organization

Edgar Schein, one of the fathers of OD, provides a workable definition of an organization.

> The rational coordination of the activities of a number of people for the achievement of some common explicit purpose or goal, through division of labor and function, and through a hierarchy of authority and responsibility.

The key words in that definition are *people, activities,* and *achievement.* These variables are all measurable at one level or another. To find out how, you have to look at the organization as a system. The organization is viewed by OD as an open system that is characterized by inputs, processes, and outputs. It exists within a larger environment. It draws resources from that environment, processes them, and returns them in a changed and value-added form. Within itself, the organization has smaller systems that act in the same manner. They draw resources from the environment and from other subsystems, process them, and pass them on in an improved form. Hence, the idea of the organizational system has these characteristics: interaction and interdependence of elements, plus the goal of creating value-added outputs. To see how this relates to OD work, we must seek a definition of organization development.

There are many descriptions of what OD is. Fortunately, they all say pretty much the same thing. Richard Beckhard offered one that I still feel is both comprehensive and efficient.

> Organization development is an effort (1) planned, (2) organization-wide, and (3) managed from the top, to (4) increase organization effectiveness and health through (5) planned interventions in the organization's processes, using behavioral science knowledge.

Please note that the goals are to increase organizational effectiveness and health. The issue of health is concerned with individuals' feelings and with interpersonal and group relationships. OD's assumption is that with improved individual work-related health, the person will become more effective on the job. This should then lead to greater organizational effectiveness and profitability.

In summary, an organization is a collection of people, activities, and objectives. It is characterized by inputs, processes, and outputs that add value. OD is a planned intervention aimed at improving individual and organizational health and effectiveness. As far as I can see, there is nothing in those statements that prohibits quantitative as well as qualitative evaluation.

OD's Opportunity

Whether they realize it or not, the world has turned in the direction of organization development. Benchmarking, reengineering, and other forms of process improvement can use OD skills. Since OD specialists understand the human element of work processes, they are the natural resource for restructuring projects. Let's face it, the hardest part of making any redesign effective is the human element. What is more threatening than reengineering your workplace?

Reengineering starts by discarding everything you know—your work environment. It says, "Forget what you were doing and start with a clean slate." Asking people to do that is like asking someone to give up their knowledge, their friends, family, even their heritage, and start life over. It's hard enough to make simple process improvements and to persuade people to go along with them, but OD can help.

Organization development is grounded in interpersonal dynamics. Teamwork, communication, and conflict resolution are the meat of OD. With their knowledge and skill in human psychology, OD pros can facilitate a smoother transition. And they won't have to worry about measuring their work. The results will be obvious. Process variables will be seen by the unit managers. Changes in production cost, process time, quantity, and quality of products or services will be monitored to learn how the restructuring has affected performance. All OD people have to do is stand up and be counted as part of the success or failure.

Why Organization Development Is Not Quantitatively Evaluated

Since measurement is clearly possible, why is it seldom attempted? There are several reasons. They are very similar to the excuses given for not measuring the HR department overall. First, some feel that since evaluation has not been demanded in the past, why offer it now? OD staffs have chosen not to pick up the signals from line managers, who settle reluctantly for subjective assessments of the outcomes. Since management has not pressed the issue, most OD staffs are content to let it lie.

The second reason is that many OD staffs simply do not know how to measure. The U.S. Department of Health, Education, and Welfare studied 34 cases of work experiments that claimed unqualified improvements. A host of critics have challenged the results, pointing out that invalid and unreliable documentation was presented.

Assuming that the reporters were not deliberately trying to deceive, we can only conclude that their knowledge of measurement methods was extremely weak. In their defense, it should be noted that opportunities for gaining knowledge and skill in field experimentation is very limited in industry. That is not a justification, it is just a small problem to be surmounted.

The third and most difficult obstacle to overcome is that many practitioners do not want to measure. The idea of measurement, proof, or the very introduction of objective methods into the field goes against the value system of a large segment of the OD profession. They believe that OD should be excused from the rigors of scientific method. Their position is that this somehow impedes the process, focuses the effort on irrelevant matters, and makes the whole thing less useful or usable. Some people who hold this position are close to being fanatic about it. Some are zealous in their love for OD, and a few are almost manic about its special purpose and value. These people love the process of OD so much that they cannot accept the constraints and expectations that science and business impose. The irony is that although they sometimes deal with the most intimate issues in the lives of their clients, they do not want to stop to look at the effects of their work. These types of persons will probably never be persuaded to measure their outcomes.

The job of the HR department manager is to convince the OD staff that there is a necessity for some type of objective evaluation of their work. Most HR professionals have reached a point in recent years where they no longer ask the business world to accept HR purely for its inherent "goodness." OD is finally moving in that direction. The following discussion should provide both sides with enough measurement alternatives that a few suitable ones can be adopted.

Measures of Effectiveness for Organization Development

The objective of the remainder of this chapter will be to demonstrate how the effectiveness of both individuals and the organization can be evaluated at points across three levels. You will see how you can start with several broadly stated criterion variables and find measurement opportunities with subsystems and with specific independent variables.

Before any OD project gets under way the first question must be, why are we doing this project? Another way of stating it is, what is the problem? A penetrating and truthful answer to this type of question

	Time period		
	Short run	Intermediate	Long run
Criterion variables:			
Production	X		
Efficiency	X		
Satisfaction	X		
Adaptiveness		X	
Development		X	
Survival			X

Figure 17.1. Criterion Variables for Organizational Development

will point out the issue, which may be measurable. If that is too simple or does not yield a satisfactory answer, the framework that follows should reveal it.

The five criterion variables in Figure 17.1 have a time aspect to them. The time dimension enters the picture when an organization is conceptualized as an element of a larger system (the environment). Over time, the organization acquires, processes, and returns resources to the environment. Accordingly, a time line with three ranges can be constructed. These ranges describe broad periods in an organization's life cycle. They are the *short run, intermediate run,* and *long run.* Some of the criteria exist across all time periods; others are primarily period-oriented.

The Xs indicate the time period of primary consideration. Clearly, issues such as productivity, quality, and service are always important. Their focus is usually on short-term measures that are continuously moving. Responsiveness and development are intermediate-term signs of organizational health. Even here there are goals and objectives which can be defined, described, and measured. One would hope that top management has at least one strategic imperative that deals with its employees.

Criteria

Here is how the five criteria can be viewed, worked on, measured and evaluated.

1. *Productivity.* Productivity is the measurable ability of the organization to generate the goods and services in the quantity and at a price that the market demands. Examples of production criteria are tons of steel, barrels of beer, dollars of sales, invoices processed, and new accounts opened. These are the dependent variables (outcomes) that are affected by an OD intervention, e.g., team building, process redesign, or conflict resolution.

The typical question asked is, "I don't see how I can relate a small OD effort in one department to the number of tons of steel my mill rolled last month." The answer is, "That depends." It depends on the business problem that drew OD in and the value of solving the problem. If it's a production problem, look for tonnage out the door. If it's an administrative process problem, look for the desired result: hiring, paying, billing, training, report generation, accidents, building maintenance, and so on. The following are two simple examples.

> *Example 1.* If you go out to the rolling mill floor and work with the crew to improve cooperation, team problem solving, or a work process—other things being equal—you can see the effect. More important, your client the process manager will see the difference. Remember, this isn't a doctoral dissertation or medical research. You don't have to prove it at the .05 level of statistical significance. So long as the client can see and appreciate it you are halfway home. Then, work out a range of value based on increased tonnage or less scrap or faster delivery, and so forth.

> *Example 2.* Moving off the plant floor to the office doesn't change anything except the output. Assume you are working in accounts receivable redesigning the work flow. That might not affect the number of tons of steel rolled, but it may affect the cash flow of the company. If helping the accounting staff reformat their work flow improves the throughput and error rate of invoices, that should speed up payments of bills and accelerate the inflow of cash. As a person who has mortgaged his next three incarnations to start and maintain a company, I can tell you that nothing is as important to a business as cash flow.

If you connect your work to the appropriate variable you will see the result. If you want to impact tonnage output, naturally you go to the place in the mill where that takes place. Look for opportunities for OD techniques to solve production-related problems. There are many people-based activities in a rolling mill that OD might be able to improve.

2. *Quality.* Quality traditionally referred to the number of errors or defects in the end product. Since the advent of the quality movement, which came to the United States in the early 1980s, the term *quality* is also being applied to measuring the cycle time of the process.

A team-building project that shortens invoice processing time may not be as exciting to the OD devotee as one that changes a supervisor's leadership style, but it is a lot easier to track and verify. It probably also has a much better chance of happening and is viewed by line management as more relevant to their goals. Nevertheless, if you are able to work with a supervisor to adopt a more effective style, it might help improve the efficiency or effectiveness of a work group. If it does, you should be able to establish that fact through interviews and quantify the benefit that ensued using the workers' own examples.

3. *Service.* Service is important to two groups of people: employees and customers. First, we are concerned with employee feelings. They are important because people are intrinsically important. Feelings are also important because they impact individual productivity and customer service. Obviously, we want our customers to be satisfied with our products and services. Without customers we have no business. The key point for OD practitioners is to see people in two ways. One is as human beings worthy of ethical and uplifting treatment. The other is as instruments of production. OD can help people realize their potential, and OD must also help people produce.

OD can measure the outcomes of its work in several ways. It should be affecting not only production and service variables but also human issues such as turnover, absence, tardiness, and grievances. It is clear that OD can do many things of value besides making people feel good. Positive attitudes, reduced stress, strong group cohesiveness, and supportive interpersonal relationships can all be related to organizational productivity, quality, and service variables. After all, if they didn't affect these variables, why would we work on them?

4. *Responsiveness.* As we move from the short run to intermediate outcomes, it becomes more difficult but not impossible to find measures. In the case of responsiveness, the only true test is when the company is faced with a need or opportunity and it rises to or fails to meet the test. OD probably can do something in this arena, but it is more difficult to show cause-and-effect relationships. The reason for the difficulty is the intervening time. You might conduct a series of very useful team-building sessions resulting in improvements in various performance criteria. A year later you might see that the company is able to shift strategies much faster than it used to. You may feel that your work had a lot to do with that improved capability, but you can only infer that. The broader the effect and the longer it takes to occur, the more difficult it is to establish a correlation. But, take heart, it is the same for all disciplines. It's just that the line functions learned it so long ago that they live with the looseness between the cause and effect.

5. *Development.* With the publication of Senge's *The Fifth Discipline*, the notion of developmental or renewal capability was recast as a "learning organization." An organization must invest in itself in order to enhance its capability for survival. The measures here are not training programs or interventions run, but competencies attained and used to achieve positive results. Much of business training is really education, as I pointed out in the previous chapter. It deals with concepts and increases the learner's breadth of knowledge. Knowledge is useful in helping people be more aware and logical, and it can give them more information with which they can improve their decision-making abilities. However, skills also have to be developed. OD teaches people skills through simulations or on-the-job experience. It helps people learn how to increase their ability to interact, supervise, and be supervised.

The types of development activities that are easiest to evaluate are the ones carried out in formal settings. OD can do some of the same type of measurement if it carefully selects some baseline data before beginning its intervention. The OD consultant has some control over the intervention environment. Most interactive change efforts are less structured than a classroom training session. Nevertheless, they are, or should be, directed toward some goal. Either the goal or a subset of the goal will be visible behavior or concrete organizational results, which are usually quantifiable.

6. *Survival.* Only in rare cases is an OD intervention close enough to a survival crisis for a cause and effect relationship to be drawn. There is enough work for OD to do among the preceding criteria that it can pass on this one.

Subsystems

Within each of the criteria just presented we can find subsystems operating. A subsystem has three phases: input, process, and output (I-P-O). As we shift from the broad criteria, through the subsystems, to the individual variables, we find an increasing number of opportunities to measure. Keep in mind that the intervention and the measure have to be related to each other. This relationship must be established at the beginning for maximum credibility.

1. *Productivity.* The inputs to the production process are

- People
- Machines
- Material   } All working together on intermediate or final
- Energy   processes to create outputs
- Capital

Traditionally, OD is concerned with how the human inputs interact during the process stage. Examples of processes and their outputs are

- Programming—an output that is a software package
- Brewing—an output that is beer
- Filling in a billing form—an output that is an invoice
- Assembling—an output that is a circuit board
- Installing—an output that is telephones/computers/washing machines
- Cashing checks—an output that is money
- Screening applicants—an output that is candidates

Some of these are the end product of a company; some are both the end product of a department and an intermediate product of the company. Since OD might be involved with people as they carry out any of these processes, how the OD intervention impacts the cost or quantity of the outputs can be demonstrated.

2. *Quality.* This is the time it takes to complete a process and the errors in the final product or service. This measurement shows how well the I-P-O subsystem is operating. The variables in the situation have values attached to them and ratios calculated for them. The formulas are self-evident. Cycle time of the process is measurable in terms of anything from seconds to years. Error rates are typically percentages of usable outputs from the process. This is sometimes called the yield rate.

An OD intervention might deal with the behavior of the input variable, people, as they interact in the process and be able to demonstrate that the group's time and error goals were met or exceeded. Surveys and interviews might also uncover data on other inputs that, if acted on, could improve ratios. OD has many faces and many tools. Measurement is possible in many different combinations. Fortunately, a plethora of data is sitting unused in organizations that demonstrates the result and implies the value of any type of work.

3. *Service.* This subsystem deals principally with feelings of customers and employees. The inputs are not only people but the things in the workplace that impinge on the people and to which they must react. The I-P-O model is shown in Figure 17.2.

Clearly, the outputs are measurable. The employee satisfaction arena is a favorite one of the OD staff. They are committed to making the workplace a more humanistic environment. If they can connect the human issues to improved feelings and attitudes and relate that to improvements in customer service variables, they can easily show the value of their work in business terms.

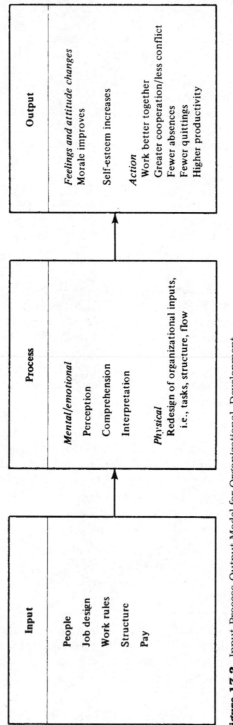

Figure 17.2. Input-Process-Output Model for Organizational Development

Input	Process	Output
People	*Mental/emotional*	*Feelings and attitude changes*
Job design	Perception	Morale improves
Work rules	Comprehension	
Structure	Interpretation	Self-esteem increases
Pay		
	Physical	*Action*
	Redesign of organizational inputs, i.e., tasks, structure, flow	Work better together
		Greater cooperation/less conflict
		Fewer absences
		Fewer quittings
		Higher productivity

Responsiveness and development utilize the same I-P-O model, but they experience it over a longer time frame. The task for the OD practitioner is to be able to connect the work being done today on the criterion variables of productivity, quality, and satisfaction with the intermediate criteria of responsiveness and development. This is difficult to prove at the .05 level of significance. However, management does not require such proof. A valid, easy to accept, inference often can be established.

Variables

Each phase in the I-P-O model has a number of variables that interact to contribute to the health and effectiveness of the individual and the organization. Many of these are quantifiable.

Assume that an OD intervention was held within a computer programming department. It could be that there had been conflict, unclear expectations, or other interpersonal issues that were affecting the output of the department. In Figure 17.3 you will find a number of vari-

Phase	Productivity/effectiveness	Health
Inputs Programmers Salaries Computers Job descriptions	Baseline data gathered before intervention on costs, timeliness, quantity and quality of work, as well as the attitudes and feelings (and maybe interpersonal skills) of the programmers.	
Processes Writing code and documenting program Writing user manuals Communications	Systematic observations and data collection which lead the organizational development consultant to design the intervention which seems most appropriate.	
Outputs Programs	Reliability, efficiency, cost, on-time completion, amount of redesign	Fatigue and stress levels
User reactions	Satisfaction with design and capability acceptance without revision	
Documentation	Readability, completeness	
Manuals	Trainees' and operators' acceptance or complaints	
Feelings and interpersonal behavior		Degree of satisfaction, stimulation, clarity about job, cooperation, accomplishment

Figure 17.3. Variables Affected by Organizational Development Intervention

ables that could be quantified on a before and after basis to measure the change which resulted from the intervention. Two types of changes are measurable. One relates to health and the other relates to productivity, quality, and service.

The variable list is obviously not all-inclusive. I am sure you can think of many more items that could be evaluated. The key is the evaluator's ability to dissect an input, a process, or an output into the many elements that constitute it. If you will take the time up front to understand the environment, just as you do when constructing the matrix, you will have no trouble finding variables to measure.

Value Chain

The four components of the value chain were introduced in an earlier chapter. Now seems like a good place to show it fully. The basic notion is that there is a linkage between work processes and monetary value. No one disputes this in sales and production. But when you bring it up in other functions people are skeptical. Figure 17.4 is an example of how the linkage works in a variety of functions.

First, if you make a change in a process you usually get a different outcome. That is simple cause and effect logic. That outcome, when compared to another outcome prior to the process change, is called the impact. The impact is the difference. It answers the question, so what? Hopefully, the change is positive. Usually it can be described as an improvement in quality, productivity, or service resulting in expense control or revenue increase. Once that is apparent, it is a simple matter to put a dollar value on it.

This linkage is the logic core of most business management measures. Perhaps I can put it this way: When you understand the value chain you can find value in practically any change. All it requires is a knowledge of the process and the ultimate values of different types of outcomes. As a staff person you might not know that. But, if you work closely with your customer partners you provide the logic questions and they provide the answers and values.

Organization Development and Productivity

In recent years there have been several attempts to correlate "enlightened" human resource management with company profitability. It is

Process/Practice > > >	Outcome > > >	Impact > > >	> > Value-Added
Centralize hiring	Lower agency rates	Lower hiring cost	Reduced operating expense
Simplify hiring process	Shortened time to hire	Jobs filled sooner	Less overtime or temps
Improve claims response	EE claims paid faster	Fewer EE follow-up calls	Higher productivity
High quality salary actions	Fewer paycheck errors	Less rework time	Reduced process cost
	Fewer unhappy employees ↗	Greater productivity	Lower product cost
		Better customer service	Fewer lost customers
Upgrade training methods	Increased ROI from training	Better Q-P-S	Lower product/service cost
Survey information interests	Improved EE communication	Higher morale/less turnover	Retention savings
Install succession planning	Fewer emergency hires	Less recruitment expense	Lower operating expense

Figure 17.4. HR Value Chain

clear from these studies that there is a relationship. How closely it correlates and which comes first are still open questions.

In a four-year research project focused on productivity carried out with over 1500 workers, we looked at 150 variables which might impact an employee's productivity.[3] Early on we used factor analysis to arrange them into 22 factors or clusters (see Fig. 17.5). Later, we

---

1. **Leader behavior** — Supervisor's way of dealing with people, work flow, and resource issues.

2. **Worker behavior** — Work-related interactions with coworkers and supervisor.

3. **Delegation** — Amount and manner in which supervisor delegates and encourages new ideas.

4. **Worker capability** — Skill, knowledge, experience, education, and potential which the worker brings to the job.

5. **Strictness** — Firm and equitable enforcement of the company rules and procedures.

6. **Equipment design** — Degree of difficulty experienced in operating equipment.

7. **Job satisfaction** — Worker's general attitude and satisfaction with the job.

8. **External influences** — Effects of outside social, political, and economic activity.

9. **Safety** — Company's efforts to provide a safe and healthy working environment.

10. **Self-responsibility** — Workers' concern for quality and their desire to be responsible.

11. **Resources** — Availability of tools, manuals, parts, and material needed to do the job.

12. **Country's situation** — Impact of national conditions on the worker and the company.

13. **Coworkers** — Mutual respect and liking among the members of the work group.

14. **Pay and conditions of work** — Performance reviews, promotions, pay, and work scheduling.

15. **Job stress** — Environmental effects, such as temperature and ventilation, plus feelings about job security.

16. **Personal problems** — Impact of overtime on personal life, and other personal life issues.

17. **Self-esteem** — Sense of self-respect and respect from others derived from doing the job.

18. **Work problems** — Physical and psychological fatigue resulting from work.

19. **The company** — General attitudes toward the company, its style of operation, and its stability.

20. **Economic needs** — Degree to which the job satisfies workers' needs for food, clothing, and shelter.

21. **Responsibility accepted** — Desired workload and responsibility versus actual workload and responsibility.

22. **Company policies** — Rest periods, training, job layout, and departmental characteristics.

---

*This list does not imply there will always be 22 factors. Each set of data will cluster according to its particular nature. The chances are more likely that the number of factors will decrease slightly rather than increase.

Figure 17.5. Productivity Factors*

regressed the factors against a productivity criterion and uncovered those factors which affected each work group's productivity.

OD can work on the belief system and the feelings of workers toward all of these factors. It can demonstrate change for the better on any of them. That in itself would be a significant achievement. Using this approach, the OD consultant can extract the factors that impact productivity in a given work group. Then the consultant can carry out the OD intervention and show management how it has positively affected the group's productivity. Unfortunately, OD people don't like to apply statistical methods, preferring to go with their beliefs based on broad theories and models.

Summary

It is clear to me, based on 25 years of contact with organizational development, that the issue of measurability is overwhelmingly one of misguided and conflicting personal values. Fortunately, more OD types are coming into the real world and accepting responsibility for business results. When you show your OD staff how they can serve both the worker and the organization by focusing on desirable outcomes, and that measuring those outcomes will prove to be a positive experience, you can overcome the value bias.

OD is a methodology of great promise. It is beginning to acknowledge that it is operating in a business organization and therefore must serve the needs of the organization as well as those of the worker. OD practitioners need only do the following things to demonstrate their value:

1. Establish partnerships with the clients.

2. Identify the business issue behind the symptom of human behavior or organizational structure/process.

3. Set clear business goals for solving the problem.

4. Use the Value Chain as a logic guide to trace change and find value.

SECTION F
The Payoffs

18

Principles of
Performance
Measurement

In the early chapters I stated that there are many payoffs to be derived from an HR department performance measurement system. They are available at all levels from the individual to the organizational. I hope you have seen many of them as you studied the formulas and figures. I want to conclude the book by reviewing the basic principles of objective performance measurement and by discussing briefly the individual and organizational payoffs which a measurement system can generate.

There are five underlying principles of performance measurement. I have covered them all throughout the book, but they bear repeating.

1. *The productivity and effectiveness of any function can be measured by some combination of cost, time, quantity, quality, or human reaction indices.* Some functions lend themselves to objective evaluation better than others. However, I have yet to find one that does not allow for any quantitative appraisal. Critics will find many reasons why something cannot or should not be measured. Nevertheless, you can find something meaningful to measure if you remember to look for observable, describable phenomena in the process or the outcome. Even such seemingly esoteric work as research and development yields opportunities for objective assessment of activities and results. In the early 1970s, Hughes Aircraft conducted an extensive study of productivity within R&D.[1] A perusal of the study report uncovers dozens of quantitative issues suitable for measurement. More recently, Sloma[2] provides examples of quantifiable issues across the entire range of functions. A broad set of indices can be found in *Vital Signs*.[3]

2. *A measurement system promotes productivity by focusing attention on the important issues, tasks, and objectives.* Over the 35 years I have worked in organizations, the single most counterproductive factor I have observed is lack of clarity about priorities. This is why I mentioned early on that the leader's vision must be to communicate. I am more interested in finding remedies than lamenting over the reasons why management doesn't make directions clear. My experience with performance measurement systems is that they help to clarify what is to be accomplished and how well it should be done. I believe that if you can get these points across to people you have carried out two of the three most critical tasks of management. The third is providing support in the form of resources: information, supplies, tools, and humanistic treatment. The value of the systems approach is that it takes into consideration the mission of the department as it relates to organizational imperatives. In doing that it leaves nothing to chance and little room for misperception of priorities. I have great faith in people. I know that if management points the way the people will meet the objectives of the organization.

3. *Performance should be measured at both individual and team levels.* As organizations shift more responsibility to ad hoc and self-directed work teams, performance measurement systems have to follow. Team measures can be constructed for both projects and permanent units. The delayering of organizations has brought teamwork to the fore. There are fewer supervisors and more opportunity for discretionary action. In order to be optimally effective a professional group has to work together. If you try to measure and compare the work of individuals and drive them against their colleagues, you are asking for trouble. Comparison leads to competition rather than cooperation. It breaks down cohesiveness because the objective shifts from group to individual performance. It's an issue of survival: When we try to measure individuals, people are smart enough to know how to protect themselves. Threat forces defensiveness, and defensiveness leads to data manipulation. If that occurs, you are sunk. On the other hand, when you build a system based on a combination of individual and group objectives you do not have to worry about laggards. Peer pressure will stimulate the low performer, and if that doesn't work you will certainly be told by someone in the group that there is a problem. I once worked for a very wise man who operated under the motto, "If we succeed there is glory enough for everyone; but if we fail there are no heroes."

4. *Managers can be measured by the efficiency and effectiveness of the units they manage.* It is true that a good group can overcome an inept manager. However, before long it will be clear that there is a managerial void. If the nature of managerial work is to get things done through other people, then it must follow that a manager's performance is reflected in the output of the group. Managers do many things, and these can be observed and objectively evaluated. However, that would miss the mark. What managers do (activity) is less important than the effects (outcomes) that they generate. This is one of the vexing problems with assessment programs. Some people look great in a work simulation. They know the theory and they are great test takers. But, often they can't manage a one-person party.

5. *The ultimate measurement is not efficiency, but effectiveness.* The highest form of organizational excellence is to create the greatest good with the least input. That is more than being efficient. It implies that resources are directed toward the objectives that are most prized. That means focusing on results, doing the right thing at the right time, and serving long-term as well as short-term goals. In order for an organization to achieve optimum effectiveness it needs a sound operating philosophy that is communicated to all employees, sound planning toward worthwhile objectives, and a monitoring system that tells it whether or not it is moving toward those objectives in an acceptable fashion. The measurement system plays a crucial part in the last step.

GEM #20   *Effective performance measurement systems make people feel good about themselves, and self-esteem is the key to productivity.*

Summary

The five principles of performance measurement provide a foundation on which to construct an evaluation system. I can tell you from years of trial and error that if you violate them, they will burn you sooner or later. But if you use them as the framework of your system, the payoffs will be many and long-lasting.

In the final analysis we are trying to measure value added. When people see how they are contributing value to the organization they feel good. Conversely, when all they see is a mountain of work with no sense of closure and no gratitude for all their well-meaning effort, they feel bad. It's simple. Put together a system that helps people see and feel how well they've done, and they will strive continuously to do better.

19

Organizational and Individual Payoffs

HR Is Free

The human resources function permeates the whole organization. Whether it is acknowledged or not, the HR department has a significant positive, or negative, effect on its organization. The HR department impacts the organization's mission or bottom line in many ways. Throughout the range of activities—hiring, paying, supporting, and developing the human asset—HR is affecting organizational costs, quality, and general competitiveness. An effective human resources department contributes far more in monetary terms than its operating expense. The following are simple examples of how this happens.

Benefits

The cost of benefits got out of control in the 1980s. After a decade of benefit giveaways, organizations found themselves in an untenable situation. Today, benefits cost is the human resource topic that most interests many chief executives. Monitoring not only costs but utilization patterns is critical to responding with a cost-effective remedy.

An attentive benefits manager makes sure that any dividends or refunds that are due the organization from the carrier are paid promptly. Tardiness and absence have to be monitored or an organization pays for people not at work. I was in a company once that did not keep track of absences of professionals and managers. Since no one seemed to care, the people got the signal that absence of any amount was acceptable, so they took advantage of what they perceived to be an uncaring management. In a contrasting case, one midwestern company saved about a million dollars annually by managing absenteeism.

Compensation

Organizations that neglect their pay system inevitably either overpay or underpay their employees. The outcome is that the overpaid incompetents stay and the underpaid competent people leave. Not only does the organization end up paying too much for what they have, they incur unnecessary turnover expenses. Compensation is important both as a cost control and as an incentive program.

Broad-banding, pay at risk, gain sharing, and team rewards are a few of the issues that compensation managers are facing. With delayering leading to fewer opportunities to be promoted, the application of incentive pay has become a fine art. Fortunately, since pay is all numbers it is easy to track the effects of various cost control and incentive programs. The good thing about pay programs is that you don't have to work hard to get everyone's attention.

Diversity

Affirmative Action is more than avoiding lawsuits. In the 1970s and early 1980s, under pressure to redress the inequities of the past, many organizations hired young, inexperienced minorities and women just to meet quotas. Often these people really were not equipped for higher-level jobs. Today, there are many highly motivated, loyal, qualified minorities and women inside companies who could handle further training and promotions.

Despite the three decades since the passage of Title VII of the Civil Rights Act, many companies have yet to wake up. Within the past twelve months alone, several discrimination awards in excess of $100 million have been made. Now, the challenge is learning how to blend the diverse talents and values of the new work force. Training and informal cross-cultural events help everyone understand the viewpoints of others. HR is leading this revolution. Saving the organization from acting in a discriminatory fashion is good. But diversity management goes beyond that to find more effective ways to use the talents of all associates.

Retention

Retention management shows its effect in several ways. Since unemployment insurance taxes are usually based on workforce turnover experience, high turnover takes money directly out of the corporate profits. Payroll unemployment insurance taxes run from 1 to about 4 percent of payroll for most companies. An effective claims management program can keep the firm's contribution toward the lower end. When I came into one company the tax rate was almost 4 percent. Over a period of 3 years we were able to lower it to less than 2 percent, which was a savings of $1 million on the company's payroll. At the time, that just about covered the entire operating budget of my department.

Some turnover is inevitable and actually healthy. Layoffs have become a common tool in downsizing and restructuring organizations for the competitive twenty-first century. Effective use of outplacement services can cut severance expense and make the outgoing employee somewhat happier. Exit interview programs can help ferret out the source of a turnover problem. Prompt counseling can turn a questionable firing or a productivity-robbing morale problem into a mutually agreeable resolution. The solution may even be a voluntary quit, which would be better than a lawsuit with all its attendant costs.

Staffing

It is a sad fact that many people hold jobs for which they are overqualified. This results in an employee who is not highly motivated, is overpaid, and is a candidate for turnover. Good recruiters learn what is really needed in the departments which they service. They persuade managers to cast the job at the right level and pay the appropriate salary. This keeps down salary expense and curbs turnover expense.

Several years ago people got scared out of testing for selection for fear of discrimination claims. Now, selection testing is more sophisticated. It does a better job of screening out people who have little chance of succeeding. A good selection system cuts down turnover. One firm I worked with was losing nearly 50 percent of their newly hired MBAs after the first year. Once we got them to pay more attention to their selection and training system, the losses dropped to 10 percent. Considering that first-year costs for salaries and training were running about $20,000, this change in the program saved the company over $300,000.

External Effects

More important than HR department efficiencies and preventive measures are proactive partnerships with line customers. HR leverages the human component of its customers' departments. When the HR staff goes into the organization to locate performance improvement opportunities and works out solutions with managers, the effects are usually quite visible. Improvements in quality, productivity, service, and sales can be found if one structures the intervention around visible outcomes. In the Value Chain I showed several examples of the many ways in which the effects of HR's work can be traced to operating and financial improvements.

Individual Payoffs

The only reason that people do anything is because they see some kind of payoff for their effort. This does not mean that they are selfish, self-centered, or greedy. It is simply normal behavior. People do not act randomly: that is, they must have a reason for doing something. That reason may be to avoid pain, or it may be to experience pleasure. It may also be just to maintain the status quo, which is a little bit of each. Only people who are suffering from some type of mental or emotional disorder act in ways that are detrimental to themselves. It is true that we all do things that do ourselves harm, but they are not intended to end up like that. We expect that we are doing what is right for us, but once in a while we make a mistake. All this is by way of saying that if you want your staff to get behind a measurement system, you need to show them what the payoffs will be.

If you ask employees of any personnel department how good a job they are doing, the chances are they will reply positively. The great irony is that their customers don't see the value added by HR. If you ask HR people to justify their existence and prove their value, most of them won't be able to do it. So here is the first payoff. Numbers can be proof, whereas words are just noise. With numbers, for the first time the staff will be able to prove that they are doing an excellent job. No one will be able to deny them. They will be able to show month after month that either they are improving or they are maintaining a high level of proficiency.

Another very important reward that stems from using hard numbers is job and self-satisfaction. Without a measurement system, all the staff are sure of is that they are working like the devil, processing a lot of people or paper, and aren't seeing any end in sight. They have no sense of accomplishment because they don't know what they have done. All they can be sure of is that they put in a lot of effort and probably got very little recognition for it. This reward is very personal and highly motivating.

The productivity research project described in the previous chapter has proven that self-esteem and self-respect, as it relates to the job, are prerequisites to high productivity. One of the major problems personnel people have always had is low self-esteem. One reason for it is that they could never show they were making a contribution to the bottom line.

A third payoff is power. HR will be able to come to prove they need and deserve more resources. As the manager you will be able to take that proof to senior management and get the resources. This is the third level of success described in the beginning of this chapter. There won't be any need to beg, threaten, or argue. The numbers will speak for themselves. At long last, your department will get the people, equipment, space, or money that it should have.

Finally, the development and use of your performance measurement system will provide the people with the organizational rewards they deserve. You will be able to demonstrate that their jobs and salaries should be leveled according to their contributions—contributions that can be substantiated. You will be able to position them properly and obtain salary increases for them that truly reflect not just their effort but their accomplishments. Then, the money, titles, and status that they have been denied in the past will come. They will have to come because they cannot be denied. The days of second-class citizenship will be over. Your people can stop acting like Rodney Dangerfield; complaining that they "don't get no respect around here." They will get it because they will prove that they have earned it.

GEM #21 *If you want to be respected, be part of someone's path to success.*

Summary

The HR department works in many ways to reduce organizational expenses and increase profitability. To consistently manage both ongoing and changing work environments you need hard data. With it you understand what is happening, can exercise some degree of control, and can make improvements. Performance measurement is essential for those who wish to make a specific, quantifiable contribution to their organization's success. The following are the key roles that quantitative measurement and reporting play in this. They:

Alert management to problems early.

Identify opportunities for greater efficiencies.

Show positive results, thereby stimulating people to do even better.

20
Conclusion: What It Takes to Be Successful in the New One-Market World

In Section A, I talked about the abilities required for a person to be successful in today's organization. The first is the ability to excel at your job. You are already doing that. Second is learning to be a businessperson rather than an HR nerd. This means you must learn enough about the technology of your organization to be able to earn a partnership with your customer. Third is acquiring fluency in financial terminology. You don't have to become a CPA, but you do need to understand basic P&L and balance sheet terms. Next you must become a change manager. That is even more than being a change agent. Stimulating people to change is a great skill, but more often than not you will have to play a major role in making the change happen. Fourth is the ability to select the issues that are important to the larger organization and to direct your efforts toward them. I hope you are doing that. Fifth and last is the ability to develop performance data from your work and to use it to inform and persuade.

Throughout the book I have focused on that last ability. The objective has been to help you develop the skill to extract objective data from the results of your work and to put it in forms that will influence the thinking of your various audiences. It is naive to believe that in an organization that may employ anywhere from a few hundred to many thousands of people, all you have to do is keep your nose to the grindstone and you will succeed. Organizations are finite institutions. They do not have unlimited resources, and there are many contenders for those resources. In order to get your rightful share, you must be able to demonstrate that there is a good business reason for giving it to you.

Although human resources work may have some intrinsic goodness about it in terms of helping people learn, grow, and advance, organizations do not tend to pay much for goodness. They are, out of necessity, most interested in return on investment. Once you can prove that something you did made a contribution to that magic bottom line, you get what you need to continue to excel at your job. Beyond that, you will get the respect that you deserve as a professional and as a member of the management team.

GEM #22 *The meek might inherit the earth, but the strong probably won't leave them much to enjoy.*

Jerry Sanders is the founder of Advanced Micro Devices, a major semiconductor company. One night over dinner he said to me, "When I was young I thought it was enough just to be right. After I got fired for being right, I realized that you have to be right and have power."

Numbers are power. Good luck.

References

Chapter 2
1. G. S. Odiorne, *Management by Objectives Newsletter*, July 1974.

2. P. Drucker, *Management: Tasks, Responsibilities and Practices*, Harper and Row, New York, 1973, p. 45.

Chapter 3
1. John Donne, *Devotions XVII*.

2. *Best in America Guidebook*, Saratoga Institute, Saratoga, CA, 1993.

3. Mary Azzolini et al., *Quality*, 1994.

4. Survey by David Ulrich.

Chapter 4
1. Valarie, Zeithaml, A. Parasuraman, and L. Barry, *Delivering Quality Service*, Free Press, 1990.

Chapter 5
1. J. L. Grahn, "White Collar Productivity: Misunderstandings and Some Progress," *Personnel Administration*, August 1981, p. 30.

2. H. Dahl and K. S. Morgan, "Return on Investment in Human Resources," in R. N. Lehrer, ed., *White Collar Productivity*, McGraw-Hill, New York, 1983, p. 282.

3. *Human Resource Effectiveness Report*, SHRM/Saratoga Institute, Saratoga, CA, 1993.

Chapter 7
1. E. H. Burack and N. J. Mathys, *Human Resource Planning: A Pragmatic Approach to Manpower Staffing and Development*, Brace-Park Press, Lake Forest, IL, 1980, p. 121.

Chapter 8
1. E. E. Lawler III, *Pay and Organizational Effectiveness: A Psychological View*, McGraw-Hill, New York, 1971, p. 59.

2. H. C. Smith and J. H. Wakeley, *Psychology of Industrial Behavior*, 3d ed., McGraw-Hill, New York, 1972, pp. 243–244.

Chapter 9
1. *Best in America Guidebook,* Saratoga Institute, Saratoga, CA, 1992.

Chapter 12
1. M. Fishbein and I. Ajzen, *Belief, Attitude, Intention and Behavior: An Introduction to Theory and Research,* Addison-Wesley, Reading, MA, 1975, Preface, p. v.

Chapter 13
1. F. E. Kuzmits, "How Much Is Absenteeism Costing Your Organization?," *Personnel Administrator,* June 1979.

Chapter 14
1. Frederick Schuster, *The Schuster Report: The Proven Connection between People and Profits,* Wiley, New York, 1986.

2. Dennis Kravetz, *The Human Resources Revolution,* Jossey-Bass, 1988.

3. Mark Huselid, "The Effects of Strategic Human Resource Management and Human Resource Planning on Firm Performance," Institute of Management and Labor Relations, Rutgers University, New Brunswick, NJ, 1993.

Chapter 16
1. R. F. Mager, *Preparing Instructional Objectives,* Fearon Publishers, Inc., Belmont, CA, 1975, Preface.

2. Jac Fitz-enz, "What Causes People to Be Productive," Saratoga Institute, Saratoga, CA, 1982.

Chapter 18
1. *R & D Productivity,* Hughes Aircraft Co., Culver City, CA, 1978.

2. Richard Sloma, *How to Measure Managerial Performance,* Macmillan, 1980.

3. Steven Hronec, *Vital Signs,* AMACON, New York, 1993.

Bibliography

Bevan, Stephan and Marc Thompson, "Performance Management at the Crossroads," *Personnel Management*, November 1991.

Boles, Elizabeth, "Increasing Organizational Return: Power From Your People," *HR Horizons*, Issue 115. Winter 1994.

Boylen, M. E., "The Four Costs of Employee Training," *Administrative Management*, March 1980, pp. 40–41.

Burton, R. and A. S. Tsui, "Human Resource Management in Complex Organizations," paper presented at the National Meeting of the Institute for Management Sciences, San Diego, 1982.

Cawsey, T. F., "Why Line Managers Don't Listen to Their Personnel Departments," *Personnel*, AMACOM, American Management Association, pp. 11–20.

Clarke, E., "Improving White Collar Productivity," *Electronic Engineering Times*, September 29, 1980, pp. 89–90.

Connolly, T., E. Conlon, and Deutsch, "A Multiple Constituency Approach of Organizational Effectiveness," *Academy of Management Review*, 1980, pp. 211–218.

Dahl, H. and K. S. Morgan, "Is Anyone Measuring Return on Investment in Human Resources?" *Upjohn Company Report*, 1981.

_____, "Return on Investment in Human Resources," *Upjohn Company Report*, 1982.

"Employment Cost Index," *Current Wage Developments*, September 1980, pp. 40–42.

Dessler, Gary, "Value-based Hiring Builds Commitment," *Personnel Journal*, November 1992.

English, Gary, "Tuning Up For Performance Management," *Training & Development Journal*, April 1991.

Fitz-enz, Jac, "The Future of Performance Management and Measurement Systems," *HR Horizons*, Issue 111, Winter 1994.

_____, "The Truth About Best Practice," *Human Resource Planning*, Vol. 16, No. 3, 1994.

_____, "Yes...You Can Weigh Training's Value," *Training*, July 1994.

_____, "The Mythology of Measuring Staff Performance," *Canadian Business Review*, Spring 1993.

_____, "Benchmarking Best Practices," *Canadian Business Review*, Winter 1992.

_____, "HR Forecasts That Will Benefit Your Bottom Line," *Computers in HR Management*, March 1990.

_____, "White-Collar Productivity, Part I: The Employees' Side," *Management Review*, May 1986.

_____, "White Collar Productivity, Part II: The Organization's Side," *Management Review*, July 1986.

Fletcher, Clive and Richard Williams, "The Route to Performance Management," *Personnel Management*, October 1993.

Greene, Robert J., "A 90's Model for Performance Management," *HR Magazine*, April 1991.

Griggs, Walter H. and Susan R. Manring, "Increasing the Effectiveness of Technical Professionals," *Management Review*, May 1986.

Kearsley, G. and T. Compton, "Assessing Costs, Benefits and Productivity in Training Systems," *Training and Development Journal*, January 1981, pp. 52–58.

Kratchenberg, A. Richard, John W. Henke, and Thomas F. Lyons, "The Isolation of Upper Management," *Business Horizons*, July–August 1993.

Lawson, J. W. II and B. F. Smith, "Cost of Benefits," *Management's Complete Guide to Employee Benefits*, Dartnell, Chicago, 1980, Chap. 3.

LeBlanc, Peter V. and Michael McInerney, "Need a Change? Jump on the Banding Wagon," *Personnel Journal*, January 1994.

Lowman, J., and T. Snediker, "Pinpointing Avoidable Turnover with 'Cohort Analysis'," *Personnel Journal*, April 1980, pp. 310–312.

McAfee, R. B., "Evaluating the Personnel Department's Internal Functioning," *Personnel*, May–June 1980, pp. 56–62.

McCarthy, J. P., "Memo to Senior Management: Is Your Personnel Department Effective?" *Best's Review*, July 1980, pp. 101–105.

McInerney, Michael, "Executive Accountability: A New Approach to Performance and Rewards," *HR Horizons*, Issue 109, Summer 1992.

McMillan, John D. and Melissa A. Lemke, "New Approaches to Paying for Performance," *HR Horizons*, Issue 115, Winter 1994.

O'Neil, Sandra, "Aligning Pay with Business Strategy," *HR Magazine*, August 1993.

Overman, Stephanie, "Labor Secretary Preaches Cooperation," *HR Magazine*, November 1993.

Paulsen, Kevin M., "Lessons Learned from Gainsharing," *HR Magazine*, April 1991.

Reisinger, Gregory S. and Cynthia Palmer Lynch, "Transitioning to Project Teams: A Prescription for Success," *HR Horizons*, Issue 107, Winter 1992.

Rivlin, Alice M., "Budgeting for Performance," *Government Finance Review*, October 1993.

Rollins, Thomas, "Two Studies Define Link between Corporate Culture and Business Performance," *Employment Relations Today*, Summer 1993.

Schneier, Craig Eric, and Cathe Johnson, "Benchmarking: A Tool for Improving Managment Reward Systems," *ACA Journal*, Spring/Summer 1993.

Solomon, Charlene, "HR Heads into the Global Age," *Personnel Journal*, October 1993.

Stone, T. H., "Absence Control: Is Your Company a Candidate?" *Personnel Administrator*, September 1980, pp. 77–82.

Thomas, Mark and Harry Brull, "Tests Improve Hiring Decisions at Franciscan," *Personnel Journal*, November 1993.

Tompkins, Neville C., "Life without Performance Summary Ratings," *HR Horizons*, Issue 111, Winter 1993.

Webb, Karen L. and Sandra L. O'Neil, "Creative Game Rewards Managers," *HR Magazine*, November 1993.

Index